Resisting Economic Globalization
Critical Theory and International Investment Law

Palgrave Macmillan Socio-Legal Studies

Series Editor

David Cowan, Professor of Law and Policy, University of Bristol, UK

Editorial Board

Resisting Economic Globalization

Critical Theory and International Investment Law

David Schneiderman
University of Toronto

First published 2013
by PALGRAVE MACMILLAN

Palgrave Macmillan in the UK is an imprint of Macmillan Publishers Limited, registered in England, company number 785998, of Houndmills, Basingstoke, Hampshire RG21 6XS.

Palgrave Macmillan in the US is a division of St Martin's Press LLC, 175 Fifth Avenue, New York, NY 10010.

Palgrave Macmillan is the global academic imprint of the above companies and has companies and representatives throughout the world.

Palgrave® and Macmillan® are registered trademarks in the United States, the United Kingdom, Europe and other countries.

ISBN: 978–1–137–00405–5

This book is printed on paper suitable for recycling and made from fully managed and sustained forest sources. Logging, pulping and manufacturing processes are expected to conform to the environmental regulations of the country of origin.

A catalogue record for this book is available from the British Library.

A catalog record for this book is available from the Library of Congress.

To Pratima,
who knows a little something about resistance

Contents

Acknowledgments

It might not be all that unusual for a book to have been prompted by feelings of dissatisfaction. What precipitated my unease was an apparent detachment from the affairs of the world in some of the literature on economic globalization, a veiled separation from the lived experiences of those subject to the disciplines of its legal framework. This book, a conjoining of critical theorists with case studies drawn from the domain of international investment law, aims to bring those experiences to bear on law and globalization studies. I am also prompted to write things that I would like to read. Some might view this as a highly self-indulgent mode of scholarship. My hope (and intuition) is that others will want to read this sort of thing too.

The book had its origins while I was a Visiting Professor at Georgetown University Law Center. I continued to pursue the project upon return to my home institution, the Faculty of Law at the University of Toronto. I am heavily indebted to former Dean Alex Aleinikoff (at Georgetown) and Dean Mayo Moran (at Toronto) for their support and encouragement and for the lively intellectual communities that they both have nurtured. They also generously provided funds for student research which ensured that I had the benefit of the research assistance of Rob Ginsburg, Kyle Gooch, Mike Johnston, Mauricio Salcedo, Chava Schwebel, Ana Turgeman and Jenny Yoo.

In addition to the astute comments of two anonymous reviewers for the press, I was fortunate to have two friends and colleagues at the University of Toronto, Karen Knop and Patrick Macklem, provide comments on a penultimate version of the book manuscript. I also benefited from comments or advice on parts of the book from: Emma Aisbett, Tom Allen, Gavin Anderson, Upendra Baxi, Jonathan Bonnitcha, Alvaro Galindo, Amanda Perry-Kessaris, Jonathan Klaaren, Ladan Mehranvar, Andrew Newcombe, Sol Picciotto, Marylyn Raisch, Boaventura de Sousa Santos, Mariana Valverde and Gus Van Harten. A number of folks kindly met with me, in person or over the phone, to discuss some of the matters under consideration here. I wish to thank Sarah Anderson, Xavier Carim, Dana Contratto, Stephen Gelb, Victor Mashabela, Polo Radebe, Jim Shultz, Randall Williams and Robert Zoellick for generously giving me some of their time. This is as good a place as any to acknowledge the growing and vibrant community of legal scholars, social scientists and non-governmental lawyers who are thinking and writing critically about international investment law and who provide intellectual sustenance for the work that I do in this area. I am also grateful to Dave Cowan for welcoming the book into the series, which he oversees, and to Rob Gibson of Palgrave Macmillan for smoothing passage for the book's publication.

Parts of the book were presented at seminars at the following institutions: Georgetown University Law Center; the Faculty of Law at the University of Glasgow; the Faculty of Law at the University of Toronto; the American Law and Society Association Meeting in Denver, Colorado; the Oñati Institute for the Sociology of Law; the International Institute of Sociology Conference in Budapest; the Mandela Institute at the University of Witwatersrand; the Faculty of Law at the University of Cape Town; the Canadian Law and Society Association Conference in Harrison Hot Springs BC; and the Legislatures and Constitutionalism Conference in Banff, Alberta organized by the Centre for Constitutional Studies. Though much in this book is new, parts of the chapters draw on previously published material which has appeared in the *Annual Review of the Law and Social Sciences*, the *University of Toronto Law Journal*, the *Journal of International Dispute Settlement* and the *South African Journal on Human Rights*.

I was blessed to have my mother Rose nearby while I completed the manuscript. My wonderful children, Kiran and Anika Mala, contributed to the happy home environment that continues to sustain me. Pratima Rao has been supporting my scholarly endeavours for a couple of decades. I am happy to be able to dedicate this book to her.

Introduction

Is economic globalization irresistible? Its agenda of insulating markets from politics, associated with the rise of neoliberal politics, has taken root in almost every part of the world. It is not that states simply have disintegrated under the excessive weight of market ideology. States continue to perform critical functions in maintaining public infrastructures, facilitating economic flows, and policing dangers of various sorts. Rather, the principal aim of economic globalization appears to have been to establish mechanisms of security for property, financiers and investors, shielding them from consequences issuing out of democratic processes deemed out-of-sync with the imagined or expressed interests of powerful economic interests. Democratic processes yielding results inconsistent with those interests are labelled extreme or declared out of bounds. Democratic processes, moreover, must get out of the way where markets fail and business firms require backstopping by states, as happened in the wake of the 2008 global financial crisis.

Legal forms, operating both inside and outside of territorial states, are important markers in establishing and enforcing these thresholds of tolerable behaviour. For these reasons, transnational legality[1] – the ensemble of rules and institutions ordinarily associated with economic globalization – pre-eminently has been a political project. The defenders of these legal ramparts mostly deny this. Consider the ensemble of treaties, rules and personnel that withdraw disputes between states and foreign investors from national contexts and deposit them in a new transnational legal arena called international investment law. By reason of the worldwide spread of bilateral investment treaties (BITs), investment disputes, it is claimed, are now 'depoliticized' (Shihata,

---

1 This is a derivation of Beck's term 'translegality' (Beck, 2005, pp. 71ff.). On the idea of transnational law, I follow Zumbansen (2006) who describes 'transnational law' as reconnecting the domestic with the international and public with private law domains (pp. 741–2). This is in contrast to Vertovec, (2009, p. 3), who prefers to confine the 'transnational' to the activities of non-state actors.

1986, p. 4; Vandevelde, 1992: p. 535). Investors have direct access to dispute resolution processes to challenge the measures of rogue states that significantly diminish the value of investment interests. Investor–state disputes, it is said, are resolved without reference to power, but only to the rule of law as applied by an impartial and independent group of lawyers (Schneiderman, 2011).

Claims about depoliticization, however, largely obfuscate the distributional effects of international investment law (Hale, 1923) – distributing power and resources as between citizens, states and investors – and elide the suppression of politics under rule by lawyers (Weiler, 2001). Such claims, furthermore, falsely universalize idealized versions of the domestic legal arrangements of powerful capital-exporting states that bear little relationship to their own paths to economic development (Schneiderman, 2008). We should understand the regime of international investment law, instead, as a means of perpetuating inequalities in wealth and power between North and South (Sornarajah, 1997). This is not to say that citizens and states previously were unhindered in regard to the regulation of economic subjects. Economic interests together with the political power of the North Atlantic economies have long sought to tame the politics of others – despite considerable diversity among nations and states – and have done so with some success (Lipson, 1985). Only the most powerful states have been able to dodge the constraints of the modern trade and investment system, shaping those disciplines in ways most beneficial to their economies (Weiss, 2005a). Rather, what is distinctive about recent trends is the way in which novel rules and institutions, like the investment rules regime, have been framed so as to obscure the operation of political power over subordinate states and peoples.[2] Following these legal lineages that make economic globalization material enables us to determine how economic globalization is being made and might even be rolled back (Rittich, 2006, pp. 249–50).

This book is an inquiry into the ways and means by which citizens and states may be able to undo some of the constraints of transnational legality. Though much of the domain of global law has been described as fragmented and pluralistic (Koskenniemi, 2007; Walker, 2008), transnational legality here refers to the compendium of rules and institutions associated with the spread of the political project of neoliberalism worldwide, having its principal object the subsumption of politics to markets. A key arena in which transnational legal norms are being simultaneously generated and contested, and which

---

2 I have explained some of the novel features of the investment rules regime elsewhere (see Schneiderman, 2008). I adopt the descriptor 'regime' from those working in international relations (Krasner, 1983; Schneiderman, 2008, pp. 26–7). I do so not for the purpose, however, of valorizing regimes (see Salacuse, 2010, p. 471) or conscripting them into a strategy for global governance (see Habermas, 2006a, p. 181). This is discussed further in Chapter 3.

provides substance for much of the book's argument, is the regime of rules to protect and promote investment, represented by over 2800 BITs and a smaller number of regional trade and investment agreements (UNCTAD, 2012, p. 84). A focus on this particular rules regime is instructive in so far as it represents the legal response of powerful economic actors and capital-exporting states intended to pre-empt and punish acts of resistance. The object is to inquire into the extent to which the investment rules regime is revisable if not reversible.[3]

The inquiry is undertaken, however, not only through episodes drawn from the arcane world of international investment law. A variety of critical theorists are also conscripted with a view to determining the degree to which theory can assist in this enterprise. It is not that theory alone is important, rather, it is that theory itself is a form of practice (Spivak, 1988, p. 275). Theory assists in identifying the 'tasks which at any given period are to be mastered' with its help (Horkheimer, 1972, p. 20). Critical theory, moreover, will have the advantage of steering us in an emancipatory direction (Guess, 1981, p. 2) where settled understandings and expectations can usefully be upset (Held, 1980, p. 5). What theorists have to say about resistance, then, is of some significance to strategies for social change. These are theorists who, it could be said, collectively are preoccupied with lessening human suffering and exploitation in the contemporary world. Lured, perhaps, by the mobility and abstract quality of global capital, many critical theorists elide the role of states in constructing transnational legality. They consequently abandon states as the locus for securing change that will countervail the deleterious effects of the free movement of goods, persons and capital. As the episodes taken up in this book reveal, however, states are critical to the maintenance and legitimacy of transnational legality and so remain salient locales for resistance. Giving up on states also seems compatible with transnational legal edicts that state actors do no more than provide security for markets. Motivating this inquiry, then, is a worry that theorists obfuscate potential pressure points operating at national levels by which transnational legality might legally be resisted or rolled back. If the book's argument urges recourse to national political systems as a means of advancing effective resistance, the book also attends to the difficulties associated with securing that sort of change. Invariably there will be blockages, setbacks and ambivalent victories. The object is to instil a 'pessimistic activism' that encourages resistance in response to recurring patterns of domination while attentive to reality that danger lurks everywhere (Foucault, 1983, p. 104).

---

3 Arguments denying globalization's reversibility are made by a variety of authors from across the political spectrum. See, for example, Castells (1997, p. 268), Hardt and Negri (2000, p. 336), Moore (2003, pp. 38ff.), Beck (2005, p. 93) and Wolf (2004, p. 96).

Methods

The book is structured as a series of discrete encounters between critical theory and practice, as a means of bringing transnational theory and legality into contact. In each chapter, the work of leading social and political theorists is contrasted with a recent episode in resisting transnational legality. The choice of theorists – Michael Hardt and Antonio Negri, Gunther Teubner, Jürgen Habermas, Boaventura de Sousa Santos, Sheldon Wolin and Michel Foucault – admittedly is diverse (there is even disagreement amongst them) but there remains an important cohering theme: they mostly view national states as marginal if not anachronistic.[4] One could say that each theorist is in search of agents – some agents will operate supranationally, others subnationally – to precipitate a Polanyian 'countermovement' of certain proportions. They are drawn variously to a restless and mobile multitude (Hardt and Negri), a plurality of self-constituting legal orders (Teubner), enlightened publics of the North Atlantic (Habermas), counter-hegemonic movements of the global South (Santos), episodic local movements that promote commonality (Wolin), and strategic resistance embedded within power relations that is perpetually in danger of being reversed (Foucault). They are also all northern theorists (Connell, 2006) and, though their theoretical orientations privilege northern history and epistemologies, this is not uniformly the case.[5] Admittedly, the selection reflects to some degree my own preoccupations and proclivities, indeed, I have learned much from each of them. Nor are they intended to exhaust the field of interesting authors worthy of discussion in this context. Rather, they each shed light on aspects of the operation of transnational legality, unsettling its presuppositions, even if that might not have been the direct object of their theoretical inquiry. The work of each can be considered a provocation to think critically along the lines that promote critical resistance.

I interrogate the work of these theorists so as to examine current conjunctures in light of their theoretical diagnoses. I contrast their theorizing with thick descriptions of particular disputes taking place within transnational legality's operative framework. A series of case studies – 'local episodes' one might say (Gordon, 1980, p. 256) – is drawn from the arena of international

---

4   Among the theorists here under consideration, Habermas is the most enthusiastic about citizens of major powers acting through formal state legal institutions. As I describe in Chapter 2, he has hopes that a new global domestic politics will emerge, operating under the auspices of a world organization such as the United Nations and intermediate regional institutions, which can overtake elements of territorial state politics.

5   Boaventura de Sousa Santos stands out as an exception in this regard (see Chapter 3).

investment law. This is a new and constantly evolving area of law that was the subject of an earlier book (Schneiderman, 2008). Though not the only area in which law is implicated in processes of economic globalization,[6] it can be said that the investment rules regime is tangible evidence of the spread of globalization (IMF, 2007). Its rules provide a particularly apt expression of the power of law to institutionalize distributive choices that impact on the ability of citizens and states to respond to economic exigencies. The case studies draw on episodes having to do with the negotiation of free trade and investment treaties, the decisions of international investment tribunals, and the responses that investor–state disputes have generated. The methodology employed in each case study varies from in-depth review of legal arguments and documentation, scrutinizing legislative debates and media reports, to unstructured interviews with key actors. The object is not to map out paths of resistance but to identify how this particular legal code operates to shrink policy space and to envisage how its structures might be undone. The principal mission is not to 'humanize transnational economic governance' (Wai, 2003) but to envisage a world without an investment rules regime. It is intended to take law to account to the extent that it contributes to the production of social and economic suffering (Baxi, 2006; Veitch, 2007).

It is not my object merely to adjust theory in light of facts. Though deepening the accounts provided by these theorists is one of my principal aims, it is, more importantly, to portray the possibilities for political change in the realm of transnational law. I would not go so far as to claim that these theorists are guilty of 'careless generalizations', deriving theory with little or no basis in empirical fact (Wickham, 1990, p. 122). After all, as Horkheimer warns, 'judgments which embrace all reality are always questionable and not very important' (1972, p. 20). Various of the theorists attempt to support their generalizations with reference to some indicia, detailed case study, or immanent critique of contemporary legal forms. They are mostly all culpable, however, of deliberately disregarding the possibility that resistance takes route via the media of state action. By denying an ability either to direct state authority, or even to ally with it, theorists disable citizens and movement actors from a means of securing meaningful, if not modest, resistance that only states can facilitate.

Nor is it, in my view, sufficient merely to imagine a different world. The prospects of advancing resistance with reference to idealism alone – by imagining that there is a direct correlation between '[k]nowing and the known'

---

6 Typically, the Uruguay-Round General Agreement on Tariffs and Trade enforced by the WTO and *lex mercatoria* are cited as instances. See Jackson (1997) and Teubner (1997a), respectively.

(Horkheimer, 1972, p. 27) – are doubtful. The case studies are intended to illuminate precisely the circumstances in and the means by which transnational legality operates. It is not enough, for instance, to show that neoliberalism plays a powerful discursive and limiting role in the contemporary world. To show, by contrast, how transnational legal norms effectively institutionalize pathologies associated with neoliberalism, thereby legally constraining alternative paths to development, is to ground the ideational within real socioeconomic and political circumstances. It is to reveal the points by which change can be achieved, even if such 'victories' will be rare.

Investment rules

Change is not easily achieved. Elsewhere, I have described the investment rules regime as constitution-like, establishing limitations on the capacity of states to take measures that may, directly or indirectly, significantly diminish the value of a foreigner's investment (Schneiderman, 2008). International investment rules prohibit a wide range of state behaviour that has the effect of substantially depriving investors of the value of their investment interest. Measures equivalent to an expropriation (in whole or in part), measures preferring local nationals over foreign ones, or measures that deny investors 'fair and equitable treatment', among other disciplines, can provide ground for damages against a host state in the range of tens to hundreds of millions of dollars.

Significantly departing from traditional international law practice, which was primarily a law only for states, investment disciplines entitle individual investors to enforce treaty norms before investment arbitration tribunals. The regime has the effect of removing disputes from local courts and elevating them to what is considered a depoliticized form of dispute resolution. Yet investor–state dispute panels adjudicate issues that determine the proper boundaries of state intrusion into markets, questions that often are crucial to citizens and their well-being. Foreign investors thus are able to thwart policy directions taken by states in circumstances where, in the past, the inter-state system would have managed disagreement via diplomacy or simply would have looked the other way. Investment tribunals exhibit their own embedded preferences, staffed by lawyers drawn almost exclusively from the cramped confines of commercial and investment arbitration, preoccupied with preserving and enhancing the economic security of commercial actors (Van Harten, 2010). As the practice area is a lucrative one, arbitrators have an incentive to grow and expand the market for their legal services (Sornarajah, 2011).

The regime can be viewed as laying down tolerable limits to state regulatory behaviour in the same way as do national constitutional rules: regulatory policy that moves beyond the threshold of what might be considered normal or acceptable is legally prohibited. The regime places legal limits, intended to last for generations, on state capacity to implement policies dissonant with the regime's embedded preference for the protection of foreign propertied interests.

There is evident disenchantment with transnational legality and this is giving rise to what can be described as resistance. This arises not only because of the decline in the power and influence of the world's leading hegemon, the US, following the debacle in Iraq and the subsequent collapse of housing and financial markets, though these likely have contributed to the atmosphere of distrust and scepticism about the benefits flowing from the investment rules regime. Disenchantment can be traced, in part, to the fact that there are over 120 investment disputes launched by investors against states currently pending before the World Bank-based facility, International Center for the Settlement of Investment Disputes (ICSID) – one of the premiere arbitration facilities in the world. Over 40 disputes alone were filed against the Republic of Argentina as a consequence of the economic meltdown of the Argentinian peso in 2001. A number of disputes against Argentina have already resulted in awards worth hundreds of millions of dollars. Investment disputes have also been filed as a consequence of big public infrastructure contracts gone awry, generating skyrocketing consumer prices and fierce local opposition, or following upon the opening of hazardous waste facility sites giving rise to public health concerns and protests from municipalities and *campesinos*. This combination of events, some of which are described in detail in the chapters that follow, together with the ambivalent evidence regarding the utility of investment rules in attracting new inward direct investment (cf. Neumayer and Spess, 2005; Yackee, 2008), has precipitated what might be called investment-rules blowback.

Countermovement?

In the wake of ongoing global fiscal calamities, it might seem impertinent to ask whether transnational legality's strictures might be undone. After all, states all over the world are taking measures in response to unregulated markets, going so far as to practically nationalize financial institutions and some factors of production; measures previously considered inconceivable (Wolf, 2009). What better evidence, then, of the capacity of states and movements to enter into a countermovement, described some time ago by Polanyi (1944), to take measures for societal self-protection in response to the operation of purportedly free markets?

Polanyi famously described a 'double movement' in the late nineteenth and early twentieth centuries, the first movement generating 'economic liberalism, aiming at the establishment of a [utopian] self-regulating market' and, the second, enhancing 'social protection ... of those most affected by the deleterious action of the market…using protective legislation, restrictive associations, and other instruments of intervention' (Polanyi, 1944/2001, pp. 138–9). Not only was intervention required, in this second movement, to salvage social and natural life but also, paradoxically, 'the organization of capitalistic production itself had to be sheltered from the devastating effects of a self-regulating market' (Polanyi, 1944/2001, p. 138). Unlike the establishment of so-called free markets – which were not free and unplanned but required the deliberate intervention of states to facilitate – the countermovement against free markets was spontaneous: 'Laissez faire was planned; planning was not', Polanyi famously wrote (Polanyi, 1944/2001, p. 147). Nor did the countermovement give expression to any particular 'intellectual fashion', rather, it was precipitated by a 'broad range of vital social interests affected by the expanding market mechanism' (Polanyi, 1944/2001, p. 151). Demands for social protection, it has been said, 'were very nearly universal' (Ruggie, 1998, p. 69). 'The legislative spearhead of the countermovement against a self-regulating market as it developed in the half century following 1860', writes Polanyi, 'turned out to be spontaneous, undirected by opinion, and actuated by a purely pragmatic spirit' (Polanyi, 1944/2001, p. 147).

Whatever the merits of Polanyi's genealogical account,[7] many have returned to Polanyi's analysis of the double movement as presaging collective responses to the current phase of economic globalization (e.g. Cox, 1992; Gill, 1995b; Birchfield, 1999; Habermas, 2001a; McMichael, 2003; Evans, 2008). For the organizers of the 2008 annual meeting of the Society for the Advancement of Socio-Economics, Polanyi's *Great Transformation* provided an organizing framework. They observed that the 'current era of globalization mirrors the era of the late 19th and early 20th centuries in many ways' and that, consequently, the 'reaction emerging today recalls the politics and policies of the Great Depression and the immediate post-war period, when the second half of Polanyi's double movement came into effect' (Piore, 2009, p. 162). At the height of the current global recession, the prospects of the double movement were made even more conspicuous. It is in this context, it was said, that the 'pendulum seems to be moving towards the interventionist pole' (Hettne, 2010, p. 48; Stewart, 2009, p. 770). The breadth of the crisis suggested, in light of the failure of existing economic models, the 'likelihood of a new paradigm' emerging (Milberg, 2009, p. 3). This could generate an 'array of standards and institutions' – a pluralism of 'economic and financial alternatives to the system-wide prescriptions of neoliberalism'

---

7 Halperin rejects Polanyi's characterization of protectionism as having universal appeal, rather, specific class interests promoted and fought for state intervention. Not all groups within society felt equally threatened by expanding markets and not all sought protection from them, she claims (Halperin, 2004, p. 265).

(Wade, 2008, p. 21) that would 'strengthen the diversity of ideas' (United Nations, 2009, p. 20).

The response of states to the current global recession, with the fiscal capacity to do so (principally those of the North Atlantic), might be characterized as fitting hand-in-glove with the Polanyian countermovement. In the US, for instance, massive government intervention focused on the financial sector (i.e. bank bailouts), subsidies to specific sectors (i.e. auto sector bailouts) and public infrastructure expenditure, and indicated a similarly pragmatic response to economic crisis. Nevertheless, in light of the breadth of programmes for social protection undertaken in the period covered by Polanyi's double movement, contemporary recovery plans look somewhat anaemic.[8]

It appears that the animating force behind recent 'rescue' plans was to return things to the *status quo ante*, that is, to restore liquidity into financial markets and profitability into key sectors of the North Atlantic economy. It was not, for the most part, about reversing course but about restoring order where there had been disorder (Summers, 2009) – which makes one mindful of Polanyi's insight that markets need states. To take one notorious instance, in the wake of the decision of US regulators to forestall the meltdown of financial markets, the Obama administration announced plans to overhaul the financial regulatory system. These plans were described initially as 'little more than an attempt to stick some new regulatory fingers into a very leaky financial dam rather than rebuild the dam itself' (Nocera, 2009). The subsequent financial reform bill, the Dodd–Frank Wall Street Reform and Consumer Protection Act, though wide-ranging, turned out not to be very far-reaching. 'Will it prevent another meltdown and future government bailouts?' asked the *New York Times'* Joe Nocera – 'probably not', he reluctantly concluded (Nocera, 2010). The Act gives regulators some power to oversee troubled financial institutions, imposes modest capital reserve requirements and some restrictions on proprietary trading by banks (the so-called Volcker rule), together with an oversight bureau for consumer financial protection. The resulting Volcker rule represents well the chastened regulatory agenda that emerged out of a US$300 million bank-lobbying campaign. Rather than reflecting its original objective, which was to bar commercial banks from speculative and risky trading activities and thereby separate out commercial banking (which would be backstopped by government guarantees) from investment banking (which would not), the resulting legislation leaves things, as Volcker puts it, 'pretty much in a holding pattern' (Cassidy, 2010,

---

8 By way of comparison, see Kennedy (1999) who summarizes President Franklin Delano Roosevelt's achievements in the first 100 days of his administration as 'impressive' by any standard (p. 153). Alter, however, describes Roosevelt and Obama as responding 'to their predicaments in similar ways' (2010, p. xvi).

p. 30). If the Act goes some distance to limiting the capacity of risk-taking by large financial institutions, it leaves the levers of control with financial regulators. These are the very same folks who were not so reliable overseers in the lead-up to the current crisis (Krugman, 2010; Stiglitz, 2010a). By providing massive funds for bank bailouts without conditioning access to these funds on fundamental reforms to the system that generated the crisis (a strategy that international financial institutions like the International Monetary Fund perfected in the 1990s), governments in the US have resigned themselves to restoring the *status quo ante* which may have little effect in reversing similar failures and bailouts in the future.[9] The Polanyian countermovement in contemporary times amounts to little more than getting the 'system back on track', as President Obama put it (Walsh and Hulse, 2009) – 'Let the comprehensive structural solution await calmer days', advises Judge Richard Posner (2009, p. 303) – a response which does little to escape the neoliberal frame that precipitated the crisis (Harvey, 2005, p. 176). Frustration with the oligarchical power of banks in stemming more meaningful reform (Johnson and Kwak, 2010) helps to explain the rise of the Occupy Wall Street movement and its diffusion to national capitals around the world (New York City General Assembly, 2011). That no further more meaningful reform was precipitated by these highly publicized remonstrations, however, affirms the durability of that neoliberal frame.

Previously colonized states, according to Polanyi, could not be expected to benefit from the countermovement against the 'backwash' of international capital. 'The protection that the white man could easily secure for himself, through the sovereign status of his communities was out of reach of the colored man', advised Polanyi (1944/2001, p. 183). Likewise in the global South, the restoration of economic order today is a goal well out of reach for some, not for reasons having to do with access to democratic institutions (as Polanyi suggested) but by reason of fiscal incapacity. Though a handful of states have weathered recent financial storms better than others (Sen, 2011) – some by pursuing developmental strategies at odds with strategies for development promoted by institutions of the global North (Ugarteche, 2012) – it seems impossible to halt the spiral of uncontrollable decline in many places around the world. According to World Bank estimates, the current global downslide will trap 'an additional 53 million people on less than $2 a day this year, a rise in absolute poverty' and this is in addition to the 130–155 million increase caused by 'soaring food and fuel prices' (Giles and Barber, 2009). The fallout from the global recession persists as high and volatile global food prices continue to vex vulnerable populations (World Bank, 2011).

---

9   For fuller discussions of the paths not taken by Congress, see Johnson and Kwak (2010) and Stiglitz (2010b).

So it is not the case that two decades of an unrelenting refrain to 'let markets do their work' has rendered citizens and states entirely incapable of responding to the exigencies of so-called free markets. Rather, there is an unevenness in the ability of states and citizens to respond and a mildly reformist mindset that tends to dominate the discourse.

Resistance

Rather than addressing appropriate responses to ongoing economic crises, this book takes up another question: by what paths might resistance to economic globalization be pursued beyond the 'restoration of order'? I do so by investigating challenges to the regime of international investment rules initiated principally by states and social movements in the 'periphery'. Despite claims that there is a virtual global consensus in support of this regime, the removal of options from the policy toolkit of states – options that were available to powerful states, such as the US and UK early on in their history (Chang, 2002; Schneiderman, 2008, ch. 9) – has given rise to recent expressions of resistance in various locales around the globe. Developing and less-developed states in the global South, in collaboration with social movement actors in both the North and South, are calling into question the utility of entering into investment treaties. There is a potential movement to revise, if not roll back, some of the strictures of transnational legality.

The concept of resistance has a ubiquitous presence in the globalization literature (Chin and Mittelman, 2000, p. 29). In the field of cultural studies, the term has an allure that is 'positively shimmering' and so is 'easily appropriated' in an indiscriminate fashion (Slemon, 1990, p. 31). My usage here is not intended to be as broad and diffuse as found elsewhere (e.g. Falk, 1999). Certainly, as transnational legality operates on various terrains, I make no effort to confine potential sites of resistance to one locale or level though, as mentioned, the case studies focus principally on states and places in the global South. For the most part, the case studies do not concern resistance at the micro-political level (cf. Drache, 2008, p. 6). Grievances against the powerful often take form via quotidian acts of resistance (Guha, 1983, p. 75; Scott, 1985, p. 290) and, while these practices of insubordination are important and worthy of study, they are not the focus here. Nor is my preoccupation with resistance focused exclusively on social movement activism or other forms of contentious politics (Keck and Sikkink, 1998; Tilly and Tarrow, 2007). Social movements play, however, an important role in the narratives I describe and remain key actors in a viable politics of resistance. Indeed, we should envisage multiple actors, including territorial states, operating in various locales that assist both in sustaining the regime and generating resistance to it.

   Though state functions have been significantly fragmented and even diminished (Strange, 1996, p. 82), states play ambivalent roles in maintaining this balance of power. States nevertheless are critical agents in the structuration of transnational legality. They are, as international law's edicts dictate (see Statute of the International Court of Justice, s. 38(1)), the principal authors of the binding constraints that constitute the orders of transnational legality (Roberts, 2010) – they are its 'primary enablers' (Yackee 2012, p. 419). I share with other theorists an appreciation that the current scene is heavily managed by states and their transnational delegates (Panitch, 1996; Hirst and Thompson, 1999; Sassen, 2006). The state retains its place, then, as a key nodal point in the continued maintenance of the regime. In which case, there is presumably much that can be achieved via states to undo these constraints (Amoore et al., 2000, p. 22). If the state does not have a rigorous homogeneity (too often presupposed) (i.e. Schmitt, 1999), but is understood as having a relation to the changing balance of forces within society – as being 'strategically selective' (Jessop, 2002, p. 40) and shot through with contradictions (Poulantzas, 1978, p. 132) – then one can envisage opportunities when a change of direction in state policy is possible, if not likely. Such a turning point might be at hand in some places.
   This emphasis on state agency can also be understood as a move away from a cartographic preoccupation with levels or scales in favour of a concern for 'jurisdiction'. It is jurisdiction, Valverde observes, that predetermines how legal knowledge operates at different scales (2009). This helps us to appreciate that the state is implicated, at various levels, in the production of transnational legality via the machinery of jurisdiction (Valverde, 2009, p. 143). A focus on jurisdiction, then, isolates an agential authority with the power to undo some of its binding constraints. From yet another angle, we could say that states, although 'losing power', have not lost their 'influence' (Castells, 1997, pp. 305, 243). Castells describes, for instance, the European project of integration as aggregating 'state power at a higher level', leaving states with some authority to direct the future of multilateral and global regulatory regimes (Castells, 1997, p. 267). Nation states and their elites, after all, 'are too jealous of their privileges to surrender sovereignty except under the promise of tangible returns' (Castells, 1997, p. 268) and so would be expected to have reserved residual authority for themselves. Influence, however, is not something exercised equivalently by all states (Braithwaite and Drahos, 2000, p. 475), neither are the 'tangible returns' of the networked society evenly distributed (Harvey, 2000, p. 81). Castells claims too much, then, by generalizing from the European case. Not all states, particularly capital-importing ones, will be part of the influential network of states and regions. All should have jurisdictional capacity, however, to reoccupy the space ceded to the investment rules regime.

This is not to say that alternative forms of transnational politico-legal action are unworthy of consideration. This is no paean to nationalism, left (Laxer, 2001), civic (MacCormick, 1999) or otherwise. Nor do I abandon the possibility that transnational legal regulation might take other forms, ones that will benefit those excluded from economic globalization's largesse. It is only to say that, at present, state agency holds out the best hope of undoing contemporary transnational legal constraints like the investment rules regime. One also should be unapologetic about this focus on states as national political systems stubbornly persist as the locus for political activity for many people in the world. While the corresponding capacity of states to change the world has been noticeably diminished, it is this disconnect between political capacity within national frames and economic power beyond (Fraser, 2003) that helps to fuel – and also to inhibit (Gauchet, 1991, p. 3) – contemporary resistance.

Turning now to the question of 'resistance to what end?', I am interested in resistance which has as its objective the opening up of new pathways for improving the lives of those marginalized by economic globalization, though contemplated by its logic (Spivak, 1999, p. 269). Following Hoy, I characterize resistance with these aims in mind as being 'emancipatory' or 'critical' (Hoy, 2004, p. 2). Agents pursuing political projects that keep open alternatives and possibilities, though admittedly context-bound, are engaging in critical resistance (Hoy, 2004, pp. 2, 232). By contrast, agents pursuing strategies that have the tendency of reinforcing existing relations of domination (Foucault, 1980c, p. 86), by expanding and legitimating transnational legality, for instance (Buchanan, 2003, p. 697), might be engaging in resistance but not of the kind I emphasize here.[10] Critical resistance, therefore, is selective with the objective of 'less domination' as the criterion of selection (cf. Abensour 2011, p. xxvi). The important distinction to maintain, though often hard to discern, is between strategies that reinforce domination and those that pursue openness or, relatedly, that between hegemonic and counter-hegemonic globalization (Santos, 2002; cf. Christodoulidis, 2009).

Jane Mansbridge helpfully distinguishes between a dominant 'resistance tradition' in democratic theory, with a focus on stopping coercion in all its forms, and uses of power to promote a 'common good', in order to get worthwhile things done, all the while acknowledging that instances of coercion can never fully meet the criterion of democratic legitimacy (Mansbridge, 2012, pp. 4–5). Both of these dimensions of democratic theory are conscripted

---

10 Critical resistance complements a model of constitutionalism, developed initially in Schneiderman (2008, pp. 13–17), that I associate with the idea of 'democratizing constitutionalism'.

into this discussion, though I engage more fully with the first than with the second. The book's modest aspiration is to stop certain forms of coercion arising via certain mechanisms of transnational legality. It is not so much about 'unleash[ing] a new movement, as to interrupt the present predominant' one (Žižek, 2009, p. 149). While no new programmatic agenda for bringing the people back in is devised, what is envisaged is a reversion to their voice being articulated principally, though not exclusively, via state power, in order to get things done. It is only within specific contexts and junctures that an evaluation of resistance as being critical, or otherwise, can best be undertaken. This is why a good part of the book is taken up with an exploration of local episodes where the possibility for critical resistance arises. If, in the course of the book's argument, I appeal to democratic processes more generally, it is for the purpose of encouraging these sorts of evaluations in specific contexts (Wickham, 1990, p. 136).

A preference for critical resistance is inspired by Foucault's genealogical inquiries in the years just before his death (e.g. Foucault, 2005). There, Foucault admonishes us to interrogate the commonplace and imagine new possibilities for ourselves. He incites us to question the taken-for-granted and unexplored ground beneath our feet (Foucault, 1979, p. 448). Refusing to submit to the arbitrary constraints posed by authoritarian edicts (such as 'there is no alternative'), this form of practical critique implores us to ask 'what has led us to constitute ourselves and to recognize ourselves as subjects of what we are doing, thinking, saying' (Foucault, 1984b, pp. 51, 53). Government, in Foucault's capacious sense of the term (Foucault, 2007, p. 108), presupposes the freedom of the governed, in which case, there is the possibility of resistance in every power relation (Rose, 1999, p. 4). Foucault's later work underscores the capacity of the governed to respond to their subjugation, even in situations of domination where power relations seemingly are blocked, frozen, or irreversible (Foucault, 1984a, pp. 27, 34, 35).[11] Critical resistance calls into question these forms of domination so that power is exercised less oppressively, with 'as little domination as possible' (Foucault, 1984a, p. 40).[12]

---

11 The 'idea that power is a system of domination that controls everything and leaves no room for freedom cannot be attributed to me', Foucault maintains (Foucault, 1984a, p. 35).

12 Dean (1999, pp. 36–8) and Brown (1995, pp. 22, 64) would deny that the appropriation of Foucault's method of critique permits the endorsement of any particular normative stance against domination (see also Gordon, 1980, p. 256). They maintain that this mode of critique only opens space in no particular direction to think about how to govern ourselves and others differently. Dean acknowledges Foucault's statements to the opposite while Brown distinguishes between his analytical strategy and political commitments (Dean, 1999, p. 35; Brown, 1995, p. 22, discussed further in Chapter 5). If they are correct (and I am agnostic about this), I am content to follow the neo-Foucauldians on this (see e.g. Connolly, 1993; Dumm, 2000; Hoy, 2004).

This sensibility – imagining a world more tolerable than the one at present – accords well with approaches to democratic theory that emphasize democracy's virtue in institutionalizing an openness to change. With democracy's 'ceaseless agitation' and 'restless activity' political power is described as an 'empty place' that is continually reoccupied by merely contingent formations (Lefort, 1982, pp. 168–9; Frankenburg, 2000, p. 13). By dissolving the 'ultimate markers of certainty', we are launched upon an 'adventure' in which foundations are called into question, observes Lefort (1982, p. 179; 1979, p. 303). Not that democracy guarantees the most tolerable form of government (Tocqueville, 2000, p. 221), only that it facilitates the politicization of contingent effects and so 'is never closed to new interventions' (Cruikshank, 1999, p. 124). Admittedly, there is a shrunken horizon of democratic possibilities by reason of the encumbering effects of transnational legality (Foucault, 1984b, p. 54; Christodoulidis, 2003, p. 415), in which case, there is always the possibility of having to start over again (Foucault, 1984b, p. 54). But critical resistance keeps open the channels of change by accepting the restless movement of democratic politics (Lefort, 2007, p. 156) and the 'permanent fever' of innovation which democratic practice invites (Tocqueville, 2000, p. 202). States remain the principal locus for this sort of activity, both lending legitimacy to transnational legality and generating a pathway through which its strictures can be overcome.

It might be thought that turning to states in order to put a halt to transnational legality is retrograde, if not downright dangerous. States, after all, brought us to this point and so are unreliable vehicles for transformative change. It is true that states have been complicit in the structuration of economic globalization but they are also the only viable *legal* recourse available to undo transnational legality's strictures. This is discussed in more detail in the course of the book's argument. Suffice it to say here that having recourse to the state is a 'blind alley' (Foucault, 1976, p. 108) only if one gives up on the task ahead: the one that arises after unlocking transnational legal commitments, namely, attending to both old and new relationships of exploitation (Foucault, 1984a, p. 27).

The 'new constitutionalism'

This book is intended to fall squarely within the growing literature addressing aspects of the 'new constitutionalism' (Gill, 2003, p. 131). The research project associated with the new constitutionalism understands national and transnational legal forms as contributing to the institutional manifestation of economic liberalism in which states are expected to both recede in the performance of certain regulatory functions while resurrecting old, or engaging in new, forms of regulation. As Gill describes the new constitutionalism, its rules and institutions are intended to 'insulate key aspects of the economy from the influence of politicians or the mass of citizens by imposing, internally and externally, "binding constraints" on the conduct of fiscal, monetary, and trade and investment policies' (Gill, 2003, p. 132). The research agenda of the new constitutionalist literature is both empirical and normative: to identify the legal modes by which the economy is cabined off from politics and to critique those institutional innovations with reference to public values associated with constitutionalism and democracy (Kelsey, 1999; Hirschl, 2004; Anderson, 2005; Fitzpatrick, 2006). My aim is to fill a gap in the literature about the modalities for undoing some of the legal constraints associated with the new constitutionalism.

The approach taken here also has affinities with the emergent literature on 'globalization-from-below'. In contrast to the singular path to economic development associated with the ideology of neoliberalism and promoted by transnational legality, globalization-from-below is conceived as the response of those most negatively impacted by globalization's strictures. This resistance is described as, most often, emanating from local movements and organizations (Falk, 1999, p. 128). Santos and Rodríguez-Garavito catalogue a 'growing grassroots contestation' to neoliberal institutionalism together with the 'formulation of alternative legal frameworks' by transnational advocacy networks and the 'populations most harmed by hegemonic globalization' (Santos and Rodríguez-Garavito, 2005a, pp. 2–3). This gives rise to a bottom-up phenomenon they describe as 'subaltern cosmopolitan legality' (Santos and Rodríguez-Garavito, 2005a, p. 5). The book also complements scholarly endeavours within international law. Rajagopal, for instance, aims to inscribe social movements into international law, arguing that third-world resistance has been central to the expansion of international institutions and the production of international law though rendered invisible by it (2003, p. 43). Both Anghie (2004) and Koskenniemi (2001) make colonial endeavours central to the construction and maintenance of international law. They each reveal how international law's institutions and doctrine were generated in response to problems associated with Europe's 'civilizing' mission abroad. This work shares with these authors a preoccupation with getting underneath taken-for-granted legal prescriptions that disenfranchise peoples and induce political passivity. With them, I share a concern with improving the conditions of those most harmed by transnational legal disciplines. This work, however, is not confined to bottom-up perspectives, though subaltern resistance is critically important in some of the stories told here. Northern and southern states, local publics and transnational social movements, all are relevant to the dense web of legal forms associated with transnational legality.

The book's emphasis on the critical role of states shares an orientation with mid-twentieth-century 'progressive realists' (i.e. Carr, 1939; Neibhur, 1944; and

Morgenthau, 1948) (see Scheuerman, 2011a). This loose and disparate group of scholars and thinkers exhibited a healthy scepticism about the likelihood of powerful nation states abandoning their self-interest in favour of global well-being. They also foresaw the urgency of moving toward a 'new and more humane postnational political and legal order', though its outlines were inchoate (Scheuerman, 2011b, p. 104). Even as the nation state was in decline – due to forces similar to those we associate today with 'globalization' (Scheuerman, 2011a, p. 54) – progressive realists appreciated the paradox that states served critical integrative functions, likely not performed by new international institutions, while blocking, in the service of its 'brutal' nationalism, movement towards a new international legal order to which they each aspired (Scheuerman 2011a, pp. 43, 47). This orientation complements well the cautious, one might even say gloomy, argument that I take up in this book; exhibiting a hope that things can improve for those marginalized by economic globalization's diktats, conjoined with a worry that this will be very difficult to do.

That much of the discussion is confined to one instantiation of the transnational legal form – the investment rules regime – also drives the tenor of this research agenda. Admittedly, there is much that can be done to trace paths of resistance against other of transnational legality's operative modes (against the World Trade Organization (WTO)-enforced Trade Related Aspects of Intellectual Property Rights regime, for instance) (Klug, 2005). It would be fruitful at some future stage, for example, to compare instances of resistance across various legal regimes of the transnational. What distinguishes this work from many others – whether in the realm of governance studies concerning public–private partnerships (Rosenau and Czempiel, 1992), related work on the privatization of public authority (Cutler, 2003), or work on cosmopolitanism and global civil society (Held, 1995) – is the continuing pivotal role of national states. Though they can be expected to work in conjunction with other partner states within a region, with social movement actors within and without of the territorial state, and through and in partnership with international institutions, territorial states continue to be the central political referent in critically resisting transnational investment rules.

What is to come

I turn, finally, to a description of each of the book's chapters. Their sequence moves from a discussion of global terrains (Hardt and Negri, Teubner), to harnessing hemispheric possibilities offered by the global North (Habermas) and then the global South (Santos), to more local and episodic forms of resistance (Wolin) and, finally, to a perspective which can move between levels (even hemispheres) all the while conscious that victories will be partial and that any resistance is fraught with danger (Foucault).

It should be uncontroversial to claim that states are active agents in the structuration of transnational legal norms and institutions. Yet Michael Hardt and Antonio Negri relegate states to a marginal place in their account of the legal order they associate with 'empire', failing to appreciate the contradictory but critical role of states in sustaining globalization's future. The 'domestic structures of domination' they associate with the nation state are irreversibly obsolete, they write, and so irrelevant to the rise of empire's legal order (2000, pp. 133, 336). Under empire, a new mobile labour force (the 'multitude') directly confronts imperial rule, generating opportunities for struggle, crisis, even revolution (2000, p. 321). Hardt and Negri's diagnosis elides the role of states in generating structural and legitimating supports for empire as expressed in transnational legal forms. States, I maintain, play critical mediating roles in rendering transnational processes workable and acceptable. I challenge their hypothesis by inquiring into the seemingly disappearing role of states despite their ubiquitous presence in the structuration of economic globalization. By reason of this paradox, economic globalization should be understood not only as a political and economic achievement but also a cultural one. It is a cultural project in so far as it has sought to frame the 'boundaries of the possible' and occupy the 'field of social vision' in much the same way as 'an army does a territory' (Corrigan and Sayer, 1985, p. 199). In pursuing this project, economic globalization has had some success in winning universal validity for its partial account of the world (Hall, 1982, p. 65). It is hard to sustain this cultural achievement, however, without the active partnership of states. I detail how the role of states is suppressed by the normative ideas of comparative advantage, consumer freedom and the rule of law – values conscripted to help legitimate new forms of non-state rule. These discursive strategies, however, prove an unstable basis for legitimation without the critical supports provided by national states in gaining and maintaining the consent of local publics. This contradictory role of states in transnational legality – placing limits on the solution to redistributive problems even as transnational legal forms rely on states to help construct and maintain the operation of that legal order – is illustrated by investment law's response to the 2001 collapse of the Argentinian economy. Investment arbitration tribunals generally have found Argentina financially responsible for sunk costs and lost profits to foreign investors who were lured by the promise of guaranteed rates of return. The Argentinian cases suggest that transnational legality threatens to undermine the very means by which globalization's legitimacy is maintained. This discrepancy between transnational legality's message and its practical effects suggests openings for critical resistance.

The international legal order, it is claimed, is highly fragmented giving rise to specialized regimes for the resolution of particular types of legal solutions having cross-border implications. While some bemoan this state of affairs and seek ways of gathering together its disparate parts into some kind of unified whole, systems-theoretical accounts encourage the spread and autonomous functioning of independent sub-systems in the realm of the transnational. In the second chapter I turn to Gunther Teubner's treatment of what he describes as multiple constitutional orders of world society 'without the state' (2011a) These 'private' constitutional orders (for example, those self-authored by multinational enterprises, international trade unions, or other non-governmental actors) operate independent of states and of each other, single-mindedly in the pursuit of their own self-governing logics. Operative sub-systems occasionally will cause friction with other sub-systems, giving rise to self-referential adjustments so as to lessen negative external effects. Adjustments are made, however, only on terms acceptable to and consistent with the sub-system's operational logic. There is, otherwise, no central coordinating agency, like the national state, that can impose unitary solutions or control systemic effects. How then, to tame the systemic effects of autonomous sub-systems, such as the investment rules regime, that undermine the capacity of states to carry out central functions, such as dampening income inequality or delivering critical public goods? Though Teubner is attuned to the imperialism of economic rationality in national and global domains, there remain few resources within systems-theoretic accounts to combat the negative externalities of investment law. In the second part of the chapter, I focus on the regime's commitment to promoting privatization, not only in facilitating and securing privatization of public enterprise but also by penalizing states that do not behave as would private commercial entities. I take up an investment dispute against Tanzania for the failed privatization of water and sewerage in the City of Dar es Salaam by way of a case study. Tanzania was found liable for damages suffered by a UK investor as a result of having stepped out of the role of private commercial actor when it sought to terminate the failed water-lease contract. The government of Tanzania was rebuked for being motivated by political logic rather than the logic of economic rationality, acting in ways that are described as 'well beyond the ambit of normal contractual behaviour'. The logic of international investment law demands that states be held liable for such deviant, non-private behaviour. By abnegating any recourse to states, the problem with system-inspired accounts like Teubner's is that they provide few resources with which to countervail these sorts of systemic effects. While sub-systems remain free to impose such disciplines, states and vulnerable citizens can be expected to do no more than make 'noise' in the hope that sub-systems, promoted by powerful economic actors, listen to their concerns.

How likely is it that powerful economic actors in the global North will begin to reverse the legal trajectory of transnationalism, away from neoliberal suppositions to more widely redistributivist ones? In Chapter 3, I take up

Habermas' claim that the leading states of the G8 and the Organisation for Economic Co-operation and Development (OECD) – those countries with deep democratic currents – will take the lead in taming global markets (Habermas, 2001a). It is the citizens of democratic states, working with global civil society actors and international organizations, Habermas claims, which will provide the impetus for a new politics that matches the strength of markets. National publics within powerful liberal democracies, such as the US, are unreliable allies, I argue, in developing the requisite cosmopolitan consciousness to reform the rules and structures that make up economic globalization. Congressional debates over the granting of trade promotion authority in 2002 to President George W Bush indicate that an institu-tionalized global consciousness in the developed world lies a long way off. The treaty modification precipitated by these debates reinforces a policy of promoting US constitutional law norms abroad while trumping local rules that regulate markets. Indeed, in light of these debates, there remains little doubt that it is US local law that is being touted as constituting the 'univer-sal'. The unreliability of northern states is underscored by an examination of failed free trade and investment talks between the US and the South African Customs Union. One of the main sticking points for the US side was South Africa's plan to generate a new black middle class via a programme of black economic empowerment. South African negotiators believed, according to a small sample of interviews, that they could secure equality-promoting excep-tions to investment treaty disciplines from US negotiators in furtherance of South Africa's new constitutional settlement. It turns out, however, that powerful OECD states like the US are less likely to tolerate divergence from their model of investment protection even where divergence is mandated by constitutional commitments to the promotion of equality elsewhere. These events also throw into doubt claims that national states remain obsolete. Rather than being relegated to the sidelines, national states continue to play pivotal roles in the future direction transnational legal forms will take.

In contrast to Habermas, Santos in *Toward a New Legal Common Sense* (2002) looks to the South rather than the North to play a leadership role in reversing the order of priority embedded within transitional legality. It is in these locales that we can expect a subaltern cosmopolitan consciousness to be articulated and non-capitalistic alternatives devised. How difficult, however, will it be for states in the global South to pursue paths of resistance in light of the rigid disciplines of transnational legality? In this period of what Santos calls 'para-digmatic transition' (2002, p. 173), state authority is significantly diminished, in which case, Santos looks to newer social movements and transnational non-governmental organizations (NGOs) for progressive, non-capitalist alter-natives to problems associated with markets – proposals associated with his notion of 'counter-hegemonic globalization' (2002, p. 459). States, in the period of transition, continue to perform important steering functions that counter-hegemonic movements will want to democratize. By experimenting with differing institutional solutions, the state becomes, for Santos, the 'newest social movement' (2002, p. 489). In order for this new social movement to do its work, it is imperative that alternatives remain open – that 'irreversible institutional options' be rejected in favour of more fluid outcomes, ones that may result in more egalitarian distribution of global wealth (2002, p. 492). Transnational legal forms look precisely like the sort of irreversible institutional options that should be eschewed in this period of seeming fluidity and transition. So as to illustrate this rigidity as well as the regime's political opportunity structures, I consider the 'water wars' in Cochabamba. This is the much-celebrated case of a popular movement expelling profiteers of water privatization in Bolivia's third largest municipality. What is not usually recounted is the second half of the story concerning a US$50 million investment claim launched against Bolivia by a subsidiary of San Francisco-based Bechtel Corporation. After examining an investment tribunal's initial decision on jurisdiction (authorizing the investor to move forward so that a tribunal could consider the merits of the claim), I trace an unprecedented campaign by a coalition of local social movement actors, the Bolivian state and NGOs operating in the global North that triggered the withdrawal of the investment dispute. Drawing on the literature on social mobilization together with a small sample of interviews with activists and lawyers involved in the dispute, I surmise that this sort of transnational campaign will not easily be replicated. Nor are transnational oppositional networks at present proving to be as durable as the contested regime.

Critical resistance will be facilitated by open and inclusive democratic practices. Just how open is contemporary democratic practice to facilitating and encouraging resistance to transnational legality? For political theorist Sheldon Wolin – whose influence on the radical democratic tradition has been described as 'profound' (Cruikshank, 1999, p. 25) – democracy is significantly dampened by the institutionalization of barriers to imagining new commonalities. The privatization of public authority, the reduction of citizenship to consumer citizenship and democracy to shareholder democracy are just some of the features that have contributed to the debasement of democratic practice. These features of contemporary democracy work to suppress the potential for ordinary people to become 'political beings through the self-discovery of common concerns', Wolin writes (Wolin, 1994, p. 11; 2001, p. 29). Though its prospects remain dim, Wolin admits that democracy remains a recurrent possibility, principally at local levels (2004, pp. 587, 603). Having previously disparaged local oppositional movements (1960, p. 430), Wolin turns to local associations that politicize the public aspects of our daily lives (Wolin, 1989, p. 81; 2008, p. 291). He has in mind those groups that fight for low-income housing, safer water or control over toxic waste dumps, for example (Wolin, 1994, p. 24). Though valorizing forms of politics denigrated by the transnational legal order (usually characterized as particularistic or rent-seeking), he discards in the process the political unit that has both capacity and jurisdiction to fight back with some effect. Moreover, by abandoning the state as a central medium for political action, Wolin muffles the impact that local resistance may be able to achieve at the national and levels beyond. In order to show how local political actors can link up with subnational and national political units, all the while attentive to the ambivalent role that states play in promoting economic globalization, I turn to an investment dispute concerning the shutting down of a hazardous waste facility site in the border state of Sonora, Mexico. The state at every level played a disquieting and facilitative role in the purchase of the site by Spanish investors, only a short distance from the large municipality of Hermosillo. Yet oppositional movements managed subsequently to convince local and national authorities to decline renewal of the licence to operate the site two years after its initial purchase. Though resisting ecological ruination on the ground (so to speak), resistance was undermined and made more difficult by an investment tribunal's decision to vindicate the investor's 'right' to continue to operate the site. As if to prove Wolin's point, the tribunal conscripted democratic theory in support of its decision. In tropes familiar to students of US constitutional law, the tribunal held that the interests of non-nationals ordinarily would not have been represented within the host state's political processes. This is despite evidence, drawn from the 'business and politics' and 'political risk' literature, of the myriad ways in which investors can influence, even pre-empt, political outcomes. The tribunal's solicitude toward investors and anxiety with the operation of democratic processes masks an attempt at legitimating controversial review by investment tribunals of high public policy matters. It also elides the role of investment rules in suppressing democratic alternatives being pursued at multiple levels.

How, then, to open up the horizon of possibility to citizens and states that can render reversible some of the constraining effects of transnational legality? In Chapter 6, I turn to the work of Foucault for guidance. While Foucault stresses the constraining techniques of power that structure possibilities, he also admonishes us to explore the ground beneath our feet. Because power operates through subjects, inside and outside of sovereign law-making via a grid of public and private relations, power affords opportunities not only for domination and stasis but also for resistance and reversals (Foucault, 1978, p. 93). Foucault emphasizes the productive side of power in perfecting the art of governing and producing governable subjects (2003b, pp. 50–1). Neoliberalism, from this angle, will be understood as produced, in part, by energetic state intervention. Power's productivity can also generate resistance – an opportunity to transform ourselves in light of possibilities previously unrecognized. Foucault's methods, however, are not about mapping paths to effective resistance but about modifying power's grip by breaking open horizons for political possibility. If the grip of normalizing power is mostly pervasive, it is imperative not to misrecognize a situation of domination for one of openness to resistance and change. This may be a problem for the government of Ecuador as it pursues strategies of resistance against investment rules strictures, going so far as to deny jurisdiction in its new constitution to international investment arbitration. In this chapter I trace the rise to power of Ecuadorean indigenous political movements in alliance with the political left, culminating in the election of the reform-minded economist Rafael Correa in 2007. Though aiming to neutralize the operation of investment rules in Ecuadorian policy space, the state remains desirous of encouraging new inward foreign investment from China, anticipating that the Chinese model of foreign investment protection will be more developmentally friendly. The People's Republic of China, however, is aggressively pursuing new investment agreements abroad on terms little different to those on offer from the global North. It turns out, then, that there is no escape from globalization's disciplines by taking up this particular path of resistance. In which case, as Foucault warns, we are in danger of being in a position of having to begin again (1984b, p. 54).

By way of conclusion, I turn to the themes of closure and openness suggested by Habermas. It might be said that doing away with this element of transnational legality (namely, investment rules strictures) – a result which cannot be predicted with any confidence – forecloses the opportunity for more inclusive futures. Foreign nationals would lose privileges which continually could have been expanded to be more inclusive (Habermas, 2001a, p. 84) so as to embrace national citizens (Schneiderman, 2006, p. 314). As others have noted, the democratic ideal of self-rule and openness to the other through deliberation paradoxically requires moments of closure in which the polity constitutes itself in order to carry out its deliberative project of self-rule (Christodoulidis, 2003, p. 419; Keenan, 2003, p. 11). Acts of closure, however, should not preclude a return to openness to the other – to the transformative possibilities engendered by encounters with those who are excluded or otherwise outside the sphere of ordinary concern (and not merely those with foreign wealth). The hope is that polities can re-engage with the democratic possibility of inclusion in the process of attending to this potential for collective self-revisability.

1
Hardt and Negri and the Immobilization of States

After the collapse of the Soviet empire, it was widely believed that humanity had coalesced around a single formula for optimal socioeconomic ordering (Žižek, 2009). The recipe for success called for less government and more markets. In the past, political authority was expected to check economic power on behalf of citizens seeking to protect themselves from the deleterious effects of markets (Polanyi, 1944/2001, pp. 79–80). Post-1989, political authority operating at the level of the national or sub-national was presumed to have dried up. States, it was said, were already doing too much; nor could they be expected to do much more.

Politics continues to have some distance to go to catch up with markets, even in the wake of the global financial crisis of 2008. According to the United Nations Commission on Trade and Development (UNCTAD), '[b]lind faith in the "efficiency" of deregulated financial markets' enabled their functioning 'with little or no supervision' (UNCTAD, 2009b, p. 13). Once the bottom fell out of the market and shock waves rolled across national borders, governments were 'caught off guard and were generally slow to respond' (UNCTAD, 2009b, p. 25). The crisis provided an opportunity, insisted a commission of experts reporting to the President of the UN General Assembly, 'to reassess global economic arrangements and prevalent economic doctrines' and to 'seize the opportunity to make deeper reforms' so as to restore a balance between markets and government (United Nations, 2009, p. 14). There can be 'no return to the status quo ante', the experts concluded (United Nations, 2009, p. 15). Though subsequent governmental response in many developed countries was 'unprecedented', fiscal incapacity and cramped policy space of developing and less developed countries was 'perceived as limited or [came] to be circumscribed in the context of IMF-supported programmes' (UNCTAD, 2009b, p. 25). Indeed, IMF lending 'surged' in the wake of the financial crisis. Poor countries received support with policy conditions attached that were 'fairly similar to those of the [conditions attached to aid in the] past, including a requirement that recipient countries reduce public spending and increase interest rates' (UNCTAD, 2009b, pp. 35–6). Financial institutions that were too big to fail, by contrast, had few strings attached to their bailouts.

So, despite easily discernible lines of responsibility for the recent crisis, citizens and states continue to find it difficult to combat contemporary modes of mobile economic production. The modern business actor continues to appear 'as an authentically global abstraction' (Dirlik, 1994, p. 350). This disenfranchisement is exacerbated by transnational legal rules and institutions intended to entrench constitution-like limits on the exercise of national and local political authority far into the future. McGinnis and Movsevian, for instance, liken the disciplinary mechanisms of the World Trade Organization (WTO) to the Madisonian checking functions of the US Constitution but 'on a global scale' (2000, p. 515). In a similar fashion, the investment rules regime, represented by over two thousand BITs and regional trade agreements, such as the North American Free Trade Agreement, has been characterized as performing constitution-like functions (Clarkson, 2003; Schneiderman, 2008). These transnational rules and institutions, an assemblage I call 'transnational legality', are intended to check popular political processes and isolate the economic from the political sphere.

National state authority, according to this line of analysis, not only is incapable of countervailing the power of transnational legality, it largely has become obsolete outside of the realms of security, policing, enhancing competitiveness and restoring financial stability (Cerny, 1999). If this is correct – that transnational legality has displaced many traditional functions served by national states – is this form of the global 'rule of law' sustainable? We might ask, as does Fraser, how power operates 'after the decentering of the national frame' (Fraser, 2003, p. 170).

This chapter inquires into the role of state agency in an age where powerful economic actors and governmental allies seek to supplant national state authority. Though transnational economic law exhibits a palpable distrust of national law-making, it also relies on state legal forms for the critical support structures that help maintain the legitimacy of transnational legality over time. Law-making under the auspices of national states, I argue below, is pivotal to the ongoing success of the rules and institutions of economic globalization. Critical theorists of economic globalization have made similar claims about the obsolescence of national legal authority that contributes to the immobilization of states. Rather than enhancing the ability of intermediate publics to resist transnational legality, such theorizing obfuscates a range of potential pressure points operating at national and subnational levels. So, if transnational law cannot be sustained without national supports, some

critical theorists help to sustain transnational legality by deeming national
states inconsequential.

In the first part of the chapter, I take up the important theoretical intervention in the realm of economic globalization by Hardt and Negri (2001; 2004;
2009). They relegate national states to an inconsequential role in the global
order they associate with 'empire'. Though they otherwise show an astute
understanding of globalization's constitutional architecture, they exhibit a
weak appreciation of the contradictory but sustaining role states will have
in globalization's future. In so doing, they theoretically close off important
avenues for the counter-power of their valorized 'multitude' to resist global
capitalism's legal order. The second part of the chapter restores the place
of states by inquiring into whether the rules and institutions of economic
globalization can maintain their legitimating force without the mediating
role of national states. Using work in social theory and international political
economy, three legitimating strategies that may sustain economic globalization in the medium to long term are identified (though they are not the only
ones) – comparative advantage, consumer freedom and the rule of law. Each
is found unsatisfactory without the 'normative and organizational supports'
of territorial states (Weiss, 2005a, p. 352). As an example of the ambivalent
role of states in the construction of transnational legality, I turn, in the last
part, to a series of recent decisions by arbitration panels established to resolve
disputes between the Republic of Argentina and a variety of multinational
enterprises. These cases illustrate well the disdain for national states exhibited by transnational legality though central to its continued maintenance.
Constituted under the auspices of the World Bank's International Centre for
the Settlement of Investment Disputes (ICSID), panels have been asked to
consider the consistency of measures taken in the wake of the 2000–2001
meltdown of the Argentinian economy with a number of Argentine BITs.
I outline here a regime that holds politics in check by punishing states for
preferring the alleviation of economic oppression over the interests of already
powerful foreign economic actors.

Empire's immobilized subjects

There perhaps has been no series of books on globalization in the social
sciences that has generated as much interest as those authored by Michael
Hardt and Antonio Negri. Their first book, *Empire* (2000), was described in *The
New York Times* as a 'heady treatise on globalization that is sending frissons
of excitement through campuses from São Paulo to Tokyo' (Eakin, 2001, B7).
Empire spawned voluminous commentary (Balakrishnan, 2003; Passavant and
Dean, 2004; Boron, 2005) as did a second book, expanding upon and modi-
fying their theses, entitled *Multitude* (Hardt and Negri, 2004). The book-end

to the trilogy, entitled *Commonwealth* (2009), articulates the mechanisms and institutions for a new political project of the commons. Highly innovative, idealistic, and intended to generate a new grammar for politics in the age of globalization, these books exhibit a tendency that is common to many theorists of globalization, that of failing to appreciate the critical role national legal orders play in sustaining the legitimacy of what they describe as empire or what I prefer to call, within a legal frame, transnational legality.

Let me first outline the main arguments in *Empire*, critique some of its elements, and then turn to its subsequent iterations in *Multitude* (2004) and *Commonwealth* (2009). Simply put, Hardt and Negri's grand thesis is that the institutional apparatus of empire – the transnational legal order of contemporary global capitalism – will collapse under the weight of its own contradictions. What precipitates its collapse is the 'multitude' – the mass of 'immaterial' labourers that 'sustains Empire and at the same time the force that calls for and makes necessary its destruction' (2000, p. 61). What emerges in their account is a 'class struggle' without limit as 'capitalist development is faced directly with the multitude, without mediation', without the mediating role of national political systems, that is (2000, p. 237). Finally, as Marx predicted, '[c]apital and labor are opposed in directly antagonistic form' (ibid.) giving rise to a revolutionary counter-empire of the multitude.

The multitude is both a productive and de-territorializing force with unprecedented mobility. This is in contrast to the geographically bound labour power of the old nation-state system. The multitude's penchant for mobility, Hardt and Negri write, 'indicates a real and powerful search for freedom and the formation of new, nomadic desires that cannot be contained and controlled within the disciplinary regime' (2000, p. 253). It is a 'desire for liberation' (2000, pp. 253, 357), the 'general right to control its own movement' which is the multitude's 'ultimate demand' (2000, p. 400) and the uncontainable threat to global capitalism.[1]

The imperial authority of empire – the powerful countries of the Organisation for Economic Co-operation and Development (OECD), operating in the institutional guises of the United Nations Security Council, G8, G20 or International Monetary Fund (IMF) (2000, p. 309) – cannot contain the multitude which is breaking down borders and destroying distance. New forms of production, giving rise to the mobility of immaterial labour, mandate that imperial authority encounters the multitude 'face-to-face' so to speak. Rule is now 'exercised directly over the movements of productive and cooperating subjectivities' and out of this emerge demands that will render

---

1 Labour's 'mobility and their commonality', they reiterate, is constantly a threat to destabilize the global hierarchies upon which global capitalist power depends' (Hardt and Negri, 2004, p. 137).

empire's constitutional order a 'site of struggle' (2000, p. 319). The resulting contradiction between the subjection and the independence of agents gives rise to a 'new social dynamic that liberates the producing and consuming subject from (or at least make ambiguous its position within) the mechanisms of political subjection'. At this point, 'a real field of struggle... can be reopened – a true and proper situation of crisis and maybe eventually revolution' (2000, p. 321).

This Marxian-inspired account of the immanent contradictions latent in the current global legal order is premised on the permanent demise of the national state. For Hardt and Negri, national legal orders represent 'positions of resentment and nostalgia' (2000, p. 218). The processes giving rise to the decline of the nation state in their account are 'structural and irreversible' (2000, p. 336). Empire, conceived as a 'universal republic', 'has nothing to do with... those state organisms designed for conquest, pillage, genocide, colonization, and slavery' (2000, pp. 166–7). With national legal orders out of the way, they can claim that borders are no impediment to labour mobility, giving rise to the insatiable demands of the multitude for greater freedom in the face of the constraints associated with empire. The alleged demise of national states, I argue below, is extravagant.

There are good reasons to doubt even the empirical basis for this hyperglobalist diagnosis of the contemporary world, where states largely are obsolete in the face of global capital. The purported post-national scene appears not to have given rise to much more worker mobility than we may have witnessed in the past. Though there are greater numbers of international migrants than ever, the percentage has remained steady at roughly 3 per cent of the global population between 2005–2010 (IOM, 2010, pp. 3, 29). By contrast, 10 per cent of the global population lived outside of their country of birth as a consequence of the waves of nineteenth and early twentieth-century migrations (Guhathakurta et al., 2007, p. 212; IOM, 2008, p. 40). It would be a gross mischaracterization, for this reason, to claim, as do Hardt and Negri, that these earlier waves of migration were 'lilliputian events' compared 'to the enormous population transfers of our times' (2000, p. 213). International migration numbers, moreover, are diminutive when compared to the dominant patterns of migration within the territorial borders of states (UNDP, 2009, p. 21). If some 214 million persons were international migrants in 2009, internal migration that same year was almost four times larger, at 740 million (UNDP, 2009, p. 21; IOM, 2011, p. 49). However large the volume of international migration, much of it (over 60 per cent) was not between developing and developed regions but primarily within regional enclaves within the same category of development (UNDP, 2009, p. 21). Poor people have far fewer resources to enable movement further abroad while legal and administrative restrictions make movement difficult if not impossible

(UNDP, 2009, pp. 24, 46). Legal mobility beyond these confines is, at present, enhanced only for the few, such as investors, whose rights of exit and entry are guaranteed by the investment rules regime, and a class of professional entrepreneurs associated with the knowledge industry – such as lawyers, accountants and financial advisors – whose services are considered essential to the operation of global economic apparatuses. Labourers around the world remain mostly trapped within the confines of geographic states and regions.

Hardt and Negri refine, even reconfigure, their diagnosis in *Multitude* (2004). They depart somewhat from their verdict that national states irreversibly are obsolete. 'To avoid confusion', they write in this second volume, 'we are not arguing here that in this interregnum nation-states are no longer powerful but rather that their powers and functions are being transformed in a new global framework' (2004, p. 163), which is a more modest and somewhat trite claim.[2] Hardt and Negri emphasize that, in *Empire*, they were observing 'a tendency' in which empire would emerge as the only 'lasting' vehicle for global power (2004, p. xiii). *In the interregnum*, they write, national states continue to perform critical functions such as creating and maintaining 'the market conditions necessary to guarantee contracts between corporations' (2004, pp. 171, 175).

Labour mobility, relatedly, is also dislodged from the central place it held in their analysis in *Empire*. If 'mobility increasingly defines the labor market as a whole' (2004, p. 133) – a point which does not to stand up well to empirical testing – their emphasis here is on the disruptive role of 'migrant' workers, who cross over and thus partially undermine 'every geographical barrier' (2004, p. 134). They cannot give up entirely though on the critical role of movement and fluidity. Mobility, they maintain, 'increasingly defines the labor market as a whole' (2004, p. 133). In the final volume of their trilogy, *Commonwealth* (2009), they continue to evince ambivalence about the capacity of immaterial labour to move about. They acknowledge that one strategy of contemporary capitalist control is to establish barriers that 'channel and halt the flows of labor' (2009, p. 147), yet they quickly return to a position where labour remains predominantly nomadic and mobile (2009, p. 244).[3] Much emphasis is placed, instead, on the denationalization of sovereignty via forms of pluralized 'governance'.

In this last volume, Hardt and Negri rely on the system-theoretic analysis of the global scene initiated by Luhmann and developed further by

---

2 Indeed, a heading in Part 2 of *Multitude* is 'Big Government is Back' (2004, p. 177).

3 See also their discussion about the 'first freedom' necessary to institute what they call 'the common' – it is 'freedom of movement' (Hardt and Negri, 2009, p. 309), which appears to acknowledge the persistence of national borders.

Teubner.[4] In their description of contemporary forms of governance without the state, they invoke Teubner's analysis of *lex mercatoria* (the customary law merchant) (Negri, 2008, p. 19) and 'societal constitutionalism' (the
establishment of autonomous transnational legal orders) (Hardt and Negri,
2009, p. 347). They go so far as to say that elements of the systems-theoretic
account 'fit so closely with our analyses of biopolitical society that they
could be seen as a summary of a string of passages in this book' (2009,
p. 374). I take up Teubner's account in the next chapter but, so as to better
contrast their theoretical orientations, I want to say a little about systems
theory in this context. Teubner has described the emergence of 'non-statal
private legal regimes' (Fischer-Lescano and Teubner, 2004, p. 1009) that are
independent of state-centred sources of law-making. The functional differentiation of new forms of law-making operating at global levels – giving rise
to the associated phenomenon labelled the 'fragmentation' of international
law (Koskenniemi and Leino, 2002) – has severed the 'structural coupling'
between law and politics previously under the supervision of national constitutional orders (Luhmann, 2004, pp. 487–8). Legal norm production can now
be observed proliferating outside of common national institutions, giving
rise to autonomous 'civil constitutions', operating in all variety of global
sectors, whether they be transnational corporations, federated trade unions
or human rights networks (Teubner, 2004, p. 8). Hence, Teubner says, we
should think of a 'global law' without the state, like *lex mercatoria*, developing
in 'relative insulation from politics' (Teubner, 1997a, p. 6). The constitutive
rules developed autonomously by these various societal actors increasingly,
however, are coming into conflict with each other, giving rise to 'irritations'.
In terms redolent of Polanyi's double movement, Teubner describes systems
as giving rise to 'counter-movements' that propose corralling the negative
effects on other sub-systems (Teubner, 2011a, pp. 213–14; Teubner, 2012,
p. 78). The strategy principally is one of devising 'internal limitations' to
sub-systems thereby inhibiting their compulsion to growth and subsequent
collision with competing sub-systems (Teubner 2012, pp. 81–3). Hardt and
Negri, however, are not so much interested in devising inter-systemic rules
for resolving conflict between functionally differentiated regimes. As states
irretrievably are obsolete, they have no expectation that national state
forms will harness global processes. They can perceive of no circumstances
in which it would be appropriate to have states intervene. Though Teubner
has acknowledged this possibility (1997a, pp. 4, 22), self-limitation strategies,

---

4 Despite Hardt and Negri's reliance on Teubner, their deep differences are canvassed in
   Teubner (2010) and Negri (2010). To the extent that Teubner's approach values the radical
   pluralism of the contemporary scene, rather than seeking to overcome it as do Hardt and
   Negri, the differences are profound and justify the separate discussion of Teubner I take up
   in Chapter 2.

he insists, can only be developed endogenously (2012, p. 85). Hardt and Negri, instead, envisage the construction of a global public space – another sort of self-constitutionalization – via the exodus of the multitude from the national institutions that corrupt and block the development of what they call the 'common' (2009, p. 247). National political power bases, in these ways, are anachronistic in the face of new mechanisms of governance that are emerging.

Hardt and Negri, moreover, do not explicate the persistent appeals of domestic movements addressed to political authority operating at national and subnational levels. For instance, their treatment of the cross-societal alliance represented by the *Coordinadora* in the Cochabamba water wars, a much heralded tale of local resistance led by a coalition of union activists and peasant leadership resulting in the renationalization of the municipal water supply (discussed in Chapter 3 below), merely becomes an instance of the multitude's political form promoting an 'altermodernity' (representing a 'decisive break' with modernity).[5] The multitude, they claim, 'has no interest in taking control of the state apparatuses' (2009. pp. 108–12, 355) and this is despite their acknowledgment that the *Coordinadora* helped to pave the way for Evo Morales to assume the Bolivian presidency in 2005 (2009, p. 108). They continue, instead, throughout *Commonwealth* (2009), to elide the critical role of national states and oppositional politics directed at actors and institutions within national states. The new empire, they reiterate, is 'qualitatively different from the previously existing imperialisms, which had been based on the power of nation-states' (2009, pp. 203, 274). National sovereignties 'are not able to organize global social space' (2009, p. 247) and so the authors consider it useless 'to search for a political form capable of supporting neoliberalism' (2009, p. 265).

Yet state forms precisely have structured global legal processes. This is not to say that states are left intact in the face of these processes, rather, the resulting experience of restructuring will be felt unevenly. Some states are better situated to exploit the structures of transnational legality. Linda Weiss has observed, for instance, that OECD states have developed a multilateral trade order that 'best suits their developmental trajectory' (Weiss, 2005b, p. 724). This form of 'strategic activism' promotes national economic interests of powerful states over the economic well-being of more vulnerable constituencies. Their interests are assisted by the oversight provided by financial

---

5 The *Coordinadora*, according to García Linera, represented a 'new territorial-type organization', one that built upon pre-existing solidaristic communities operating at local levels that gave expression to the demands of the 'multitude' (2004, p. 75). He is referring to the concept of 'multitude-form' as developed by René Zavaleta (Linera, 2004, p. 85, fn. 10) rather than to Hardt and Negri's 'multitude'.

market actors, who are less interested in scrutinizing the policy choices of developed countries than in policing developing ones. Financial investors, observes Mosley, 'consider many dimensions of government policy when making asset allocation decisions' in the less developed and developing world, considerations which do not apply in the developed world (Mosley, 2006, pp. 92, 96). This double standard in the surveillance of developed economies' finances was highlighted as the complicity of rating agencies in events leading up to the economic crisis of 2008 became apparent (US Senate, 2011, ch. 5).

Economic globalization, from this angle, is about preferring certain local interests over others. The transnational legal order should be understood, then, as concealing, in the guise of universality, the fact that particular national projects successfully have gone global. This is a manifestation of what Santos calls 'globalized localism', where a 'given local phenomenon is successfully globalized' (2002, p. 179). Complementing this process of exportation is one of importation, what Santos calls 'localized globalism', where local conditions are transformed as a result of adopting the imperatives associated with the transnational legal order (Santos, 2002, p. 179). By eliding these interests – by repressing, in Bourdieu's terms, the conditions of access that give rise to the universal – theorists give cover to the most 'unjustifiable of monopolies' (Bourdieu, 1997, p. 70). Others are more attentive to this phenomenon. Dezalay and Garth (1996) describe a transnational struggle centred in the international arbitration centres of Paris and Geneva, driven by global law firms, between a flexible, case-by-case determination in accordance with the traditional law merchant (*lex mercatoria*) and a rigid, more predictable, rule-bound approach favoured by Anglo-American trade lawyers. The US rule-of-law side, Dezalay and Garth report, is in the ascendance (1996, ch. 4). Sell has documented the 'stunning triumph' that was secured by US-based pharmaceuticals in institutionalizing their preferred version of intellectual property rights in the Trade-Related Intellectual Property Rights (TRIPS) regime of the Uruguay-round General Agreement on Tariffs and Trade (Sell, 2003, p. 163). Sassen has theorized how the local can go global via non-state actors operating in very specific, even peripheral, localities but 'constituted at multiple scales' in global networks (Sassen, 2004, p. 650). We might better understand, in this light, how the transnational movement of HIV/AIDS activists, health, consumer and development non-governmental organizations, working in co-operation with developing states, have had some success in improving access to patented drugs in the face of a recalcitrant pharmaceutical industry and their allied national states (Klug, 2005, p. 119). Hardt and Negri's analysis does not account well for these sorts of struggles over interpretive monopolies. Hardt and Negri misrecognize that the legal regimes of economic globalization are expressions of particular interests that are intended to suppress other alternative formulations of competing interests that take shape, and often are articulated, at national and subnational levels (Buchanan and Pahjua, 2004, p. 76; Bourdieu, 2005, p. 230).

Their highly formalistic account of transnational legality ignores the ways in which states are deeply implicated in the very process of their presumed marginalization. Rather than bypassing the state, globalization amounts to a drastic reorganizing, and in some instances an augmentation, of state authority (Panitch, 1996, p. 85; Weiss, 2005a). The institutional resilience of the state is made manifest by the responses of leading OECD states to the global financial crunch of 2008. Though governmental support largely (but not exclusively) was confined to financial institutions deemed 'too big to fail', it resulted in 'an unprecedented scale of governmental intervention in many developed countries' (UNCTAD, 2009b, p. 25). There is no global stimulus package to speak of in this context because national decision-making continues to be in the driver's seat of global economic policy-making (Stiglitz, 2009, p. 4). To date, 'no form of extra-economic power has yet been devised that can fill these needs apart from the territorial state' (Wood, 2003b, p. 25). Even in the regional European context, a small sub-set of powerful northern states calls the shots concerning the future of the monetary union in the face of an impending European-wide fiscal crisis (Streeck, 2012). Narrowing the rules of engagement along the lines suggested by Hardt and Negri, outside the scope of the inter-state system, ignores both the agency of states in producing transnational legality and the capacity for collective action that states facilitate for people to countervail that global legal order in the interregnum.

As I argue next, states are active players in the structuration of economic globalization. They play multiple and even contradictory roles as home and host state to global business interests, regulator, enforcer of contracts and property rights, and legitimator-in-chief of transnational legal forms (Wood, 2003a). Without the legitimating processes promoted by national political systems, these forms of domination, it has been said, 'could quite easily collapse like a house of cards in the tiny breeze created by public curiosity' (Beck, 2005, p. 148). Ulrich Beck unnecessarily overstates the point. Even if, as Hardt and Negri describe it, imperial authority acts only to discipline and oppress the multitude in negative relations of repression, states play critical mediating roles in rendering transnational processes acceptable, if not desirable. By rendering invisible the role of the domestic in globalization's structuration, Hardt and Negri also negate the points at which globalization might legally be resisted or rolled back. The counter-power to empire, thereby, is disabled in the very specific locales at which economic globalization is taking legal shape.

Legitimacy problems

The establishment of national state forms, according to work in histori-cal sociology, was not only a politico-economic-military and legal achievement but also a cultural one. Critical to the successful construc-tion of formal state apparatuses – unified political institutions, with capitalist modes of production secured by sovereign law-making capaci-ties – were cultural changes accompanying state formation. Corrigan and Sayer, for these reasons, describe English state formation as a 'cultural revolution' (1985, p. 191). The structure of national political author-ity institutionalized relations of production and generated the 'fictive community' associated with the English as a nation. This was a project of 'social integration' through 'moral regulation':[6] state authority certi-fied the validity of certain forms of memory and suppressed competing sites of allegiance and memory in the 'active organization of forgetting' (Corrigan and Sayer, 1985, p. 195). State formation becomes 'an ongoing cultural project', its existence in 'constant jeopardy from the very facts of material difference' (Corrigan and Sayer, 1985, pp. 195, 197; Gramsci, 1971, p. 246). This smoothing over of difference – material, political, and cultural (Colley, 1992) – results in what Corrigan and Sayer call a 'violent disruption of human personality, a crippling restriction of human capacity', continuous with a 'more or less violent suppression of alterna-tives' (1985, pp. 198–9):

> The ordinary procedures of state inflate to become taken-for-granted boundaries of the possible, occupying – in the same way an army does a territory – the field of social vision (1985, p. 199).

One might want to take issue with this description of the state as a unified force field. The state is better understood as a complex ensemble of insti-tutions with only a formal, rather than a substantive, unity (Jessop, 1990, p. 256). Bourdieu, for instance, has distinguished between the 'left hand of the state' – agents of the 'spending ministries' associated with the promo-tion of social welfare – and the 'right hand of the state' – officials from the ministries of finance or international trade who hold inordinate sway over the direction of state policy (1998, p. 2). In so far as these dominant branches within the state operate in a 'strategically selective' manner – wherein certain social forces are privileged over others – state forms structure political possi-bilities along the lines that Corrigan and Sayer suggest (Jessop, 1990, p. 260).

---

6 They associate the idea of moral regulation primarily with Durkheim (1957) rather than with Foucault (1990). See Ruonavaara (1997).

To the extent that transnational legality has reconfigured states, we might similarly consider economic globalization as being a cultural project with the normative object of actively forgetting alternatives. Without denying the elements of fixity and security that make material the felt experience of economic globalization, there are important discursive elements that help contribute to the success of the globalization's imaginary (Fairclough and Thomas, 2004; Fairclough, 2006; Steger, 2008, p. 184). The integrating and homogenizing aspects of economic globalization, premised upon a single path for economic development fictitiously experienced by the developed countries of the North, is about constituting thresholds of normalcy (Coward, 2005, p. 868). Deviations from the normal are simply forbidden (Tarullo, 1987). This well represents the constitutive and negative role law plays in the structuration of economic globalization: legal disciplines erect barriers that cabin political possibilities and suppress alternative futures. If there is a seeming diminution in national state authority, can this form of legality maintain its legitimacy without the mediating role served by the states and local democratic processes? Can these legal forms solely secure the cultural transformation of the sort that Corrigan and Sayer describe in the context of English state formation?

Neoliberalism, Harvey has observed, is a theory of political economy which hypothesizes that human well-being will be advanced by the practices associated with free markets. It is the role of the state to 'create and preserve an institutional framework appropriate to such practices' (Harvey, 2005, p. 2). States are expected, for instance, to entrench property rights, guarantee contractual obligations, and perform security and policing functions so as to ensure the smooth operation of free markets, as Hardt and Negri admit. The degree to which states have diminished their capacity to regulate remains in question, however (Peck, 2010; Harcourt, 2011). States have retained, after all, some scope for policy diversity – they are not entirely disabled by the legal regime associated with empire (Hay and Marsh, 2000, p. 5; Hirst and Thompson, 1999). A variety of studies suggest that, on matters such as welfare reform (Hay, 2005) and industrial, technological and export subsidies (Weiss, 2005b), there is room for policy difference in spite of the convergence effects of economic globalization. As already suggested, the power to develop rules better suited to national interests is distributed unevenly. For many states in the world, there is little or no room to deviate from the touted paths to economic development taken up by powerful developed states. Less powerful states typically will resile from taking measures – particularly redistributive ones – that will appear out of step. Legal capacity at the national and subnational levels, then, remains unused, even if available. Legal reforms that facilitate market processes are welcome – innovative policy positions less so.

There is a crack, however, in the legal forms that aim to secure the rights of global capital. Stephen Gill notes, for instance, that the movement toward remaking the state along neoliberal lines 'lacks moral credibility, legitimacy and authority' (2003, p. 140). Ulrich Beck, similarly, asks what legitimizes these new forms of legality *'in the absence of* state democratic authority?' (Beck, 2005, p. 120). If political authority is the 'fusion of power with legitimate social purpose' (Ruggie, 1998, p. 64), what legitimate social purposes are advanced by adhering to the regimes of transnational legality? States are considered incapable of taking 'abnormal' measures to protect the mass of its citizens without incurring retaliation from powerful global economic actors – the drying up or withdrawal of investment, for instance – in addition to running up against the disciplines of transnational legality. Unable to harness mobile capital for taxation purposes, states cannot be expected to deliver critical public goods, particularly redistributive ones (Rodrik, 1997; Cerny, 1999, p. 127). If there is a disjuncture between economic globalization and 'the political institutionalization of new social relations' (Robinson, 2001, p. 601), how can transnational legality maintain its legitimacy without the active partnership of national states? We can identify at least three powerful discursive strategies that purport to solve this legitimacy problem: (i) the pursuit of comparative advantage; (ii) the advancement of consumer freedom; and (iii) the promotion of the rule of law.

Comparative advantage

The promise of neoliberalism is that state functions become obsolete as the mass of citizens are better served by greater liberty, gains from economic efficiency and enhanced social well-being. Comparative advantage speaks to the idea that there are structural differentiations in economic capacity around the globe, and that nations should specialize in that which they produce most efficiently and import that which they do not. In this statically efficient version of the long run, it can be expected that all – consumers and producers, workers and owners – will be better off (Unger, 2007, p. 30). Contemporary international economic law is premised on this powerful idea associated with David Ricardo (1912) in the nineteenth century and modified by later developments in econometrics. Former WTO head Mike Moore describes the 'compelling logic' of comparative advantage as the 'best established and the most profound observation in political economics' (2003, p. 52), while Martin Wolf of the *Financial Times* describes it as 'perhaps the cleverest [idea] in economics' (2004, p. 80).

It is a powerful idea not only in the world of economics and trade law. According to the Pew Research Centre 2011 global attitudes survey of public opinion in 23 nations, 'majorities in all parts' of the world viewed growing international trade and business ties as a 'good thing'. In the US, 67 per cent of respondents believed it either 'somewhat good' or 'very good' (Pew Research Centre, 2011, p. 42). National states conduct themselves accordingly, opening up their economies and binding their governments to the constraints of transnational legalism, anticipating the promised gains from trade and investment. Yet these gains will not be felt the same everywhere. As Joseph Stiglitz notes, economic liberalization can 'wreak havoc on small emerging markets' (2002a, p. 59). Jobs can easily be destroyed with no corresponding economic growth and the transition costs associated with economic globalization – including externalities and market failures – are left for markets to resolve. Despite comparative advantage's favourable press, Michael Trebilcock and Robert Howse postulate that, absent a global hegemon imposing its will on weaker partners, more intensive trade policy harmonization is unlikely to unfold without 'a reasonably egalitarian distribution of political influence and a common interest in overarching political objectives' – conditions which seemingly will not apply in the near future (1998, p. 10). Moreover, there is some doubt that real economic benefits flow to many people in the world as a consequence of open borders in trade and investment as accompanying the growth of liberalized markets has been a growing inequality between the rich and poor states such that 'global inequality remains at extraordinarily high levels' (UNDP, 2005, p. 33; UNDP, 2010, p. 43). If Sen had reason to say that *homo economicus* is 'close to being a social moron' (1990, p. 37) – premising social and economic policy exclusively on rational, self-interested and self-maximizing individuals – then there is equally good reason to say that a global political order premised primarily on competitive advantage is kind of moronic.

Consumer freedom

The notion of consumer freedom – the ability to consume goods and services from any place and to travel anywhere (Lash and Urry, 1994, p. 58) – best represents how comparative advantage becomes subjectivized. Consumerism offers a space of 'freedom' to those who face obstacles in most other areas of life (Hall, 1996, p. 234). Despite this emphasis on individual agency, consumers are not so much actors as, at best, 'choosers' (Appadurai, 1996, p. 42). Citizens, nevertheless, appreciate the significance of this form of self-realization (Rose, 1999, p. 164), choosing greater purchasing power over social welfare by reducing taxes and the size of public expenditure (Williams, 1961, p. 325). At the same time, public subsidies to capital are considered unquestionably beneficial (what Harvey calls 'accumulation by dispossession') (Harvey, 2000, pp. 162–3).

We should expect the legal order of economic globalization to actively constitute subjectivities, like the consumer citizen (Silbey, 2005, p. 334). Forbath, for example, shows how working-class consciousness was influenced by the possibilities and limitations offered by popular understandings of US constitutionalism in the *Lochner* era (*Lochner* v *New York* (1905)). The myopic limitations of nineteenth-century US constitutionalism silenced dissent and elicited the consent of the labour movement 'to the dominant groups' version of the natural and the good', observes Forbath (1991, p. 170). Habermasian 'constitutional patriotism' might be considered in a similar light though operating at a regional, rather than a national, scale. The integrative effect of the European liberal legal order, Habermas maintains, can be expected to generate an allegiance to a new non-national constitutional order, in which case, legality would beget legitimacy (Habermas, 1998b). Whatever the causes of the stalled European constitutional project (Walker, 2005), it probably is the case that citizens 'need to be motivated by solidarity, not merely included by law' (Calhoun, 2002, p. 275; Grimm, 2005, p. 199). Sovereign debt crises among numerous EU member states precisely have tested the limits of legal solidarity. Ulrich Beck, for this reason, insists that the '*masochism of economic self-interest* running amok amid the delights of the consumer society' lends only a 'fragile consent' to global capitalism (2005, p. 60). The ideological backbone to neoliberalism's orthodoxy – the 'culture-ideology of consumerism' (Sklair, 2002) – might not be sufficient, then, to sustain globalization's systemic features over time.

Rule of law

Even if consumer freedom cannot be expected to do the necessary legitimating work, consumerism necessitates national legal orders guaranteeing liberties of contract and property and the civil rights to participate equally in markets – legal principles associated with the idea of the 'rule of law'. These retain an independent discursive power that cannot lightly be disregarded (Thompson, 1975, p. 265). They also buttress the message that economic globalization is good for you and that, in any event, there is no alternative. Rule-of-law reforms are usually promoted within national legal institutions and structures, optimally, argue its proponents, via national constitutional change (Buchanan and Tullock, 1962). There are transnational variants that seek to restrain state regulatory capacity that, for instance, impedes the flow of trade and investment or upsets unreasonably expected returns on investment. This rule-oriented approach is 'preferred for its stability and predictability of governmental activity', writes John Jackson (1997, pp. 109–11). This partly has been achieved, he writes, with the establishment of a world trade constitution under the WTO secured, above all, by 'an intricate set of constraints imposed by a variety of "rules" or legal norms' (Jackson, 1997, p. 339). The rule of law is deployed here to cabin 'the tendency of governments to stray from the range of acceptable responses' (Kennedy, 1994, p. 78).

The critical supports to the rule of law – heightening protection for property rights and guaranteeing the obligation of contracts – call on states, as much as they do agents operating within the transnational legal frame, to actively stand with economic globalization's strategy of accumulation. They have done so with gusto. National states, acting as consensual intermediaries, would seem critical, then, to the success of the normalizing project of neoliberalism (Beck, 2005, p. 148; Gill, 2008). In which case, 'what we describe as global, including some of the most strategic functions necessary for globalization', is by definition nested within national legal systems (Sassen, 1996, p. 13).

The national is implicated in the structuration of legal economic globalization in a number of ways. First, state participation is critical to erecting the scaffolding upon which the rules and structures of economic globalization operate (Panitch, 1996). That is, states will have authored the legal regimes of pre-commitment that limit room for policy manoeuvrability. Second, states are expected to restructure domestic legal relations to augment the norms of transnational legality. The shift from public to private regulation and provision, in the realm of the family, for instance, necessitates the reorganization of legal relations that penetrate deeply into political and social life (Harvey, 2000, p. 65). The 'underside of reprivatization' in these realms, Brodie notes, 'is reregulation' (1996, p. 390; Brenner, 1999, p. 65). Accompanying judicial reforms pave the way for the 'post-structural adjustment state' where the rule of law is converted 'into just one more technique of regulation' (Santos, 2002, pp. 339, 341). The rulings of international investment tribunals, for instance, must be rendered enforceable within domestic legal structures as if they were the decisions of national courts. Lastly, states are expected to undertake legal reforms that smooth the operation of market processes generally. The UNCTAD has annually monitored national policy measures that improve the climate for foreign direct investment. Taking the 10-year period 2000–2010, it reports that, of a total 1944 regulatory changes introduced by 1417 countries, about 85 per cent had the effect of 'liberalizing' investment policy while almost 15 per cent were investment restrictive (UNCTAD, 2011, p. 94). The number of restrictive changes has increased proportionately throughout the 2000s, precipitated in part by disenchantment with rules to promote and protect foreign investment.

The transnational legal rules and institutions of economic globalization aim to normalize legally binding constraints by drawing on the normative ideas of comparative advantage, consumer freedom and the rule of law. The object is to achieve a cultural transformation of the state and the subjectivity of its citizenry in much the same way that Corrigan and Sayer describe the cultural achievements of English state formation. Yet this seemingly cannot be achieved without relying on state legal forms in both structuring these legal orders and in gaining and maintaining the consent of national publics. If alternative futures that disrupt dominant understandings are to be discouraged or forestalled, then economic globalization needs the assistance of state forms to help occupy the fields of social vision.

The operative rules and structures of transnational legality, however, suggest a great deal of ambivalence, if not outright disdain, for state partners. Perhaps this should not be surprising, given the contradictory path transnational legality is expected to navigate – both decentring national states yet relying upon state legal forms in order to maintain the high priority accorded to the rights of global capital. This suggests that the legitimation strategies embraced by the proponents of transnational legality may be weaker than thought and, perhaps, unsustainable. So as to illustrate this difficulty, in the next part I examine the take-up of neoliberal policies in Argentina, the subsequent economic meltdown, and the response of international investment tribunals in disputes between multinationals and the Republic of Argentina. I do not attempt here to evaluate the impact of these rulings on Argentinian legislators or their publics, nor do I mean to determine how successfully economic globalization at present limits the horizon of expectations in Argentina. The more modest aim is to draw the outlines of the agenda I associate with transnational legality and the cramped residual role left for states and citizens in its design.

Immobilized states?

Hardt and Negri presume a 'single' juridical model that 'structures' economic globalization 'in a unitary way' (Hardt and Negri, 2000, p. 9). The model promotes neoliberalism's values via supranational law that 'directly or indirectly...penetrate[s] and reconfigure[s] the domestic law of nation states' (Hardt and Negri, 2000, p. 17). Though neoliberalism has, at base, working ideas about the relationship between politics and markets, it also has been described as a messy, 'shape-shifting' project that is 'associated with institutional promiscuity and ideological sprawl' (Peck, 2010, p. 30). That is to say, neoliberalism has gone through differing stages and will continue to mutate as its proponents navigate through various global financial stresses. Indeed, neoliberalism has given rise to so much political volatility as to constantly require the production of new modes of regulation (Sawyer, 2004, p. 93; Zamosc, 2004, p. 132).

Divesting Argentina

There is perhaps no better example of this promiscuity than the variety of regulatory innovations taken up by Argentina resulting in one of the most dramatic economic collapses in recent history. Described as the 'poster-child of globalization, Latin style' (Bello, 2005, p. 123) and an 'A-plus student of the IMF' (Stiglitz, 2002b), Argentina enthusiastically followed directives issuing out of Washington and the IMF in pursuit of the developmental path promoted by international financial institutions (Blustein, 2005, p. 23). It is true that the IMF did not actively promote one of the main pillars of Argentina's economic transformation: the 1991 convertibility plan pegging the Argentinian peso to the US dollar at an exchange rate of one-to-one. If the IMF initially 'expressed misgivings' about Argentina's currency board, it soon thereafter joined in the chorus of support (IMF, 2003, pp. 8, 66). After years of hyperinflation, convertibility halted the printing of money and stabilized prices, sparking a four-year period of impressive economic growth. This was the first in a series of 'regime shifts' (IMF, 1998, p. 4) that would lead the country down the path to economic ruin. Other 'regime shifts', enthusiastically described by the IMF in a 1998 staff report, were trade reforms (eliminating export tariffs and non-tariff barriers to trade), deregulation (i.e. abolishing regulatory and marketing boards), privatization (of 90 per cent of all state-owned enterprises yielding about US$20 billion in revenue) and financial system reform (banking deregulation and accelerated foreign ownership) (IMF, 1998, pp. 5–6). Argentina regrettably was a laggard in labour market reform, observed IMF staff (IMF, 1998, p. 7). State authority effectively was conscripted, nonetheless, so as to enable these regime shifts to occur.

Divestiture of key state assets particularly required ongoing state complicity. According to the prevailing wisdom, privatization is necessary to reduce public expenditure, increase foreign investment, produce economic efficiencies and enhance technology transfers (Schneiderman, 2000, p. 88). The bulk of Argentinian state enterprises touching on almost every important sector in the economy, including airlines, electricity, highways, natural gas and telecommunications, were sold in short order, without public consultation, mostly to foreign investors (Teubal, 2004, p. 181). Though generating a windfall to pay down public debt, these processes lacked transparency, were tainted with corruption and often resulted in sales of assets below market value (Blustein, 2005, pp. 24–5; Cooney, 2007, p. 19).

The process resulting in the privatization of water and sewerage services for metropolitan Buenos Aires was emblematic of the difficulties associated with the 'privatization spree' (Teubal, 2004, p. 182). Rates charged by the state-run Obras Sanitarias de la Nacion, whose operating system had fallen into serious disrepair, were increased five times in the year leading up to the bidding process. This resulted in a 62 per cent price increase, not inclusive of an 18 per cent value-added tax (Solanes, 2006, p. 154). The concession contract then would be awarded to any company that offered the largest tariff reduction in light of the new higher base-line tariff. In the case of Aguas Argentina, part of a consortium led by the French-based multinational water companies Suez and Vivendi, it was proposed that water tariffs decline by 26.9 per cent in the first ten-year period, resulting in the awarding of a contract for a term of 30 years (Loftus and McDonald, 2001, p. 185). Though the World Bank praised the bidding process as evidence of how privatization 'has been effective in reducing costs' (Crampes and Estache, 1996), and analysts for the Inter-American Development Bank pointed to this experience as a model for 'managing' consumer responses to water privatization (Wenyon and Jenne, 1999, pp. 197–8), this patently was a 'manufactured' process of price reduction (Loftus and McDonald, 2001, p. 190). After the initial tariff reduction, water rates rose significantly, with the government's co-operation (Schneier-Madanes, 2001, p. 50; Cassarin et al., 2007, p. 238). This turned out to be inconsistent with the terms of the concession contract: price increases were, in fact, banned during the first ten years (Solanes, 2006, p. 159). Increases were also well beyond the ability of poor people to pay, amounting to about 23 per cent of their monthly wages (Cassarin et al., 2007, pp. 239, 241). The investor provided little new inward capital: only a modest 2.6 per cent of total funding between 1993 and 2001 (Castro, 2008, p. 68). This experience, common to water privatization contracts around the world, belies one of the principal claims of its promoters that privatization attracts fresh private investment (ibid.).

Not only was this a contract for the world's largest water concession, it was also one of the world's most profitable, according to *The Economist*, approaching a 40 per cent rate of return (Artana et al., 1998, p. 21). If the concessionaire succeeded in connecting new users to its water service, it severely underperformed in connecting existing users to city sewers. In both cases, the poorer districts of Buenos Aires were left out. According to Cassarin et al., there was a statistically significant relationship between high levels of poverty and unfulfilled water targets (Cassarin et al., 2007, p. 238). Compliance with targets was more likely to be highest in those districts where the costs of expansion were low and 'economic well-being of users offered the most attractive income stream' (ibid.). Unhappy with the rate of progress, the municipal government asked Aguas Argentina to accelerate expansion ahead of schedule and to expand connections beyond the original plan. Rather than cross-subsidizing new connections or injecting new capital, the company preferred further rate increases and borrowing, incurring indebtedness in excess of that contemplated in the concession contract (Cassarin et al., 2007, p. 245).

The extensive state activity in this sector is emblematic of what Morgan calls 'global water welfarism', where 'public aid supplements the private investment of multinational corporations' (Morgan, 2004, p. 11). This represents just the sort of state activism that is intended to render neoliberalism sustainable.

Though the subsequent downturn of the Argentinian economy was sparked by financial instability in Russia and then in Brazil, high foreign indebtedness, increasing capital outflows and currency inflexibility meant that few policy options were available. A combination of 'bad luck', slow fiscal adjustment and 'enormous political uncertainty' intensified the country's economic vulnerability (Powell, 2002, p. 2). Once the economic depression got under way in 1999–2000, 'there was no easy way out', the IMF later observed. Terminating convertibility might have eased the economic shock that would later be felt but this, the IMF surmised, would not have been sufficient without more fiscal discipline in regard to the public debt. Even '[g]reater structural conditionality', an IMF policy review concluded, 'would have been less damaging to the Fund's credibility' (IMF, 2003, p. 66).

The Argentinian economy became unglued as the trade deficit, capital outflows and unemployment shot up and stock prices plunged. Protestors took to the streets after the government, by decree, froze bank deposits and prohibited cash withdrawals of more than US/Arg.$250 per week (labelled the *corralito* or 'little fence'). Thirty civilians died after one day of riots in December 2001. Also that month, Argentina defaulted on its sovereign debt by announcing deferral of over US$100 billion of external bond debt that was owed to both domestic and foreign creditors. In January 2002, Argentina enacted Emergency Law No 25.561, pulling the plug on convertibility, unpegging the peso to the dollar ('pesification'), resulting in sovereign debt default and an all-around meltdown of the Argentinian economy. By decree, all bank deposits were 'pesified', resulting in an unprecedented wave of 210,188 *amaparos* (injunctions) filed with Argentinian federal courts (Spector, 2008, p. 139). With the collapse of the peso, thousands were thrown out of work and foreign investors lost hope of reaping high returns on their investments which had been guaranteed in the heyday of privatization. Those at the bottom suffered the most: the population living in 'extreme poverty' more than tripled between 2000 and 2003 (UNDP, 2005, p. 36). In *The Economist's* assessment, this was 'an economic collapse to match the Great Depression of the 1930s' (Emmott, 2003).

A 'powerful weapon'

As it was divesting the state of assets in the 1990s, Argentina signed 57 BITs with leading capital-exporting states, including one with the US in 1991 (*Suez and Others v Argentina* (2010), para. 29). The BIT tracked closely the 1987 US model investment treaty and so promoted high standards of protection intended to vindicate the rights of US-based investors. This signalled the end of an era for Argentina, observe Alvarez and Khamsi. Despites its 'penchant for declaring national emergencies', Argentina could no longer escape liability owed to foreign investors in the wake of any future economic crisis (Alvarez and Khamsi, 2009, p. 415; *Suez* (2010), para. 234). Lawyers awakened to the possibility that BITs could be a 'powerful weapon' against the Republic of Argentina as investors sought to recoup some of the losses suffered as a consequence of the economic collapse (Peterson, 2002, p. 6). Holding Argentina fast to these commitments proved to be the preferred strategy for foreign investors who were given no special regard in its wake. From this angle, foreign firms should not have been expected to share in the burden of the economic crisis, instead, they should have expected a compensation windfall of sunk costs and lost profits in the depression's wake (Argentine Republic, 2005, paras 20–1). As Stephen Gill describes this phase of economic globalization, it would be a case of 'oligopoly and protection for the strong and a socialization of their risks, market discipline for the weak' (Gill, 2008, p. 131).

At one point, there were 42 cases filed before the dispute resolution arm of the World Bank, ICSID, against the Republic of Argentina based on BITs' legal disciplines. There are, at present, about 18 disputes still pending, the others having been settled, resolved, or suspended (Embassy of Argentina, 2011). These actions were launched by some very large multinational corporations based on contracts for the provision of water and sewerage services, gas or oil production and transmission, information services, telecommunications and electricity. In most of these cases, the companies contended that the collapse in the value of their holdings in privatized Argentinian utilities were triggered by Argentina's use of fiscal emergency measures in the wake of the collapse of the peso. They claimed that these measures amounted either to the indirect expropriation of their investment interests or the denial of 'fair and equitable treatment', entitling them in either case to a large damage awards.

In contemporary times, international arbitration is the preferred mechanism for the resolution of these sorts of legal disputes. Tripartite arbitral panels, established under the auspices of ICSID or another such facility, operating under ICSID rules or those prescribed by the United Nations Commission on International Trade Law (UNCITRAL), set up shop in one of a number of global venues (i.e. Washington, Geneva, or Paris), with one neutral chair and two sides-persons appointed by the parties to the dispute. Drawn from a narrow field of trade law specialists (Sornarajah, 1997), panels are moving away from resolving discrete commercial problems with reference to *lex mercatoria* to answering broader public policy questions ordinarily associated with the field of politics (Zumbansen, 2002; Van Harten, 2007). Indeed, the capacity of state action in a wide array of policy fields is being brought into question in these disputes – precisely the aim of the investment rules regime, its supporters would admit (Vandevelde, 1998).

Taking up Polanyian measures for societal self-protection in the wake of a severe fiscal crisis appears to cut against the grain of transnational legality.

One should not presume, however, that the Argentinian state was repudiating fully globalization's legal order. Argentina, instead, energetically challenged the jurisdictional bases of each claim. At every step in the various proceedings, the state argued that creditors were obliged to first seek remedies under Argentinian law and in Argentinian courts and not in global arbitration centres relying upon BIT rights. It was local law that applied to such privatized enterprises and not non-local 'minimum standards of justice' guaranteed to investors in these treaties. This happened to be the claim articulated by Argentinian jurist Carlos Calvo in the late nineteenth century. Calvo argued that the countries of Latin America were entitled to the same degree of respect for their internal sovereignty, as were the US and the countries of Europe (Calvo, 1887, p. 266). Among Calvo's precepts was the proposition that states should be free, within reason, from interference in the conduct of their domestic policy. From this, he could argue that foreign nationals could not lay claim to greater protection in their disputes with sovereign states than the citizens of these same countries. The arbitration panels established to resolve these disputes have, for the most part, rejected Argentina's arguments.

The decision of the panel in the *CMS* case exemplifies the manner in which these disputes would be resolved (*CMS Gas Transmission Company v República Argentina* (2007)).[7] The case also illustrates how economic globalization's legal order is intended to check national legislative action in regard to markets, despite the fact that national states continue to provide critical legitimating supports to the global project. CMS initially participated in the 1995 privatization of the public company Transportada de Gas del Norte (TGN), purchasing almost 30 per cent of the company's shares (para. 58). Tariffs collected by the company were to be recouped in US dollars, adjusted periodically, and converted into pesos at the time of billing (paras 58, 85). The economic crisis precipitated a variety of measures for societal self-protection – in the case of natural gas, this involved a temporary suspension of prices and then freezing of profits converted into dollars. The Argentine government by emergency decree in 2001, as we have already seen, limited the capacity to withdraw funds from bank deposits, abolished dollarization and, because of devaluation of the peso, refused to convert tariffs into US dollars (para. 66). As the Republic of Argentina's legal brief explains things, the redenomination of all contracts into pesos 'ensured that all participants in the economy [in the wake of economic collapse] would share the necessary burden collectively' (Argentine Republic, 2005, para. 20).

CMS, however, together with many other foreign investors was not willing to share in this burden and so, in July 2001, filed a dispute under ICSID

---

7   Further references are to the paragraphs in this decision.

auspices invoking the 1991 US–Argentina BIT. The company claimed that it had a guaranteed rate of return on its investment, regardless of the financial hardships being experienced by Argentinians and the fiscal crisis experienced by the state. On the basis of this reliance expectation, CMS had invested almost US$175 million in the purchase of shares in TGN (para. 68). Having reneged on its commitment, the Argentinian government's action precipitated a 92 per cent drop in the value of CMS shares. This, the company claimed, amounted to the indirect expropriation of the company's assets without compensation and, additionally, a failure to comply with the standard of 'fair and equitable treatment' mandated under the treaty (para. 88). The government responded with a variety of arguments – including that the company received a reasonable rate of return in the face of a bona fide emergency – not all of which will be canvassed here. Central to the Argentinian defence, however, were arguments defending the usual capacity of states and citizens to change policy direction: that government's should be 'free to change such policies' in order to take into account 'needs of social importance' (paras 91–3). Argentina, in other words, should be free to take Polanyian measures for societal self-protection – it was free to revise its economic policies in order to protect citizens from the 'relentlessness of the market' (Rodrik, 1997, p. 36) – and that no public utilities licence or BIT could be read as freezing that regulatory environment. This particularly should be the case where the economic harm suffered by the vast majority of Argentinian citizens was exacerbated by adhering to IMF directives (Stiglitz, 2002b).

Advancing an argument made in a law review article by professor and then Justice Minister Horacio Rosatti (2003), Argentina argued (though not very forcefully) that the BIT and the ICSID system of arbitration were inconsistent with Argentinian constitutional commitments to basic human rights (paras 114, 119). Human rights, the state argued, were compromised by transnational commitments to guaranteed profits. The tribunal rejected the constitutional submission based upon the tribunal's own reading of the Argentinian Constitution. First, provisions in the constitution assert the primacy of treaties under Argentinian law. Moreover, the constitution 'carefully protects the right to property, just as the treaties on human rights do' (paras 121, 239).

In so doing, the tribunal weighed in on a debate then occurring at the highest levels of the Argentinian judiciary. It might reasonably have been anticipated, based on then settled constitutional law, that the mass of *amparo* filings by Argentinians, challenging both the *corralito* and pesification, would be unsuccessful. The Argentinian Supreme Court, however, chose to depart significantly from previous jurisprudence by ruling in *Smith* (*Smith, Carlos Antonio v PEN/medidas cautelares* (2002)) (affirmed again in *Provincia de San Luis v Estado Nacional/amparo* (2003)), that the emergency measures amounted to a 'flagrant violation' of constitutional property rights (Spector, 2008, p. 140).

This constitutional violation by emergency decree has been likened to the resurrection of a vested rights doctrine that is commonly associated with the *Lochner* era in the late nineteenth-century US. It amounted to a repudiation of the court's settled doctrine that had validated, according to Spector, 'the most diverse invasions of private property and contractual freedom' (2008, p. 141). Spector explains the court's turn pejoratively as being 'guided mainly by political factors' (2008, p. 141). A majority of the court finally reverted to its earlier doctrine in *Bustos* (*Bustos, Alberto Roque v Estadio Nacionale/amparo* (2004)), describing its turn in *Smith* as an 'unfortunate' decision. It has since maintained this course (Spector, 2008, pp. 142–3). Weighing into this debate on Argentina's Supreme Court about the constitutionality of the emergency decree, the tribunal preferred the ruling by the discredited court in *Smith* and *Provincia de San Luis* (*CMS Gas* (2005), para. 216). Acknowledging reversion to the earlier doctrine in *Bustos*, the tribunal declared that *Bustos* 'does not over-rule other decisions of the Supreme Court' (*CMS Gas* (2005), para. 215). In any event, the dispute did not affect fundamental human rights, the tribunal concluded, without any further explanation (paras 121, 203).

Having found constitutional harmony, the panel moved on to the company's claims. The tribunal found no indirect or regulatory expropriation of the company's assets (paras 259–63) as CMS was still in control of its invest-ment (para. 263). Argentina, however, had denied the company fair and equitable treatment. The company, after all, had invested in Argentina on the basis that the state would guarantee the stability of its investment interest (para. 134). The panel concluded that the Argentinian programme of priva-tization was 'successful' – over US$10 billion was raised – precisely because the state offered commitments in a manner that would not allow 'for their reversal within a few years' (para. 138). Because the licence was in the nature of a 'guarantee', the state was obliged to honour this commitment (para. 161). Freezing and then reducing the rate of return via pesification was not in keeping with this form of commitment through licensing. The state was ordered to pay CMS US$133.2 million.

Argentina subsequently filed an application for annulment of this award under an extraordinary procedure available at the World Bank to set aside ICSID panel rulings (Argentine Republic, 2005). The application was denied by the ICSID Annulment Committee, though it did find errors in the tribunal's decision, including a mix-up of the treaty defence of necessity and the defence available under customary international law (*CMS Gas* (2007), paras 130–4). This, however, did not amount to a 'manifest excess of power' and so did not provide grounds for annulment under the ICSID Convention (*CMS Gas* (2007), para. 36). Argentina has not fared much better in the other cases aris-ing out of the 2001 financial crisis. Though there has been some variation as regards the defence of necessity and calculation of damages (e.g. *LG&E Energy*

Corporation v Argentine Republic (2006); *Enron Corporation and Ponderosa Assets v Argentina* (2007)), there has been virtual unanimity that Argentina breached the requirement of fair and equitable treatment by diminishing expected rates of return for investors (Alvarez and Khamsi, 2009; Schneiderman, 2010a).

What of the concession awarded to the consortium led by French-based Suez and Vivendi for the delivery of water and sewerage services to the denizens of greater Buenos Aires? That investment, too, collapsed in the aftermath of the economic crisis, precipitating an investment dispute under French, Spanish and UK BITs signed with Argentina in the early 1990s. Once, again, the investment tribunal sided with the investor, finding that Argentina had been denied fair and equitable treatment (*Suez* (2010)). The tribunal seemed oblivious to the investment's early profitability:

> As is customary in long-term concessions implying substantial investments in early years, the Concession's investment requirements exceeded the amounts that might be gained immediately from tariff revenues; consequently, the Concessionaire sought loans from local and international sources, primarily from multilateral lending agencies whose loans were denominated and payable in U.S. dollars (*Suez* (2010), para. 35; also para. 124).

Nor would the tribunal accept that the concessionaire had offered an unrealistically low bid in order to secure the concession (*Suez* (2010), para. 40). Instead, the tribunal considered the investor to have acted entirely reasonably, even as it sought tariff increases just as the Argentinian economy plunged into nosedive. In March 2001, by which time the economy was experiencing some difficulty, again in January 2002, by which time the economy's downward trajectory seemed unstoppable, and again in March 2002 and December 2002, tariff adjustments were sought as Aguas Argentina began to suffer significant losses (*Suez* (2010), paras 42–50). These requests were unreasonably refused, the tribunal ruled, while Argentina 'abruptly' terminated the concession in March 2006 (*Suez* (2010), para. 146). Having failed to live up to the terms of the 30-year concession contract, Argentina undermined the investor's 'legitimate expectations'. This was a legal framework upon which the investors' specifically had relied and, the tribunal was certain that 'without such belief in the reliability and stability of the legal framework the Claimants – indeed no investor – would ever have agreed to invest in the water and sewage system of Buenos Aires' (para. 231). Moreover, Argentina could have adopted 'more flexible means' in responding to the requests for tariff increases, such as relieving the concessionaire of further investment commitments, passing on tariff increases to consumers who could pay, and having governmental bodies pay overdue tariffs to the concessionaire (*Suez* (2010), para. 235). To have done otherwise was an abuse of regulatory discretion (*Suez* (2010), para. 237). Yet

Argentinians experienced a serious decline in household income after May 2001 and a subsequent 'collapse' after October 2001, ranging from 23 per cent to 41 per cent (Corbacho et al., 2003, pp. 12, 32). Fifty-four per cent of the population was living below the poverty line (Mortimore and Stanley, 2006, p. 25). By the end of 2005 this number remained at a high of about 31 per cent despite strong gross domestic product growth (Galiani et al., 2008, p. 30). The tribunal nowhere addressed the proportion of the paying population of Buenos Aires that could have offset these losses. The tribunal also takes for granted that it was more appropriate, in the face of a US$100 billion sovereign default, for the state to give priority to investors, by requiring them to pay overdue tariffs, than addressing other economic priorities, such as assisting economically desperate Argentinians. IMF staff admitted, after all, that it was difficult even for non-poor households to have managed the economic shocks in Argentina. '[S]ocial intervention' – including public works programs and direct transfers – is "useful"', IMF staffers frankly admitted, 'to assist households during macroeconomic crises' (Corbacho et al., 2003, pp. 27, 33).[8] It simply was beyond the capacity of the tribunal to acknowledge even the possibility of reversing the investment law regime's order of priority.

Fundamental contradictions

One gets the sense that these tribunals believed that Argentina not only contributed to its own demise, it actually benefited from its aggressive embrace of market disciplines (Blustein, 2005, p. 25) – it was, in Birdsall's contemptuous characterization, the 'spoiled child of the Washington Consensus' (Birdsall, 2002, p. 3). Moreover, its politicians and citizens were not 'wholly innocent' victims in setting the country's economy on a collision course, though, Blustein notes, they got plenty of help from the IMF and the US Treasury Board (2005, p. 6). In so far as Argentina acted imprudently, in tying the peso to the US dollar, for instance, then it was expected that the state should pay for the consequential economic harm suffered by foreign investors. Following the logic of the tribunals' rulings, investment treaties have the effect of freezing regulatory environments when new policy initiatives have an inordinate negative impact on investment interests. Stable and predictable rates of return – synonymous, for these tribunals, with the guarantee of fair and equitable treatment (*CMS Gas* (2005), paras 266–84) – mandate state

---

8 As did other tribunals, the *Suez* panel concluded that Argentina could not take advantage of the customary international law defence of necessity (there was no treaty defence for the tribunal to consider as in the 1991 US BIT). Because it could have taken less drastic measures and also contributed 'substantially' to the circumstances giving rise to the crisis, two of the requisite four conditions for invoking the customary international law defence had not been satisfactorily proven (*Suez* (2010), paras 260, 64).

immobilization in certain sectors. There would be no concomitant stability and predictability granted to the citizens of Argentina, however. Following many of the edicts laid down by the 'Washington consensus' and directly benefiting companies like CMS, LG&E, Enron and Suez that participated in the programme of denationalization (each of whom have successfully sued for damages), Argentinians were expected to pay for these missteps long into the future despite constitutional commitments to the contrary. Though foreign investors insist on equal treatment with citizens (represented by the BIT standard of 'national treatment'), this is tolerated only so long as treatment does not fall below certain minimum levels, at which point investors cannot be expected to share in the burden of a failed economic experiment – one, albeit, that companies like CMS et al. would have actively endorsed.

The cases illustrate the ways in which the rules and institutions of economic globalization are intended to place limits on the capacity of states to solve redistributive problems. According to the logic of *CMS*, foreign investors are to be granted priority in the wake of the financial collapse of the state; citizens cannot expect to receive similar solicitude. Not only are rates of return guaranteed, citizens and their states are made fiscally responsible for these prior commitments – in *CMS*, to the tune of US$133.2 million – irrespective of fiscal capacity. The cases illustrate the cramped role to which states are confined when they act to protect citizens from the deleterious effects of markets, even when they act in the advancement of the collective project represented by the state's constitutional order.

States, moreover, are expected to give due solicitude to and immediate enforcement of these awards. According to Article 53 of the 1966 ICSID Convention, awards are 'binding on the parties' and cannot be the subject of any appeal outside of the ICSID system. States 'shall abide by and comply with the terms of the award' and, according to Article 54, shall 'enforce the pecuniary obligations imposed by that award within its territories as if were a final judgment of the court of that state'. If the outstanding disputes at ICSID and elsewhere against the Republic of Argentina are resolved in favour of multinational companies, there simply is no way that Argentina could compensate all of these firms for future lost profits. Argentina, for this reason, has so far refused to pay out on any of these awards, claiming that in order to be a final award of an Argentine court, it must comply with certain 'administrative procedures' (Inside US Trade, 2011).

Despite the strict legal obligations flowing out of the investment rules regime, however, the system is unlikely to collapse. Rather, Argentina is probably holding out hope that it can negotiate with foreign investors as it did with foreign bondholders in the wake of its debt crisis. In 2005, 76 per cent of Argentine bondholders agreed to take an unprecedented 'hair cut', reducing to approximately 70 per cent monies owed with a lengthened maturity date (Helleiner, 2005, p. 959; Mortimore and Stanley, 2006, p. 19). In 2010, a second set of bondholders exchanged debt, resulting in over 90 per cent acceptance. Unresolved debt claims against Argentina, however, can now be channelled via ICSID, according to the tribunal decision in *Abaclat* (*Abaclat and Others v Argentina* (2011)), upsetting expectations about negotiated settlements. Some 180,000 bondholders are entitled to proceed with their claims alleging expropriation, discrimination and denial of fair and equitable treatment (among other things), under an Italian–Argentine BIT so long as they hold the requisite Italian nationality at the relevant time (para. 422). The *Abaclat* tribunal concluded that it is capable of responding to a mass claim of this sort, though unprecedented in the annals of investment arbitration (para. 491). Whatever leverage Argentina had against bondholder indebtedness now will have been erased by the disciplines of transnational legality.

* * *

Though transnational capital's desire for profits seems insatiable, there are limits to what can be extracted from states and their populaces. The overriding objective, perhaps, is the cultural one: to lower citizens' expectations of state capacity. Governments are expected to be accountable first and foremost to investors and not to their citizens (Gill, 2003, p. 131). The investment rules regime, in this way, aims to establish thresholds of tolerable behaviour promoting a culture of markets seemingly freed from the control of politics. Local policy initiatives are expected to conform to this culture of limited and constrained government and any public that rebukes the regime's precepts can anticipate punishment with an award of damages in the range of tens to hundreds of millions of dollars. This is so because of the fact that the investment rules regime is critically reliant on stable national legal orders to protect fixed and immovable investment interests. At the same time, national states are expected to take the difficult and contradictory path of succumbing to economic globalization's legal edicts while resisting demands for non-market-based solutions to contemporary social problems. This seems a shaky foundation for a sustainable legal order with pretensions of globality.

All of which seems far removed from the diagnosis Hardt and Negri offer of the global scene. States largely are expunged from this arena. Having installed the apparatuses of transnational law, states, they maintain, have receded into the background. By rendering states' inconsequential to the maintenance of transnational legal order, Hardt and Negri contribute to the fog that is globalization where what is made material by hard law is rendered non-national and abstract. By closing off pressure points for change, they help to immeasurably prolong – until such time as the multitude rises up and seizes the machinery of empire – an unjustifiable form of transnational legal domination.

2
Teubner and System Liberation

Polanyi famously maintained that markets are always embedded within society, that is, markets are not self-regulating but the product of political instrumentalities (Polanyi, 1944/2001, p. 60; Dale, 2010, p. 193). Eighteenth and nineteenth-century liberal economists sought to inverse this relationship, rendering politics subordinate to the logic of markets. If early liberalism was about having the economy act as an internal check on government, twentieth-century formulations were about the marketization of all relations, including those of government, a case of disembededness running amok, so to speak (Foucault, 2008; Tribe, 2009, p. 694). This is the point of view promoted by neoliberal thinking and continues, to this day, to shape public policy in many states around the world. This is despite Polanyi's insistence that disembedded markets are an impossibility; a 'stark' and unrealistic 'utopia' (Polanyi, 1944/2001, p. 3).

According to prevailing wisdom, it is not enough merely to insist that states privatize public enterprise, social security and the provision of basic necessities such as water – IMF 'regime shifts' associated with the 'Washington consensus'. Instead, transnational legal norms are structured to ensure that states behave as would private-economic actors. States are expected to mimic rational economic behaviour – they should manage their affairs in ways that give priority to commercial relations and maximize private wealth accumulation. Only those measures that ensure the 'self-regulation of the market' will be countenanced (Polanyi, 1944/2001, p. 72) – public policy is expected to function merely as an adjunct to the exigencies of the economy. Doing anything other than facilitating market rationality is pejoratively characterized as 'political' (Chang, 2002). This miserly view of the state is precisely the one advanced by principles of international investment law that I discuss in part two below, 'Systemic effects'.

Systems theory takes a somewhat different view of the economy than does the Polanyian account. Markets are not so much embedded as a distinctive organizational form. Systems, according to Luhmann, are self-referential, or autopoietic, forms that both create and maintain differences from the environment in which other systems operate (Luhmann, 1995, p. 17). The rise of various sub-systems corresponds to the increasing complexity of societies and their division into functionally differentiated organisms (Teubner, 1983, p. 270) – law, politics, science, religion, education and economy develop systemic properties which are internal to the logic and rationality of each sub-system (Luhmann, 1989). Such proliferation inevitably gives rise to conflict. Sub-systems can be made aware of the 'perturbations' and 'irritations' emanating from other sub-systems and can selectively choose to respond to such noise. Though sub-systems police their own boundaries, they are, in Luhmann's felicitous phrasing, 'normatively closed but cognitively open' to these signals (Luhmann, 1992, p. 1427).

The economy is one such autonomous sub-system that operates independently – it is 'a rigorously closed, circular, self-referentially constituted system' (Luhmann, 1989, p. 52). Though independent, the economic sub-system communicates on an ongoing basis with the political system within the constitutional systems of national states via a continuous operation of 'structural coupling' (1992, p. 1432). As a consequence, the economic system is not free to maximize its own logic within national states. Instead, it is continually subject to the threat of steering by political systems. Since politics has not been able to keep up with markets, there is no such structural coupling in operation beyond the confines of states. The global 'economy cannot be controlled politically', Luhmann emphatically declared (2004, p. 480).

Building on Luhmann's account, Teubner situates these considerations within the global legal context, arguing that there have arisen multiple constitutional orders 'without' the state (Teubner, 1997a; Teubner, 2012). Teubner has in mind international organizations, multinational enterprises, international trade unions and non-governmental organizations that, cumulatively, represent the 'constitutionalization of a multiplicity of autonomous sub-systems of world society' (2004, pp. 6, 8). This diagnosis complements well recently expressed concerns about the 'fragmentation' of international law (ILC, 2006): that discrete specialized regimes within international law have arisen each giving expression to their own embedded preferences (Koskenniemi and Leino, 2002; Koskenniemi, 2007). Each of these societal constitutional orders operates independently of the other but, in the pursuit of their own distinctive purposes, potentially is on a collision course with other operative sub-systems. The appropriate response to these sorts of collisions, Teubner maintains, is to have sub-systems develop responses on terms most consistent with the internal logic of the sub-system.

As differing autonomous legal orders collide with the normative orders of states, sub-systems effectively can reward and punish states according to the sub-system's own exigencies. Though it remains a possibility, it is not appropriate for states to respond by interfering or destroying the normative universe within which sub-systems, like international investment law, operate (Teubner, 1997a, pp. 4, 22). At best, what can be hoped for is 'weak normative compatibility' (Fischer-Lescano and Teubner, 2004, p. 1004) – a tug of war between sub-systems and states – achieved by the reflexive internalization of each regime's system effects.

Such an approach significantly dampens possibilities for resistance. It ensures that transnational legal orders remain autonomous, self-regulating and mostly resistant to political pressure. Indeed, the state is sidelined, if not largely absent, from this account of transnational legality. There are reasons to worry, then, about the normative implications of systems theory in a global context. If transnational legality facilitates the marketization of all aspects of collective life such that states are expected to mimic the behaviour of market actors, however much Teubner might find the single-minded logistics of the market abhorrent, there are few resources in his account to minimize, much less eradicate, these effects. I attend to these and other difficulties associated with a systems-theoretic approach in part one of the chapter ('Systems emancipated') before turning, in part two (Systemic effects'), to a disturbing aspect of international investment law's systemic effects.

Systems emancipated

The principal claim advanced by systems theory is that, as society has become more complex and functionally differentiated, autonomous sub-systems have emerged to perform distinct social functions. These are self-referential or autopoietic sub-systems: systems police their own boundaries on their own terms (Luhmann, 1995, p. 17). As sub-systems pursue their own institutionalized rationalities, they invariably will run up against the operating logic of other sub-systems. This causes 'irritations' and 'perturbations' that likely can be observed by the agitating sub-system. This is because sub-systems are open to 'communications' from other sub-systems. Autopoietic sub-systems can respond to this noise, however, only with reference to their own operating elements (or media of communication) rather than those of other (outside) competing sub-systems (Teubner, 1988, p. 3; Luhmann, 2004, pp. 80–1). These perturbations then are capable of being internalized according to the language and logic of the sub-system causing negative external effects. This is unlike the 'structural coupling' between law and politics within national states, which has the effect of channelling influences between these two sub-systems on an ongoing basis (Luhmann, 2004, p. 382). Without the benefit of structural coupling, sub-systems are not open to the direct influence of other operating sub-systems. Instead, they can listen and adapt, if they so choose, in ways consistent with the purposes and in the language of the listening sub-system. Systems, for this reason, are normatively closed but cognitively open (Luhmann, 1992, p. 1427; 2004, p. 110).

Teubner's version of 'societal constitutionalism' moves the discussion up one level, describing the proliferation of autonomous legal orders on a global plane. Various transnational actors are authors in the construction of societal constitutions, what[s] described as a constitutionalization of separate global sub-systems without the state (Teubner, 2004, pp. 8, 15). Drawing, for instance, on the transnational commercial law of *lex mercatoria* (customary law developed by commercial arbitration and practice), Teubner theorizes the provocative claim that a 'global law' has developed in 'relative insulation' from (or 'without') the state (Teubner, 1997a, p. 3), a claim that attracted Hardt and Negri to Teubner's systems-inspired account of globalization discussed in Chapter 1. These sectoral constitutions have been developing for a long time (2011a, p. 212) 'in underground evolutionary processes' (2004, p. 18). They are now beginning to have a presence on a global scale, though 'invisible to the naked eye', due to the increasing complexity and functional differentiation of society on multiple scales (ibid.).

The constitutive rules developed autonomously by these various societal actors are, however, increasingly coming into conflict. What has sometimes been described (benignly) as 'global legal pluralism' is actually 'the expression of deep contradiction between colliding sectors of a global society' (Fisher-Lescano and Teubner, 2004, p. 1004). It is only a matter of time, writes Teubner, before liberated energies of autopoieitic systems 'have destructive consequences of such proportions, that the resulting societal conflicts push for drastic change of constitutional politics' (2011a, p. 213). Echoing Polanyi's idea of double movement (Polanyi, 1944/2001, pp. 138–9), Teubner envisages 'counter-movements...now appearing which form limitative rules, in order to countervail self-destructive tendencies and to limit damage to social, human and natural environments' (2011a, p. 213; 2011b, p. 23; 2012, p. 78). The task today is to 'identify the real structures of the existing global constitutionalism, to criticise its shortcomings and to formulate realistic proposals for limitative rules' (Teubner, 2011a, p. 214; 2012, p. v). This is a strategy of devising 'internal self-limitations' to sub-systems, inhibiting their compulsion to growth (Teubner, 2011b, p. 13). They can then suitably correspond to, and so do less damage to, their social environments (Teubner, 1983, p. 273).

As did Luhmann, Teubner considers it futile to attempt to unify fragmented operative social systems. 'Centralized social integration is effectively ruled out today', he observes (1983, p. 272). This is because the 'structural coupling' between law and politics under the supervision of national constitutional orders now 'ha[s] no correspondence on the level of world society' (Teubner, 1997a, p. 6 quoting Luhmann, 2004, pp. 487–8).

It is worth pausing to underscore here that Teubner's prescriptive account does not include doing away with any of these fragments of constitutionalism, rather, the impulse is reformative: it is not about building up something new, but 'transform[ing] what is an already existing constitutional order' (2011a, p. 214; cf. Frankenberg, 1992). The constitutional plurality of transnational legality offers an 'opportunity' to 'maintain...even increase...conflict', Teubner insists (Teubner, 1997b, p. 158). The overriding consideration is to render functional transnational regimes 'sustainable' in the long run (Teubner, 2012, p. 173). Luhmann offers that there is 'no conservative bias in such a theory'. He nevertheless admits that there is 'no choice' but to have systems maintain an equilibrium of 'dynamic stability' (1992, pp. 140–1).

Having described some of the key elements of a systems-theoretic account, we can now assess how this account links up to the regime of international investment law. First, it could be said that the account complements well the commonsense view of many actors operating within the field of international investment law. The regime appears to be an autonomous, norm-producing sub-system that is focused principally on its own self-production and, in this way, appears normatively closed but cognitively open. The regime is not entirely closed to external influences (the various instances of resistance I describe in this book suggest that there is a fair amount of 'noise' being produced), only that, in so far as the regime is responsive to its own short-comings, those responses will be determined by the regime's own principal players (namely, lawyers, arbitrators and academics). These actors will typically respond in accordance with the regime's own embedded preferences employing the regime's terminology and, typically, not according to the logic of competing sub-systems, such as international environmental or human rights law. So, as a descriptive matter, a systems-theoretic account corresponds well to the perceived functioning of international investment law.

It cannot be said, however, that the regime is uncoupled from the state and politics. We should qualify the immediately preceding paragraph by acknowledging that states that are party to investment treaties, generating the constitutional architecture for the regime's operations, shaping the sub-system's operations by negotiating specific treaty text and modifying those texts, or, as in the case of the North American Free Trade Agreement's (NAFTA) Free Trade Commission (FTC) (an interstate cabinet-level body), issuing interpretive directives (Roberts, 2010). Even here, however, state influence in the ongoing operations of the system is limited. Though investment treaties exhibit some variance (Muchlinski, 2011), and despite their vaunted flexibility (Schneiderman, 2009), there remain a standard set of core constraints that almost every investment treaty will exhibit. Nor have interpretive notes, such as those issuing out of the NAFTA FTC, proven entirely effective in taming the exercise of arbitral discretion. Indeed, in the case of an interpretive note intended to narrow the scope of the minimum standard of treatment requirement to that provided under customary international law, NAFTA tribunals have been resistant to being so confined (*Mondev International Ltd v United States* (2002), para. 124; *Pope & Talbot v Government of Canada* (2002), para. 59; cf. *Glamis Gold Ltd v United States* (2009), para. 616). It cannot be said, then, that the investment rules regime is a species of global law without the state. States are deeply implicated in the construction of the regime – with some 2800 bilateral investment treaties (BITs) signed, they are its principal architects and authors – and, to the extent that they continue to tolerate incursions into policy domains previously unchecked by international institutions, are key to sustaining the regime's operations. Nor are legal norms that fill in the content of investment law generated outside of national legal experiences, rather, they issue out of specific locales and tout as 'global' particular national experiences (Schneiderman, 2008, pp. 44–5). They are a prime example of what Santos calls 'globalized localism' (Santos, 2002, p. 179) – local rules that have had global lift-off. Even Teubner's claims about the autonomy of *lex mercatoria*, the system of international commercial law and arbitration that has served as a device for measuring the existence of global law, seem extravagant. There is no question, for instance, that *lex mercatoria* has had a 'productive relationship' with national law (Calliess and Zumbansen, 2010, pp. 32, 59), that state law has been key to its success (Cutler, 2003, p. 237; Kadens, 2012), and that its shape has been determined partly by national states (Trakman, 1983, pp. 24–7; Zumbansen, 2002, p. 402).

We might acknowledge, nevertheless, that the investment law regime, as understood by its relevant actors, generates a version of what Teubner calls societal constitutionalism. Constitutionalism, admittedly, is a plastic term and serves conflicting purposes in the contemporary literature on global law. For Teubner, it would appear that constitutionalism refers principally to the capacity of autonomous groups to organize themselves into self-functioning associations in ways the British political pluralists characterized associational life in the early part of the twentieth century (Hirst, 1989; Schneiderman, 1998). For instance, Teubner describes the 'constitutional emancipation' of the World Trade Organization (2011a, p. 221), which suggests a deepening of the more formal constitutional system outlined by John Jackson (1997). Teubner speaks of systems that not only engage in norm production but that also exhibit certain 'constitutional properties' (Teubner cites Peters, 2006, p. 585; see also Walker, 2002, p. 343 and Cass, 2005, p. 19). There are limits to the constitutional analogy, Teubner admits, however. They are confined to specific sectors within transnational domains and so have no correspondence to the constitutional aspirations of national states. They have no capacity to 'constitutionalis[e] other global spheres' (Teubner, 2011a, p. 219) and instead are characterized as 'islands of constitutionality' (Teubner, 2011a, p. 220). There are only 'occasional couplings [rather than structural couplings] as and when social problems demand' (ibid.).

Yet the investment rules regime has significant effects beyond the reproductive operation of the system itself. The regime exhibits features I have associated with a constraining model of constitutionalism (Schneiderman, 2008, p. 37). This is a classical model of constitutionalism distrustful of exercises of power by public (but not private) authorities (McIlwain, 1947, p. 21) and in which, more specifically, the state is expected to recede from regulative and redistributive functions (Hayek, 1982, p. 148). It is this diminished version of constitutionalism that has been described as emerging at the transnational level in the form of a 'new constitutionalism'. New constitutionalist proposals, writes Stephen Gill, are 'intended to "lock in" commitments to liberal forms of development, frameworks of accumulation and of dispossession so that global governance is premised on the primacy of the world market' (Gill, 2008, p. 254). It is a form of government without a genuine demos other than a regime for conferring on economic actors – citizens 'proper' – privileged rights of mobility and access denied to most people – 'imperfect' citizens of the world (Schneiderman, 2008, pp. 187–91).

With no single overarching checking mechanism, there will be few constraints on the centrifugal tendencies of sub-systems associated with transnational law. In which case, they get to 'maximize' their own partial rationalities and respond autonomously and selectively to communications received from other sub-systems. The normative and institutional implications of this account necessitate that politics within and without of states be conducted in accordance with the demands of these sub-systems, such as international investment law. Though occasional collisions between sub-systems will result, the theory insists that responses be generated by each sub-system and in accordance with the 'logic specific' to it rather than by outside actors (Teubner, 2011b, p. 14; 2012, p. 172).

Proliferating transnational legal orders impose market discipline on state actors. International investment law, more precisely, entails not only ensuring that politics facilitates markets and entrepreneurial values; it also mandates that state actors behave as if they were market participants. If the systems-theoretic account I have just described principally is about liberating operative sub-systems from the constraints of national state authority, then there seem few resources available – other than making some 'noise' – to resist those effects. Democratic polities, in sum, are expected to be responsive to international investment law and its edict of market rationality. Resistance, if not ruled out of bounds, is rendered increasingly difficult. I turn next to a more detailed discussion of the mechanisms by which international investment law insists that market rationality guide state action.

Systemic effects

The commercial state

The fantasy of disembedded markets continues apace. If the state previously 'defined' the economic space rather than was 'defined by it', Schill observes, economics now has primacy over politics (2012, p. 96) – politics is now embedded within markets. States and their agents are expected to behave as do economic actors in the marketplace and will be rewarded when they so act. Should they step out of that role, their behaviour will be characterized as 'political' and vulnerable to legal punishment. This disciplining effect emerges most clearly in the investment law context where there are allegations that there has been an expropriation or a denial of fair and equitable treatment. Where states behave 'normally', that is, as would commercial actors, states are more likely to escape the charge. If they purport to act as if they are a 'sovereign' authority, they are less likely to.

The ubiquitous binary between sovereign state and market actor therefore continues to perform important functions. The doctrine of state immunity observed by many national courts in the Western world, for instance, distinguishes between states acting in their sovereign capacity (*jure imperii*) and states acting as market actors (*jure gestionis*). State immunity doctrine differentiates between those acts for which the state is immune in domestic courts (in the former cases) and acts for which it may be liable in domestic courts (the latter cases) (Higgins, 1982, p. 266). The doctrine is premised on the idea that the states should not be immune from suit when they engage in ordinary 'commercial transactions' (Hess, 1993, p. 272). All else is considered extraordinary and so labelled an exercise of sovereign authority. This distinction has taken on global pretensions: it has been embraced in the United Nations Convention on Jurisdictional Immunities of States and their Property to apply in the context of states facing civil suit in foreign courts (2004).

The contribution of international investment law in this domain is to radically extend the notion of state liability across a range of host-state actions that run afoul of investment treaty disciplines, including those where states act in their sovereign capacity. The transnational legal order complements the law of state immunity by expecting the resolution of *jure gestionis*-type claims by national legal systems (though, in practice, they are as likely to fall within international jurisdiction) while extending liability for *jure imperii* to the realm of international law. The assumption of jurisdiction by international law draws upon the customary international law of diplomatic protection articulated by the American–Mexican Claims Commission in the *Jalapa Railroad* case (*Jalapa Railroad and Power Company* (1937)). In *Jalapa Railroad*, the legislature of the State of Veracruz declared void certain payments owed to Jalapa, derived from federal petroleum tax revenues, for the purchase of

Jalapa's title to railroad and electric light equipment situated within the state. Judicial review (*amparo* proceedings) within Mexico yielded no initial remedy for the investor. The Mexican Supreme Court sanctioned the legislature's actions, finding that the state governor exceeded his authority in pledging tax revenues to pay for the purchase price. The Claims Commission took the view that, in so doing, the Mexican Supreme Court violated Mexican federal constitutional law (thereby engaging in a curious form of appellate review). The legislative decree, moreover, violated international law in so far as the legislature had acted 'arbitrarily', giving rise to 'confiscatory breach of contract' and a 'denial of justice' (*Jalapa Railroad* (1937), para. 540). This was not an 'ordinary breach of contract', the Claims Commission ruled, rather, the government 'stepped out of the role of contracting party and sought to escape vital obligations under its contract by exercising its superior governmental power' (ibid.).

The Claims Commission derived the content for its standard of arbitrariness from the work of Frederick Sherwood Dunn, who had drawn a similar distinction between government 'acting as a private individual' and 'as a sovereign and supreme power' (Dunn, 1932, p. 165). International law would not provide succour to private contractors when government acted in the former capacity, he observed, but when government 'steps out of that role and takes action that a private contractor could not take, in order to escape its obligations under the contract, then it upsets the contractual basis and pursues a course of action that is quite incompatible with normal business relations' (Dunn, 1932, p. 166). Dunn identifies three categories of government action that have given rise to international liability: (1) a 'failure to provide adequate remedies' in local courts; (2) 'arbitrary annulment...without recourse to a judicial determination of the terms of the contract or of the legality of the government's act'; and (3) 'various other "arbitrary" acts' (1932, p. 167; *Jalapa Railroad* (1937), para. 541). The first two classes of cases appear to fall within the rubric of denials of justice, when foreign persons have been denied access to impartial courts or have suffered unfairness in the administration of justice (Paulsson, 2005). The investor, however, did have recourse to the courts but failed to secure interim relief via *amparo* proceedings. The investor succeeded subsequently: the Supreme Court reversed a reduction in the purchase price and elimination of interest by the Veracruz legislature. At that point, it did not pursue its claim any further in Mexican courts – it did not, in other words, exhaust local remedies.

The Claims Commission, nevertheless, concluded that state behaviour amounted to an arbitrary breach of contract and a denial of justice. This is not necessarily the case for a number of the other authorities cited by the Claims Commission (*Jalapa Railroad* (1937), para. 542). Edwin Borchard, for instance, refers to state responsibility for arbitrary annulment of contracts by foreign governments when there is no 'recourse to a judicial determination' and 'without a resort to the courts' (Borchard, 1915, pp. 292–3). Alwyn Vernon Freeman implores us to distinguish between a breach of contract and a failure to 'provide adequate judicial protection against the non-observance of its contractual undertakings' (Freeman, 1938, pp. 112–13). It is only in the event of the subsequent failure to provide judicial protection that 'an international obligation may have been violated' (ibid). There was no denial of access to courts or to judicial determination of legal obligations in this instance and so the case does not fit easily within the first two classes of cases described by Dunn.[1] It appears that the state's behaviour fell within the third class of case, the amorphous category of 'various other "arbitrary" acts' that result in loss to the private contractor (Dunn, 1932, p. 167). Whether this nebulous standard – which turns on whether a state has relied on its superior governmental authority – had something to with the Claim Commission's broad jurisdictional scope, concerning claims regarding 'losses or damages suffered by persons or by their properties' and government actions 'resulting in injustice' (*Jalapa Railroad* (1937)), the arbitrators did not say.

Jalapa Railroad complements well the systems-theoretic claim about the centrifugal tendencies of specialized transnational regimes – it also anticipates developments within contemporary international law that have moved significantly beyond these doctrinal confines. For this reason, *Jalapa Railroad* has been invoked as persuasive authority by modern investment tribunals (*Compañía de Aguas del Aconquija SA and Vivendi Universal SA v Argentina* (2007), para. 7.5.9; *Siemens AG v Argentina* (2007), para. 251). International investment law is concerned now not only with 'sovereign' acts but extends its reach to state action of any kind (unless treaty text suggests otherwise) (Crawford, 2008, p. 356). Breach of simple commercial contracts can give rise to international liability via investment treaty law (for example, contract rights are susceptible to expropriation claims or contracts can become 'internationalized' via an 'umbrella clause'). This too is consistent with the operational logic of the regime, which is intended not just to complement national state law but overtake and supplant it with obligations of a higher and stricter order.

Such transnational legal norms reinforce policies pursued by allied international institutions like the World Bank and International Monetary Fund (IMF). Though it is not entitled to meddle in the internal political arrangements of states, it is entirely within the World Bank's mandate, observed its

---

1 The Claims Commission characterized the Mexican Supreme Court's actions as amounting to a denial of justice and approved the legislatures confiscatory breach (*Jalapa Railroad* (1937), para. 543). This likely provided some cover for the arbitrators as they went on to expansively interpret state liability for acting 'arbitrarily' (*Jalapa Railroad* (1937), para. 543).

General Counsel Ibrahim Shihata, to assist states in developing their own laws so 'long as it is based on considerations of economy and efficiency' (Shihata, 1991, p. 86). Shihata's interpretation of the World Bank's legal mandate presupposes, as does systems theory, that markets are independent of politics. Appropriate legal frameworks are required to facilitate the spread of markets which can then operate free of political constraints (Santos, 2006, p. 271). Institutionalizing the 'depoliticization' of markets, therefore, is within the World Bank's purview. According to this logic, the privatization of state functions, such as the provision of water utilities, serves the objective of separating out politics from utility management which can then be driven more by commercial considerations (WaterAid, 2008, p. 17).

The depoliticized state

Vulnerable states in the global South have been under pressure to embrace precisely such initiatives. Tanzania, for instance, is one of the poorest countries in the world. According to a 2000 report by World Bank and IMF staff, half of the population lives below the poverty line (65 US cents per day) and about 40 per cent may be living in abject poverty (IMF, 2000, p. 9). Water and sewerage services in Dar es Salaam, its largest city, are highly unreliable, if not unavailable, for swathes of the rapidly growing urban centre. In a city of 2.5 million people, 98,000 households have access to running water (Greenhill and Wekiya, 2004, p. 5) with many having to rely on provision by enterprising water vendors charging exorbitant rates.

The free provision of water, initiated after independence by the government of President Julius Nuyrere, was condemned by the World Bank and IMF for being 'unsustainable' (IMF, 2000, p. 5). Under pressure from these international financial institutions, Tanzania embarked on a comprehensive programme of structural adjustment in 1986, 'aimed at dismantling the system of state controls and promoting the private sector' (IMF, 2000, p. 5). An element of the structural reform agenda was the privatization of public utilities, including water services provided by the state entity Dar es Salaam Urban Water and Sewerage Authority (DAWASA) (IMF, 2000, p. 11; World Bank, 2003, p. 12).[2] Privatization turned out to be a principal condition for obtaining sovereign debt assistance via enhanced Heavily Indebted Poor Country relief in 2000.

Tanzania had some difficulty attracting appropriate operators for its proposed water concession, however (IMF, 2000, p. 23, box 3). It took five years and three different tendering processes in order to finalize a ten-year

---

2 The World Bank proudly described its role in 2003 as 'probably the only financing agency that has been actively involved in supporting the "privatization" of WSS [water supply and sanitation] operations in Africa during the last two decades' (World Bank, 2003, p. 4).

leasing contract with the only available tenderer, Biwater Gauff (Tanzania) Ltd. Biwater, a UK-based company under the sole ownership of Adrian White (who made his fortune in the heyday of UK privatization initiated by Prime Minister Margaret Thatcher), in a joint partnership with German-based HP Gauff Ingenieure, would operate under a local subsidiary, City Water Services Ltd (World Bank, 2011, p. 7). The process was described as 'competitive' and one that was 'satisfactory' to the World Bank (2003, p. 7). Yet Biwater Gauff significantly underbid in order to secure the concession nor was it required to invest much of its own capital (Centre for International Environmental Law et al., 2007, pp. 36–8). Most of the project's funding came from the World Bank (US$61.5 million), the African Development Bank (US$48 million), the European Investment Bank (US$34 million) and DAWASA itself (US$12.6 million) (World Bank, 2011, p. 18). Biwater Gauff had only to invest a 'modest' US$8.5 million as working capital, mostly in 'removable assets' like computers (Rice, 2007). In addition to its own capital injection, the company would have access to a US$5.5 million sub-loan provided by DAWASA on which it could draw down proportionate to City Water's investment (*Biwater Gauff (Tanzania) Ltd v United Republic of Tanzania* (2008), para. 139). Such modest amounts of new private inward investment are common in priva-tized water and sanitation projects (as we saw in the case of Aguas Argentina in Chapter 1 (*Suez and Others v Argentina* (2010)) (Castro, 2008). In return, City Water was required to make monthly rental payments, transfer a portion of the collected tariff to DAWASA, and contribute to a first-time connection fund which would subsidize water connections for poorer customers (Biwater Gauff, 2008, paras. 124–8). Financial projections indicated that City Water would continually lose money until the seventh year of operation (Biwater Gauff, 2008, para. 137).

Water rates immediately rose without any appreciable improvement in service, households having to 'pay twice' for their water – first to City Water and then again to water vendors at even higher rates (Greenhill and Wekiya, 2004, p. 14). As would have been anticipated, customers began to 'complain' (World Bank, 2003, p. 21). Interviews conducted in 2004 by the non-governmental organization (NGO) ActionAid indicated that 'custom-ers are angry' and that bill collectors are being 'chased away with dogs and knives' (Greenhill and Wekiya, 2004, p. 14). Residents who failed to pay their tariffs were cut off, even in circumstances where little water had been provided to a neighbourhood for some period of time (Dill, 2010, p. 615). Despite the many incentives provided to City Water, including potentially lucrative plant equipment contracts and a holiday from value added tax (VAT) until at least year six (ibid., p. 12), City Water quickly fell into finan-cial difficulty. Though its business plan was deemed 'acceptable' to the World Bank (World Bank, 2003, p. 19), within the first 12 months, admitted Bank

President Paul Wolfowitz, 'City Water Services was in breach of many key provisions of the Lease Contract' (World Bank, 2006, p. 2).

An application for tariff adjustment contemplated by the lease agreement was approved in August 2004 (*Biwater Gauff* (2008), p. 129). A follow-up request, also in 2004, for a more comprehensive tariff review and increase was rejected by Tanzania. Following the advice of auditors PriceWaterhouseCoopers and the consulting engineers Howard Humphreys, Tanzania concluded that City Water's request was without foundation (*Biwater Gauff* (2008), p. 135). There simply was not sufficient information available, advised PriceWaterhouseCoopers, to confirm City Water's allegation that a reduction in water available for distribution necessitated an increase in water rates (*Biwater Gauff* (2008), para. 173). Pending further renegotiation, City Water's tariff transfers and lease payments to DAWASA were suspended in December 2004 (*Biwater Gauff* (2008), para. 184). The subsequent appointment of a mediator, TRC Economic Solutions, resulted in further stalemate between the parties. The mediator concluded, nonetheless, that City Water 'was not in compliance with the terms of the lease contract' (*Biwater Gauff* (2008), p. 196). By 9 May 2005, DAWASA's board of directors endorsed taking steps to terminate the contract. The chair of DAWASA so informed the Minister of Water and Livestock Development, Edward Lowassa, by letter dated 12 May 2005, a letter that was tabled before Cabinet and approved the following day.

The water concession seemed doomed to fail from the start. A group of three Tanzanian-based and two international NGOs obtained amicus curiae status to file a legal brief in the subsequent investment dispute, to which I turn shortly. The amicus brief astutely argued that Biwater Gauff engaged in a deliberate strategy of 'renegotiation': the company offered an opportunistic bid in order to secure a concession contract only to then seek renegotiation when the concessionaire's leverage was much greater (Centre for International Environmental Law et al., 2007, pp. 36–8). This strategy, J L Guasch warns, has the effect of undermining all of the benefits of 'competitive' bidding processes (Guasch, 2004, p. 33). Though this particular process was not so competitive, the lease was granted on the best terms that Tanzania could obtain in the circumstances. It turned out, of course, that the terms were not so favourable to either party as Biwater failed to pay rental fees, transfer tariffs or even contribute to the first-time connection fund as required by the contract (*Biwater Gauff* (2008), para. 227). Its performance was so poor that average monthly collections were 21 per cent lower than its state-run predecessor in 2002–2003 (World Bank, 2011, p. 19).

With repeated contractual failings and further pleas from City Water to 'talk about it' (Biwater, 2005; Ford, 2005), Minister Lowassa announced the contract terminated at a press conference on 13 May 2005, the same day

Cabinet approved termination of the lease by DAWASA (*Biwater Gauff* (2008), paras. 207–8). Minister Lowassa, candidate for Prime Minister in the upcoming election, censured City Water for performing so poorly (Vidal, 2005). '[W]ater supply services...have deteriorated rather than improved since this company took over two years ago', he declared (IRIN, 2005a). 'The revocation was made following persistent complaints by city residents over the incompetence of the firm' and non-payment of tariff and rental fees (IRIN, 2005a). All of which, in the circumstances, hardly sounds controversial or impeachable. Minister Lowassa subsequently addressed a meeting of DAWASA staff to declare that Cabinet had approved termination of the lease contract but that they would be assured of holding onto their jobs (IRIN, 2005b), an event that is described derisively as a 'political rally' by the investment tribunal (*Biwater Gauff* (2008), para. 499).

City Water countered that the contract was 'still intact' (IRIN, 2005b), though it was reported that top executives had left the country three days after the minister's press conference (IRIN, 2005a). At City Water's own press conference, managers insisted that no proper notice of contractual termination had been received and that the company would continue to provide water and sewerage services (*Biwater Gauff* (2008), para. 217). The next day, government withdrew City Water's VAT exemptions (24 May 2005), took control of City Water facilities (1 June 2005) and, on that same day, deported three City Water senior management staff, all UK nationals (*Biwater Gauff* (2008), paras. 223–4). In the interim DAWASA had issued a notice to terminate the lease contract on 25 May 2005. If contractual failures were left uncured, DAWASA warned, the contract would terminate effective 24 June 2005 (*Biwater Gauff* (2008), para. 219).

Biwater's press release on the day its executives were deported challenged the government's account. According to chief executive officer (CEO), Larry Magor, the company met all of its investment obligations and, hinting at wrongdoing of some sort, that '[w]e won't speculate on the motivations of Mr Edward Lowassa' (Biwater, 2005). The company again shot back in late June 2005, buying advertising space in African weekly publications declaring that 'When aid flows through political pipes, it sometimes leaks.' (White, 2005) The investor had already triggered an arbitration mechanism under the lease contract on 16 May 2005 and in August 2005 initiated investment arbitration under a 1996 UK–Tanzania BIT. The investor alleged that there had been an expropriation, unreasonable and discriminatory treatment, and a denial of fair and equitable treatment. The theory of the case would be, as the advertisement campaign implied, that politics had tainted commerce: that the company had been sacrificed on the altar of political expediency rather than on the basis of rational economic calculations. The wager was that investment arbitration's logic would punish political actors operating under a different rationality than one based on a market model, that is, one having to do with an estimation of the best interests of the residents of Dar es Salaam.

The resulting tribunal decision is an exemplar of the system's objective of separating out politics from commerce. States that step out of the shoes of the market actor and into those of the political actor will be disciplined for their behaviour, though the tribunal ultimately did not award damages to Biwater Gauff. At the moment when Tanzania departed from the profit-seeking behavioural model, the tribunal determined that the economic value of City Water was 'nil'. No quantum of damages would be awarded where the state had caused no damage to the value of the investment (*Biwater Gauff* (2008), p. 797). Also of some significance was that Biwater Gauff had earlier launched arbitral proceedings on the basis of the lease contract under the United Nations Commission of International Trade Law (UNCITRAL) rules, this apart from its investment treaty claim. The UNCITRAL tribunal revealingly dismissed the company's claim and granted DAWASA'a counterclaim, awarding the government operator US$13.7 million in damages and costs (less City Water's performance bond of US$6 million) (Vis-Dunbar and Peterson, 2008). This could not bode well for the pending investor–state arbitration.[3] The investor, nevertheless, had its way with the investment tribunal in several critical respects.

First, the tribunal acceded to the company's request in 2006 that the proceedings remain closed to the public until release of the final award. In an extraordinary interim order, disclosure of discussions and documents to any third party concerning the proceedings were barred (excepting, of course, the tribunal's own order prohibiting disclosure). The tribunal accepted the investor's claims that Tanzania had been leaking documents to third parties, helping to precipitate NGO activity. The World Development Movement campaign against Biwater, launched under the banner 'Dirty aid, dirty water – Hands off Tanzania: Stop UK company Biwater's attempt to sue', asked supporters to email Biwater Gauff (Tanzania) CEO Larry Magor directly so as to persuade him to discontinue the International Centre for Settlement of Investment Dispute (ICSID) proceedings (a social movement strategy I discuss in greater detail in another context in Chapter 4) (*Biwater Gauff* (2006), para. 16). Yet Biwater Gauff, Tanzania replied, had not hesitated in using advertisements and press releases to advance its own cause in the arena of public opinion (*Biwater Gauff* (2006), para. 41). The tribunal accepted, nevertheless, that:

> prosecution of a dispute in the media or in other public fora...may
> aggravate or exacerbate the dispute and may impact upon the

---

3   The investment tribunal, however, claimed that it did not find it 'necessary' to rely on the UNCITRAL award (*Biwater Gauff* (2008), para. 478).

integrity of the procedure. This is all the more so in very public cases, such as this one, where issues of wider interest are raised, and where there is already substantial media coverage, some of which already being the subject of complaint by the parties [sic]. (*Biwater Gauff* (2006), para. 136)

In such circumstances, the tribunal concluded that:

[g]iven the media campaign that has already been fought by both sides of this case, by many entities beyond the parties to this arbitration, and the general media interest that already exists, the Tribunal is satisfied that there exists sufficient risk of harm or prejudice [to the integrity of the proceedings], as well as aggravation [of the dispute], in this case to warrant some form of control (*Biwater Gauff* (2006), para. 146).

The tribunal was compliant in putting a halt to the company's reputational bleeding, stifling further public discussion about a case concerning a critical public resource for which Tanzania potentially was on the hook for US$20 million. The systemic logic of investment arbitration was fruitfully exploited. Modelled on a system intended to resolve private commercial disputes, investment law's mechanism of dispute resolution aims to keep proceedings closed, as if it were a dispute between two private commercial entities (Van Harten, 2007, p. 58). The order of confidentiality also had the perverse effect of undermining participation in the dispute by third parties, a possibility contemplated by amended rule 37(2) of the ICSID rules of procedure. The tribunal, as previously mentioned, granted standing to a group of five environmental NGOs to file an amicus brief in the dispute. They could do so, however, without the benefit of having access to any of the arguments either side would be making in the case. This would severely hamper their ability to contribute to the tribunal's resolution of the dispute (Marshall, 2007, p. 185). Handcuffing public interest input, where matters of a 'wider interest are raised', seems a perverse outcome.

Second, the tribunal agreed with many of the company's allegations. The tribunal found an expropriation of the investment had taken place – that Tanzania's actions substantially deprived the investor of an investment even though there would be no causation and no resulting quantifiable sum of damages (*Biwater Gauff* (2008), para. 464). An expropriation had occurred even though state officials initially were as enthusiastic as could be about the privatization of their water and sewerage services. Even Water Minister Lowassa, at a handing over ceremony, described City Water's involvement as 'seriously welcome' (Greenhill and Wekiya, 2004, p. 8). The tribunal acknowledged that the government's positive attitude eventually turned sour as City

Water began to renege on its commitments. It was understandable that the 'normal contractual termination process' would have been well underway, the tribunal admitted, when the Republic of Tanzania turned against the company. It was at this moment, in May 2005, that the state behaved in ways that departed from 'normal' contractual behaviour giving rise to state liability under international law (*Biwater Gauff* (2008), paras. 487, 460). Here, the tribunal brings to the surface the systemic rationality of international investment law, which mandates that states behave as if they were commercial entities.

For the purposes of its analysis, the tribunal drew on the distinction between circumstances where the state acts 'merely as a contractual partner' and those circumstances where it acts '*ius imperii*, exercising elements of governmental authority'. For the latter, the tribunal preferred to rely upon the French public law notion of '*puissance publique*' (*Biwater Gauff* (2008), para. 458), attributed to the French constitutional theorist Maurice Hauriou (1923, p. 187), describing prerogatives for which there is no individual analogy (Jones, 1993, p. 199). In circumstances where the state intervenes as might a 'private shareholder', the state would not be liable under treaty. By contrast, in those circumstances where the state acts on its 'prerogative of *puissance publique* to perform acts which exceed the normal course of conduct of a State shareholder', then the state is more likely to be liable (*Biwater Gauff* (2008), p. 460). At the beginning of May 2005, the tribunal acknowledged that 'the normal contractual process was underway', but by 13 May 2005, the 'normal course of contractual termination was disrupted' (*Biwater Gauff* (2008), paras. 487, 489). Termination of the lease contract itself was not, for this reason, an expropriation as termination had been 'foreshadowed'. This constituted 'ordinary behaviour of a contracting counterparty' (*Biwater Gauff* (2008), para. 492).

It was Minister Lowassa's press conference of 13 May 2005, announcing termination of the lease contract, that was 'outside the ordinary activity of a contracting counterparty'. This was an act that 'inflamed the dispute, thereby undermining City Water in the general public's eye, and disabling it from progressing the contractual process in an ordinary fashion [sic]' (*Biwater Gauff* (2008), para. 498). Why a private party might not, in analogous circumstances, similarly have held a press conference or issued a press release, announcing termination of a contract, the tribunal does not explain. Nor does it explain why it pejoratively characterized as a 'political rally' a general meeting of City Water staff, communicating the Cabinet decision on 17 May 2005, amounting to an act of *puissance publique* by the republic which was unreasonable and 'motivated by political considerations' (*Biwater Gauff* (2008), paras. 499–500). The unilateral withdrawal of VAT exemptions on City Water purchases was also 'unreasonable and unjustified' and an act of 'sovereign executive authority' (*Biwater Gauff* (2008), para. 502). The occupation of City Water facilities and 'usurpation of management control' were 'well beyond the ambit of normal contractual behaviour', 'unreasonable and arbitrary, unjustified by any public purpose (there being no emergency at the time) and the most obvious display of *puissance publique*' (*Biwater Gauff* (2008), para. 503). Lastly, the forced deportation of City Water staff on 1 June 2005 was an exercise of *puissance publique* and 'without any satisfactory justification' (*Biwater Gauff* (2008), para. 511). Taken together, the cumulative effect of these acts of state, prior to the expiry of the notice of termination, amounted to an expropriation violative of treaty obligations (*Biwater Gauff* (2008), para. 519). Arbitrator Gary Born, partially dissenting, described this as a 'classic instance of expropriation' (*Biwater Gauff*, Concurring and Dissenting Opinion (2008), para. 3). The tribunal also found that there was a denial of fair and equitable treatment given these same circumstances, relying on almost identical language (*Biwater Gauff* (2008), para. 605).[4] In order to make all of these findings, the tribunal invokes the adjectives 'normal' or 'ordinary' 16 times in the course of its reasons.

It can be said that the operational logic of international investment law aims to tame states by legally requiring that they behave as if they were profit-seeking commercial enterprises. Any other behaviour is deemed 'political' and likely to give rise to liability under investment law strictures. Without any award of damages in this instance, however, could it be said that the regime operates as a meaningful constraint on politics? Though investment tribunals are one-off affairs that do not control the outcome of future similar investment disputes, arbitrators aspire to offer reasons that are persuasive, not only to the parties but to future arbitrators, investors, states and their lawyers (Paulsson, 2008, p. 247). In this way, it could be said that investment arbitration offers a system for resolving disputes resembling judicial review within national states (Schneiderman, 2010a). Moreover, the tribunal's reasons fit well with larger trends occurring within the regime, shores up pressures generated by capital-exporting states and international financial institutions, and complements developments within international economic law more generally. For these reasons, the *Biwater Gauff* arbitration will remain an important statement of the law in the area. Moreover, there is little reason to think that, in circumstances where a subsidiary was making some sort of profit or where a lease/concession had some sort of value, that an award of damages would not be forthcoming. Arbitrator Born in his separate opinion says as much, suggesting the company did not fail for lack of failing to show causation but because

---

4   The tribunal accepted that there was denial of 'full protection and security' based on these same facts (*Biwater Gauff* (2008), para. 731) and preferred to deal with the claim that the republic took 'unreasonable or discriminatory measures' under the fair and equitable treatment requirement (*Biwater Gauff* (2008), paras 696ff).

the company was worthless at the time it suffered injuries at the hand of the state's sovereign exercise of authority (*Biwater Gauff*, Separate Opinion, (2008), para. 23).

*   *   *

We can now return to a consideration of the systems-theoretic account of transnational legality and the possibilities it generates for resistance. I have already mentioned that this account complements well the self-understandings of many of the principal actors within international investment law. That is, systems theory generates a plausible account of how the system operates as a normatively closed system (closed, that is, to logics other than that of economic rationality). As argued above, however, the account is flawed to the extent that it excises the state from its norm-generating operations. States are essential to the operation and ongoing legitimacy of the regime. They are both authors of the regime and provide critical supports for maintaining its limited success over time.

To the extent that systems theory normatively fortifies the very regimes that it empirically identifies, it offers few resources for critical resistance. Which is not to say that Teubner and others are not attuned to the detrimental effects of the operation of transnational legal orders (Teubner, 2012, p. 31). It is only to say that this theoretical intervention enables sub-systems to learn, if not regenerate, in response to their negative effects (by way of communications received from other 'irritated' sub-systems such as weakened political orders). Systems can only 'mutually reconstruct, influence, limit, control, and provoke one another' without having to arrive at 'one final collective decision on substantive norms' (Fischer-Lascano and Teubner, 2004, p. 1018).

The account, finally, elides the hierarchy of norms reinforced by the institutions of transnational legality. Transnational legality is the product, and serves the interests, of powerful capital-exporting states – it does not merely represent spontaneous and autonomous self-ordering. I turn to a deeper discussion of this point in the next chapter. What I wish to underscore here is the degree to which systems-based theorization tolerates, even promotes, regime liberation. This system-inspired account enables transnational legality to intensify its pathologies, placing limits on the capacity for critical resistance to do its work.

3
Habermas and Global Power Policy

If economic globalization is shrinking the authority of the state – if states appear to have less of a capacity to preserve social standards and to address social inequities – how might politics be expected to catch up with markets? In contrast to the theorists discussed in Chapters 1 and 2 who consider it futile to have national states harness global political processes that are autonomous and self-reproducing,[1] Jürgen Habermas expects the leading states of the G8 and Organisation for Economic Co-operation and Development (OECD) – those countries with deep democratic currents – to take the lead in taming global markets via new transnational legal institutions. It is the citizens of democratic states, working with global civil society actors and international organizations, who will provide the impetus for a new politics that matches the strength of markets.

Vulnerable to the disintegrating pressures arising from widespread markets, networks and modes of production, states and citizens increasingly are exposed to the exigencies of economic power (Habermas, 2001a, p. 83; 2007, pp. 339–40). Not only is the redistributive state under threat, social policy 'in the broadest sense' is 'threatened with collapse' (Habermas, 2001a, p. 77). Politics must once again 'catch up' with markets, but not through the agency of the failing inter-state system, Habermas maintains. Rather, this is best achieved by fostering the 'consciousness of an obligatory cosmopolitan solidarity' that can generate vigorous countervailing global institutions (2001b, p. 55). Resisting the possibility of a 'renewed closure' – the old protectionism and policed borders associated with the 'nostalgic attitudes of the losers of modernization' – Habermas conceives the expanded options offered by the circuits of globalization as providing an opening for the 'inclusion of citizens

---

1 Habermas describes this 'postpolitical world' as 'Hobbesian': 'Its vanishing point is a completely decentred world society that splinters into a mass of self-reproducing and self-steering functional systems.' (1998b, p. 125)

of every background' (2001a, p. 73). It is this openness to others, characteristic of democratic political cultures, that can generate new transnational forms of will formation beyond the civic nationalism of nation states. Habermas does not envisage closure in the form of world government, rather, he foresees a 'global domestic policy' that is generated through a dynamic interchange between national states, international institutions and global actors. It is at the transnational level, via the collective decision-making of regional or continental authorities together with powerful nation states, that binding global domestic policy can be generated with the requisite legitimacy.

We are expected to look to global powers, such as the US or the EU, to lead this effort of correcting the inequities engendered by globalized markets. It is within these leading democratic societies that public spheres remain open to the 'renovative impulses' of 'informally developed opinion' (Habermas, 1996, p. 357). Once taken up in legislatures, the authors of law become simultaneously its addressees (Habermas, 1996, p. 104). The problem, however, is that in an age of globalization 'there is less and less congruence between the group of participants in a collective decision and the total of all those affected by their decision' (Habermas, 2001a, p. 70). This is why Habermas looks to leading democratic polities to broaden their perspective 'on what counts as the "national interest"' beyond their own civic communities to include a global citizenry. Citizens and states can then participate in the production of global domestic policy generated by a new transnational legal authority.

I suggest in this chapter that, currently, national publics within the powerful capital-exporting states, such as the US, are unreliable associates-in-transnational law. They are unlikely to develop the requisite cosmopolitan consciousness to reform the rules and structures that make up economic globalization. This is not to disprove Habermas' predictive capacity – his work is an idealized formulation for a global world order – rather it is to suggest that we can reliably look elsewhere in the world for leadership in this field. After filling out a bit more of Habermas' proposal for transnational governance ('Global mindset'), I turn to 2002 debates in the US Congress concerning 'trade promotion authority' ('Global pretension') and then to failed negotiations between the US and the South African Customs Union (SACU) toward a new trade and investment agreement ('Global failure'). Each of these case studies illustrates that an institutionalized global consciousness in the developed world lies a long way off. In the first instance, congressional initiative resulted in the modification of current US investment treaty practice. The fear was that treaty language, particularly the prohibition on expropriation and nationalization (the 'takings rule'), hampered the potential for self-government within the US. The change of policy, however, reinforced the goal of promoting US constitutional law abroad and trumping local rules that regulate markets. Indeed, in light of these debates, there remains little doubt that it is a particular version of US local law that is being promoted on the global scene. In the second case of negotiations leading toward a trade and investment treaty with the states of southern Africa, it increasingly became clear to negotiators on both sides that it would be difficult to accommodate aspirations to promote economic equality via a programme for black economic empowerment (BEE) in post-apartheid South Africa. Rather than creating exceptions to an otherwise rigid US model treaty, the parties abandoned negotiations. Both instances suggest that we might have to look elsewhere, other than to the citizens of powerful liberal democratic states, to assume a leadership role in revising transnational legality in ways more favourable to those who benefit least from them.

Global mindset

Encouraging for transnational legal prospects, Habermas claims, is the capacity within capital-exporting north-Atlantic states to develop allegiances beyond crude ethnic formulations that have dominated much of the twentieth century (1998b). In thinking about systems for the production of global domestic policy, Habermas appears to be extrapolating from his discourse-theoretic account of contemporary democratic practice. It makes sense, then, to begin with a brief review of his discourse-theoretic account before turning to recent proposals for global law-making structures that gain their legitimacy from democratic sources within nation states.[2] It is via multi-level chains of legitimation that Habermas foresees the global community interrupting the ways of transnational legality.

Habermas describes legitimate constitutional authority as predicated upon the institutionalization of procedures that enhance deliberation regarding public matters in both institutionalized (i.e. parliament) and informal (i.e. social movements) public spheres. It is in these places that citizens exercise communicative freedom and make laws to 'steer' or 'balance' systems of economic or administrative power (1996, pp. 150, 169). This vibrant public sphere, however, is dependent upon the private domains of the 'lifeworld' (1996, p. 417). Core basic rights secure autonomy in the private sphere and guarantee the requisite independence for the exercise of political freedom in the public sphere.[3] These rights allow for the identification (or 'spontaneous inputs') of mischiefs that call for resolution through the legal code. In this way, the subjects of law (its 'addressees') become, simultaneously, its 'authors' (1996, p. 104). It is the guarantee of both private

---

2 I have discussed Habermas' discourse-theoretic account elsewhere (see Schneiderman, 2004a).

3 These are described, roughly, as rights securing 'equal individual liberty', 'status' or membership rights, due process rights and, lastly, political rights. These are four 'absolutely justified categories': the first three consider individuals in their private capacity as 'addressees' and the fourth as 'authors' of the law. The core rights also imply a fifth category: basic social rights that enable individuals to access the other core rights (Habermas, 1996, pp. 122–3).

and public autonomy (they are 'co-original,' Habermas writes[4]) that generates the foundations for self-rule in modern democracies.

Though Habermas insists on a minimum core, rights become meaningful only after they are subjected to interpretation and expansion under the rules of particular constitutional systems (Habermas, 1996, p. 123). Rights, under a discourse-theoretic account, seem infinitely revisable. 'The constitutional state', he writes, 'does not represent a finished structure but a delicate and sensitive – above all fallible and revisable – enterprise, whose purpose is to realize the system of rights anew in changing circumstances, that is, to interpret the system of rights better, to institutionalize it more appropriately, and to draw out its contents more radically. (1996, p. 84) The progressive elaboration of existing fundamental rights not only enables democratic self-government, it also facilitates political inclusion by inviting others to join in the project of self-government (2001a, p. 73). The practice of rights in Western democracies becomes, in this way, universalizable.[5]

From a functional angle, Habermas notes, the discourse of individual rights cannot be resisted. Rights perform critical functions in 'modern economic societies', including generating the 'necessary conditions' for commerce and 'the achievements of an individualistic legal order' (2002a, pp. 207–8). From a normative angle, the Western ideal of legal persons as bearers-of-rights resonates globally. All of which complements well the seeming exigencies of our increasingly economically integrated world. The concern is that it might leave little room for citizens at either national or transnational levels to challenge the exercise of private power under conditions of economic inequality prevailing in most parts of the world. This is an ambivalence about private power issuing out of Habermas' account that has been noted by others. An 'ambitious radical democratic' project is outlined, Scheuerman observes, yet it is one 'in which democratic institutions exercise at best an attenuated check on market and administrative processes' (Scheuerman, 2002, p. 63). Regrettably, this account of rights might assume only 'trampling...at the edges' of markets (Rosenfeld, 1995, p. 1173).

In more recent work, Habermas has been developing a proposal for multi-level global law-making authority, without world government, that

---

4   The idea of co-originality has got Habermas in some trouble for departing from his proceduralist moorings and finding ground in a pre-existing contractualist consensus on basic rights (see Michelman, 1996). For our purposes, it is sufficient to note that Habermas has responded to these critiques by saying that he is describing a two-stage process in which rights are accorded and then filled out in concrete ways via legal mechanisms (1996, p. 457; 2006e, p. 122).

5   The correspondence between Habermas' account here and Hardt and Negri's rhapsodic account of the US Constitution at its origins is striking (Hardt and Negri, 2000, pp. 165–7) ('an expansive project operating on an unbounded terrain', occupying a space that is 'always open').

yields, I argue, a similar ambivalence. Inspired by Kant's sketch of a 'perpetual peace' based on a federation of republican states (1795), Habermas insists that global law be managed not by a new global state but by institutions such as a reformed United Nations and new transnational institutions represented by regional or continental alliances and single global powers. Turning first to the level of the supranational, Habermas perceives global legal authority confined jurisdictionally to a few subject matters, namely, war, peace and the protection of human rights (2006a, p. 136). These are the few items on which, in his view, a global consensus can be envisaged (2007, p. 335; 2008, p. 449) as they are rooted in the core moral contents of all of the major world religions and in the cultures they have shaped (2012, p. 65). Consensus on the application of universal moral standards in particular circumstances seems highly unlikely, however (Lafont, 2008; Scheuerman, 2008, pp. 144–5). Overloading a supranational institution such as a reformed United Nations with additional jurisdiction over subjects with 'distributive implications' (Habermas 2012, p. 68), such as the economy or the environment, worries Habermas as it would stretch the legitimacy of this superior law-making authority and jeopardize its capacity for peace and human rights promotion (Habermas, 2007, p. 336). In which case, he reserves these highly politicized sorts of subjects for an intermediate transnational legal authority that can produce 'global domestic policy'. It is at this transnational level that global economic institutions like the World Trade Organization (WTO) can be made subject to 'institutionalized negotiation between some legitimate continental regimes' (2007, p. 339). That is, he envisages a global law-making authority that is made up of regimes based on continental or regional alliances – building on extant intergovernmental institutions like the EU and regional agreements such as the Asia-Pacific Cooperation Agreement and the North American Free Trade Agreement (NAFTA) – which could then generate consensus around critical public policy matters of global concern (2007, p. 337). In an addendum, he envisages the transnational level taking direction from, and under 'continual adjustment' of, the supranational authority (2008, pp. 449, 452). Regional regime authorities, as in the case of Europe (from which he clearly generalizes[6]), would represent member states and so generate chains of legitimation from the local to new institutions for the production of global

---

6 The EU is his 'exemplary case' for testing the conditions for democratic politics beyond the nation state (Habermas, 2001a, p. 88). On the inadequacy of generalizing from the particular regional experience of Europe, by Habermas' own reasoning, must entail further diversification of forms', p. 109). On Habermas' appreciation of the achievements of the European social state that 'directly repudiate' his earlier critiques regarding the infantilizing effects of state welfare supports (i.e. 1996, p. 407), see McCormick (2007, pp. 198–201).

domestic policy. Not all states need be part of a continental or regional alliance, however. Though he mentions NAFTA as a continental regime that
could be party to transnational law-making, he privileges the US (together
with China, India and Russia) with having sufficient 'predestined' weight to
not be party to a regime alliance (2007, p. 336; 2008, p. 446). 'At any rate',
he admits, 'the improbable constellation with which the whole construction stands or falls calls for a certain concentration of political power in the
hands of a few global players.' (2008, p. 446) How then to move away from
the asymmetries generated by great power politics to which Habermas is
evidently attuned? The hope – and there is a lot riding on this – is that citizens and their representatives will develop the 'enlarged mentality' necessary to make these institutions work (Nedelsky, 2000).

The edifice is dependent, then, on developing the requisite cosmopolitan
consciousness. It is one of the considerable achievements of modern constitutional democracies to have expanded the capacity to have rights beyond
the local to an ever-growing number of civic strangers (Habermas, 2006d,
p. 105). Why couldn't this notion of civic solidarity premised upon the
abstract rights of citizenship, Habermas asks, gain momentum beyond
national state borders? The effect of institutionalizing mechanisms for global
governance beyond the state might very well initiate processes that internal-
ize an enlarged sense of civic solidarity (2006a, p. 177). If, as Habermas claims,
constitutional patriotism overtook the place occupied by ethnic nationalism
(1998b, p 118) – a controversial claim to be sure (McCormick, 2007, p. 197) –
so might a new cosmopolitan consciousness overtake parochial expressions
of national self-interest (Habermas, 2001a, p. 74; 2008, p. 453). According to
this constructivist account, innovative legal change comes to 'permeate the
consciousness of the broader population ... as result of practical experiences'
(2008, p. 454) and cosmopolitanism thereby becomes a 'self-fulfilling proph-
ecy' (2007, p. 334). Legally constructed solidarity, however, alone is insuf-
ficient. Habermas anticipates a 'learning process' analogous to that which
paved the way to a European-wide civic solidarity (2006c, p. 87; 2006d,
p. 105). There is 'no reason to assume', then, 'that the formation of this kind
of civic solidarity must come to a halt at the boundaries of the nation-state'
(2006c, p. 101).

Is this merely wishful thinking – a 'best case scenario' (2006a, p. 185)?
Habermas admits that 'states and nations as we know them are still *far from*
satisfying this normative expectation' (2008, p. 452). The overriding response
of powerful European states to the Greek debt crisis, for instance, displayed
more national self-interest than European-wide solidarity for 'those in need'
(Fernandes and Rubio, 2012). Habermas maintains, nevertheless, that this
proposal builds on 'currently existing structures' (2006a, p. 135; 2007, p. 333)
by supplementing them and so closing the legitimation gap between existing

institutions and demands for transnational justice. Here arises an ambivalence regarding the regulation of markets, just as it did in Habermas' account
of national constitutional rights. Might it be that the problem begins with
the premise of having politics 'catch up' with, 'follow the lead' of, or 'make
up ground' lost to markets (Habermas, 2001a, p. 123; 2006c, p. 6), which
relegates politics to a subsidiary role vis-à-vis markets? Does Habermas give
up too much by having, as one of his objectives, the legitimation of transnational networks and institutions?

It is plain that the goal of global governance at the transnational level
is to curb the pathologies of transnational legality (2006a, p. 181; 2007,
pp. 339–40). Habermas bemoans, after all, the threatened marketization of
the social functions of democratic states by undoing the mechanisms that
secured public and private life (2001a, p. 77), 'forfeiting' the capacity for
autonomous action (2006c, p. 77) and 'robbing' future generations of the
capacity to reverse course (2007, p. 341). As we saw in Chapter 2, transnational investment law aims to discipline states that depart from the norms
of market behaviour – precisely the sort of *'postpolitical* world' bemoaned
by Habermas where the 'multinational corporation becomes the model for
all conduct' (1998b, p. 125). On the other hand, Habermas understands
that 'capitalism made possible the fulfilment, rather than the frustration,
of the republican promise of the equal inclusion of all citizens' (2006c,
p. 74) and that, post-1989, there is no escape from its beneficence (2009,
p. 228). Unilateral resistance to these developments would be nothing more
than futile: 'any such attempts must expect to meet with sanctions' (2002b,
p. 224). Indeed, there might even be less of a legitimation problem for global
capitalism, he admits. The fruits of economic globalization, via the exchange
of political sovereignty for participation in transnational agreements and
organizations like the WTO, are not wholly without merit. Arrangements
like the WTO, Habermas insists, were 'the product of political voluntarism',
not imposed unilaterally by any one state but the consequence of 'negotiated path-dependant cumulative decisions' (2006c, p. 81; 2002b, p. 224).
The WTO derives its normative substance, after all, from 'constitutions of
the republican type' and 'increasingly take[s] into account the protection of
human rights' (2006a, p. 140) (the latter a dubious claim: Vázquez, 2003).

His embrace of 'regime' theory (2006a, p. 181; 2007, p. 339),[7] beyond
mere description, further deepens suspicions that this proposal for
multi-level governance pastes over the imbalance of contemporary transnational legality. Regimes, as developed in a vibrant US literature, consist of
implicit or explicit 'principles, norms, rules and decision making structures

---

7 Habermas credits Zürn with prompting his thinking on intermediate regimes that compensate for diminished state capacity (see Habermas, 2001a, p. 70).

around which actors' [namely, states] expectations converge' (Krasner, 1983, p. 2). They are intended to render predictable the behaviour of states in a range of specific policy domains – they are not intended to upset or disturb those expectations. As Cox describes this line of inquiry in the international relations literature, it 'takes the existing order as given, as something to be made to work more smoothly, not as something to be criticized or changed' (1992, p. 509; also Strange 1982, p. 488). The resulting structure, in Habermas' account, resembles the consolidation of dominant networks that institutionalize unequal access to the normative inputs of transnational legality.

This benign neglect of global power politics is curious. After all, Habermas has suggested that his Kantian project for multi-level global governance has the merit of meeting reality 'halfway' (Habermas, 2007, p. 337). If the US is one of the only presently 'viable' political units capable of participating in the development of global domestic policy, it is mystifying why Habermas would think that global power politics would be abated when it operates at transnational levels. He proclaims to be appealing to America's better self (and the likelihood of cognitive dissonance[8]) (2006a, p. 185), but what is the likelihood of progressive, countervailing global legal policy to be led by a few powerful global actors when the 'concentration of political power' remains in their hands (2008, p. 446)?

Subsequent to the debacle in Iraq, Habermas expressed some anxiety about the role the US unilaterally has assumed as defender of human rights and democratic culture. 'The normative authority of the United States lies in ruins', Habermas wrote in the aftermath of the Iraq invasion (2003, p. 703). Yet, he credits the pre-invasion US as being the 'pacemaker for progress' that is pursuing a 'cosmopolitan path' (ibid.). Even after the global economic downturn, Habermas concluded that we have no alternative but to bet on this 'draft horse' of the new world order (Habermas, 2009, p. 233). What his proposal for multi-level governance omits, then, is an account of asymmetric structural power that, one reasonably anticipates, will continue to operate on the transnational plane (Gill and Law, 1988, p. 75; Strange, 1988, p. 25).

The exercise of that power will be guided, in great measure, by national economic forces within capital-exporting states. Economic interests operate on a terrain larger than those typically of concern to the territorial interests of nation states and so are apt to conscript home states to their cause (Wallerstein, 1974, p. 348). Consequently, 'the political battle within

---

8   The 'fact that the superpower has a liberal constitution is indeed important. Citizens of a democratic political community sooner or later become aware of cognitive dissonances if universalistic claims cannot be squared with the particularistic character of the obvious driving interests' (Habermas, 2006a, p. 185).

structurally influential states becomes a battle with global consequences' (Strange, 1997, p. 242). If it is correct to say that domestic structures help to determine foreign policy outcomes (Katzenstein, 1976; 1978), we then will want to take note of the vulnerability of political systems to business influence. As discussed in much greater detail in Chapter 5, the empirical evidence within the US, not surprisingly, reveals that corporate actors will endeavour to effect political change. Adopting the premise of profit maximization as an explanation for corporate political activity (Grier et al., 1994), studies reveal that corporations making their home within the US will use political activity to modify costly regulations or to secure government contracts (Hansen and Mitchell, 2000, p. 892). Corporate political activity will also make itself felt in foreign policy domains. This helps to explain Sell's observation that the US-based proposal that got taken up in the Trade Related Intellectual Property Rights regime closely mirrored 'the expressed wishes of the twelve chief executive officers of US-based multinational corporations who spearheaded the effort' (Sell, 2003, p. 13). Lang attributes international trade law's preoccupation with effects-based trade 'barriers' and 'distortions' to the rise of the neoliberal mindset in 1970s US trade policy spearheaded initially by American business interests (Lang, 2011, pp. 224–6). As a consequence of this shift, he explains:

> [e]ntire categories of domestic governmental action which had once been relegated to the background as self-evidently outside the domain of trade policy were now foregrounded, reconstructed as potential impediments to trade, and therefore made objects of legitimate international scrutiny and discipline (Lang, 2011, p. 239).

It also lends support to Shaffer having observed close relations between private business and the Office of the United States Trade Representative's (USTR) in US-initiated WTO litigation, which is intended to be the sole preserve of states (Shaffer, 2003, p. 151). Capital-exporting states, Lipson reminds us, have long sought to control international legal outcomes in ways that promote economic success of their home companies and investors (Lipson, 1985, p. 20). This is unlikely to change any time soon.

In which case, we might not expect capital-exporting states to take the lead in reframing transnational legality. Habermas suggestively hints elsewhere that it is those places 'exposed to the full force of the imperatives of an increasingly globalized economy', namely capital-importing states of the global South, that might be better poised to precipitate reform (Habermas, 2008, p. 453). I take up this possibility in later chapters. First, I turn to instances where US trade and investment policy failed to exhibit the requisite cosmopolitan consciousness.

Global pretension

Despite the strong consensus in favour of investor rights, there has been momentum to peel back some of its unremitting standards. Canada, on the frontlines of NAFTA investor-initiated disputes, was among one of the first to seek 'clarification' of NAFTA's takings rule (discussed further below) (Pettigrew, 2001). This followed a series of claims being made by foreign investors from within the US challenging measures in Canada, such as a ban on the gasoline additive MMT, the allocation of logging licences in British Columbia and a prohibition on the cross-border movement of hazardous waste (see, generally, Schneiderman, 2008, ch. 3). At first, the other NAFTA parties were resistant to the initiative (Scoffield, 2000; Jack, 2001). A proposal to modify the transnational takings rule was taken up in the US Congress in 2002, however. President George W Bush was seeking 'trade promotion authority' from Congress, and the congressional response was initially cool. This chill was precipitated, in some part, by proposals emanating from the public sphere. According to Inside US Trade – the online trade news resource – it was journalist Bill Moyers' 'hard-hitting' documentary on NAFTA, broadcast on PBS (*Trading Democracy*) (Moyers, 2001), which helped to mobilize congressional leadership (Inside US Trade, 2002a). Moyers' documentary shed light on the 'secret' tribunals established under NAFTA that could hamper the ability of states to regulate in the interests of protecting workers or the environment. Particular emphasis was placed on a dispute launched against the US by the Canadian company Methanex arising from losses suffered by the phasing out of the gasoline additive MTBE by the state of California (*Methanex v USA* (2005)). California claimed that it had banned the additive in the interests of promoting the environment; Methanex countered that the decision was based on bad science, protectionism and discrimination (Schneiderman, 2008, pp. 92–5). Those California legislators interviewed by Moyers for the documentary described themselves as shocked that the state measure could be the subject of a suit for damages against the US under NAFTA.

   Concerns that NAFTA's takings rule hampers state capacity to take environmental, health and welfare measures had been advanced prior to 2001 by organizations like Ralph Nader's Public Citizen (Wallach and Sforza, 1999), a handful of academics (e.g. Robinson, 1993; Schneiderman, 1996; Wagner, 1999) and other groups comprising the 'anti-globalization' movement (e.g. the International Forum on Globalization). Warning shots had been fired in publications like *The Nation* (Greider, 2001) and, on one occasion, even in the *New York Times* 'Money & Business' pages (De Palma, 2001). Moyers' PBS broadcast, in which critics like William Greider of *The Nation* figured prominently, helped to move the discussion from the periphery – contained largely within the social movement community – to the centre of the institutional public sphere (Habermas, 1996, pp. 380–2).

Of particular concern were provisions in bilateral investment treaties (BITs) that prohibit expropriation or measures tantamount to expropriation (the takings rule), the 'international minimum standard of treatment' and the 'fair and equitable treatment' requirement. The Democratic chair of the Finance Committee, Senator Max Baucus (D-Montana), endorsed proposals that would have qualified the phrase 'tantamount to expropriation' in any future investment protection agreement (Inside US Trade, 2002a). This proposal would have limited the scope of regulatory measures subject to dispute under NAFTA, accompanied by a 'non-exhaustive list' of measures that either would conform with or violate the takings rule. A second proposal would have 'screened' investor claims, interposing political and foreign policy considerations in the determination of when an investor would be entitled to launch a dispute under any future investment treaty. Typically, investors cannot enforce the terms of international instruments directly so, in this way, Baucus's proposal would have reverted matters to traditional inter-state practice. A screening mechanism, on the other hand, would have been a radical departure from the trajectory of US trade and investment policy. Since at least the 1980s, the US has pursued a strategy of 'depoliticizing' these disputes and imposing 'rule-of-law' disciplines on state actors who discriminate or take measures tantamount to expropriation (Vandevelde, 1998). The object of both of these proposals, Baucus explained, was to ensure that foreign investors received no greater entitlements than US investors under US law (Cong. Rec. S4267, 13 May 2002).

Similar proposals were picked up in amendments proposed by Democratic Senator and future presidential candidate John Kerry (D-Massachusetts). In addition to screening investor claims, Kerry's amendment would have limited the scope of takings claims to those that qualify under the US Constitution (Inside US Trade, 2002b). Kerry's amendment purported to mirror the US constitutional law of takings, as 'murky' and 'messy' as that law may be (Levmore, 1990, p. 287; Poirier, 2002). The amendment would have limited compensable takings 'by ensuring that payment of compensation is not required for regulatory measures that cause mere diminution in the value of private property'. It also would have ensured that the 'minimum standard' of treatment required by international law grants 'no greater legal rights than United States citizens possess under the due process clause of the United States constitution'. No foreign investor could succeed in challenging a federal, state or local measure 'that protects public health, safety and welfare, the environment or public morals' unless it was demonstrated that 'the measure was enacted or applied primarily for the purpose of discriminating against foreign investors or investments' or violated 'due process' (Cong. Rec. S4504, 16 May 2002).

In speaking to the amendment, Senator Kerry noted that '[w]hen we passed NAFTA, there wasn't one word of debate on the subject of the chapter 11 resolution – not one word'. 'Nobody knew what was going to happen', he claimed (echoing a recurring theme in Moyers' documentary (Moyers, 2001)). The proposed amendment would ensure that investment protection was 'consistent with US Supreme Court holdings' (S4595) – the standard applied 'should not be less than the standard applied by the Constitution of the United States' (S4596). What the proposal did was 'seek to define over 80 years of Supreme Court decisions as to what is not an expropriation' (S4601).

Also on the Senate floor, Republican Senator Phil Gramm (R-Texas) traced the origins of investment protection agreements, taking note of the 45 BITs that the US had signed to date. These protections, Senator Gramm noted, 'were modeled on familiar concepts of American law, [and] became the standard for protection of private property and investment around the world' (S4595). There was little need, then, to redefine rights that already reflected US constitutional experience. Also speaking against the Kerry amendment, Republican Senator George Allen (R-Virginia) noted that: 'Chapter 11 does not provide novel rules on what constitutes an expropriation beyond that covered by traditional investment agreements or by U.S. Courts.' (S4599) 'Proper trade agreements', he proclaimed, 'foster adherence to the rule of law and protect private property and intellectual property rights.' (S4599) These senators opposed defining investment protections with any further precision. This was an 'evolving standard' (Gramm, S4597). The Supreme Court's 'definition of what constitutes a taking, and, therefore, requires compensation is extremely complicated…extremely complex' (Baucus, S4600). 'We can't define what a taking is', agreed Senator Baucus: 'The Supreme Court says what takings is [sic].' (S4600)

Though the proposal for a screening mechanism did not fare so well (Inside US Trade, 2002c), reformers got pretty much what they wanted in the resulting Trade Promotion Authority Act of 2002. The Act required that foreign investors be accorded no greater rights than US investors in the US. The USTR immediately began modifying investment treaty practice. In agreements with Chile, Singapore and Morocco, the takings rule would now encompass only interference 'with a tangible or intangible property right or property interest in an investment'. Though investment agreements protect a wide variety of interests, this is seemingly an attempt to limit the prohibition to what Kelman calls the 'the sort of entitlement that law students study and name in first year property classes' (1999, p. 19). The agreements identify criteria which will aid in determining whether an indirect taking has occurred. This requires 'a case-by-case, fact-based inquiry' that considers, among other factors, the 'economic impact' of measure, the extent to which it interferes with 'distinct, reasonable investment-backed expectations' and the 'character of the government action' – mirroring criteria applied by the US Supreme Court in *Penn Central Transportation Co. v New York City* ((1977), para. 124) (USTR, 2004). An 'adverse effect on the economic value of an investment, standing alone, does not establish' an indirect expropriation. 'Except in rare circumstances', the texts declare, 'nondiscriminatory regulatory actions by a Party that are designed and applied to protect legitimate public welfare objectives, such as public health, safety, and the environment, do not constitute indirect expropriations' – an attempt at carving out of the treaty prohibition traditional exercises of the state police power authority in the US (Rose, 2000). USTR has sought, then, to capture the messy and inconsistent but constituent elements of the Supreme Court's jurisprudence on takings (Sampliner 2003; Parvanov and Kantor, 2012, p. 778). It is this core qualification to the takings rule that the Obama administration retained in its 2012 model investment treaty (USTR, 2012).

In the case of the 2004 US–Australia trade and investment agreement, however, investors have no ability to launch disputes to enforce the agreement other than through the auspices of their home states. Though it appears that it was Australia that objected to the model US rule (TEPAC, 2004, attachments 1, 2), the Australian Department of Foreign Affairs and Trade explained this omission on the basis of 'the Parties' open economic environments', their 'shared legal traditions, and the confidence of investors in the fairness and integrity of their respective legal systems' (though exclusion of investor–state dispute mechanisms is a policy the government of Australia has since endorsed for all future treaties (Australia, 2011)). Other legal systems – Chile, Morocco, Jordan, and presumably the states of southern Africa – are considered less trustworthy by the US. Moreover, they were not members of the 'coalition of the willing' that participated in the 2003 US invasion of Iraq, unlike the more reliable Australia. They are also less likely to be home to foreign investors filing troublesome suits for regulatory takings against the US.

Not long after congressional debates ended, the Bush administration proudly announced in 2003 that negotiations toward a new trade and investment treaty with the SACU – comprised of the states of Botswana, Lesotho, Namibia, Swaziland and South Africa – would be commenced (Zoellick, 2002). Building on momentum initiated by the Africa Growth and Opportunity Act 2000 (AGOA),[9] unilaterally admitting goods from Africa duty free into the US, it was anticipated that economic relations with the states of southern Africa would be significantly deepened and liberalized. On the South-African side, the US was considered a 'strategic partner' for post-apartheid South Africa, where 'a clear

---

9   The AGOA 2000 removes import duties on goods such as apparel and footwear from 37 sub-Saharan countries. The Act was due to expire in 2008, but was extended in time by President George W Bush until 2015.

convergence of interests' dictated an 'intensity of engagement' (Ismail et al., 2002, pp. 7, 10). By late 2004, SACU–US negotiations were at an impasse. Talks ended in failure in 2006 because of what the USTR described as 'differences' that 'will require detailed examination over the longer term' (USTR, 2006).

There were a number of issues over which the parties were deadlocked in these complex, multi-party negotiations. Of particular concern to the US side were deviations from standard investment treaty language intended to advance the goals of BEE.[10] This is an African National Congress (ANC)-government initiative intended to generate a new indigenous class of black entrepreneurs. The programme insists that economic actors operating within South Africa promote black managers, hire black suppliers and divest a significant amount of minority control to black-controlled enterprises. Deputy USTR Karan Bhatia complained, for instance, that 'the South African government is unwilling to provide equitable access [to government procurement] for foreign firms as this could negatively impact on its black economic empowerment initiatives' (*Sunday Times*, 2004). BEE remains highly controversial, having, in its first phase, benefited only a small group of well-connected former ANC activists like Cyril Ramaphosa (former ANC Secretary General and Chair of the Constitutional Assembly) (Jack, 2006). It remains, nevertheless, one of the few ANC-initiated programmes aimed at reversing the economic legacy of apartheid. South Africa, as lead SACU negotiator, for this reason sought to exempt from the requirement of national treatment (or non-discrimination), as it had in an earlier BIT, measures 'taken pursuant to Article 9 of the Constitution ... the purpose of which is to promote the achievement of equality in its territory, or designed to protect or advance persons, or categories of persons, disadvantaged by unfair discrimination' (2000 South Africa–Iran BIT, Art. 4 BIS, § 2).

This was a matter that attracted concern early on in the negotiations. The 'United States seems wary of South Africa's black economic empowerment (BEE) programme, which could jeopardise free trade talks', a South African business daily reported (*Business Report*, 2003). According to Inside US Trade, negotiations were 'plagued over questions on investment and how US companies will comply' with BEE (Inside US Trade, 2004a) – this amounted to a 'major obstacle', it reported (Inside US Trade, 2004c). Negotiators state-side surely would have been emboldened by US-based companies who 'indicated they could not meet empowerment criteria' (Inside US Trade, 2004b). The results of a 2004 survey by the American Chamber of Commerce in South Africa suggests that 74 per cent of US companies in South Africa viewed divestiture under BEE as having 'negatively affected their investment decisions' (Rose, 2004). According to the State Department, though US companies 'support the broad goals' of BEE, they expressed concerns about the 'lack of clarity and

---

10   The next few paragraphs draw on Schneiderman (2009).

consistency' in BEE rules, having a 'major concern' with the requirements of equity ownership (US Department of State, 2005). This discomfort with BEE strictures is confirmed by interviews with a sample of senior executives in South Africa from 25 foreign-owned firms in diverse sectors, 16 of whom identified BEE as having a negative impact on investment (Thomas and Leape, 2005). Polo Redebe, then head of BEE, admitted that US-based multinationals remained one of her 'greatest challenges', having not 'fully embraced' BEE.[11]

There admittedly were other obstacles aside from BEE that helped to bog down negotiations, such as controversies over intellectual property and agriculture (Inside US Trade, 2004b). Nevertheless, it appears that South-African negotiators believed that they could extract concessions from the US. Negotiators may have proceeded on the basis that they could capitalize on global public opinion, even a cosmopolitan consciousness of the Habermasian sort. Emerging out of the ruins of apartheid, many – from ordinary citizens to heads of state – wish the democratic and multiracial experiment of South Africa to succeed. South Africans may have expected to trade on this moral authority so as to extract concessions from powerful economic actors as they have, for instance, in gaining access to lower-cost drugs to combat HIV/AIDS (Klug, 2005). South Africans also would have been emboldened by the positive response of some transnational firms to BEE's programmatic objectives. This would have encouraged the belief that the private sector would not stand in the way of empowering previously disadvantaged economic actors (e.g. Mbeki, 2005). Even the International Monetary Fund (IMF) jumped on board, indicating its support for broad-based BEE as it helps to foster 'social cohesion and consolidate an environment favorable to sustained economic and social progress' (IMF, 2006). Lastly, there is the shadow that Zimbabwe casts on events in South Africa and the largely unspoken possibility of other, more radical, forms of redistribution, such as expropriation and nationalization. The government, perhaps, viably could threaten to derail negotiations with the US in light of alternative models for redistribution elsewhere in sub-Saharan Africa. Concessions from the US side, on this and other matters, seem not to have been forthcoming, however.[12] Negotiations stalled and then were terminated.

---

11 Personal interview with Polo Redebe, 28 May 2007, Johannesburg.
12 After US–SACU talks collapsed, South Africa offered to exempt foreign investors operating outside of the mining and resource sectors from having to divest equity ownership to black enterprises in cases where equity equivalents are in place (Schneiderman, 2009). Wholly owned firms that do not have a 'global practice' of selling equity in their subsidiaries may propose alternative equity equivalents to make up for lack of minority ownership (Southey, 2007). Such programmes might entail a substantial commitment of funds (25 per cent of the value of the investment over ten years) and so investors have been warned to weigh expected returns from an equity equivalent against returns on the sale of equity in the company (Lalu et al, 2007).

In light of these and other events, the South African Department of Trade and Industry (DTI) revisited its model investment treaty language so as to correct the misalignment between investor rights and 'the necessary safeguards to preserve flexibility in a number of policy areas' (South Africa DTI, 2009, p. 5). As a result of the 'inexperience of negotiators' and 'lack of knowledge about investment law in general', South Africa had entered into agreements 'that were heavily stacked in favour of investors' (ibid.). Given that investment law extends 'far into developing countries' policy space', it is now prudent, the DTI proposed, to ensure that '[a]dequate policy space is [available as] a key developmental tool for developing countries' (ibid., p. 54). An inter-ministerial Cabinet committee largely agreed with the DTI assessment, concluding that South Africa should 'refrain from entering into BITs in future, except in cases of compelling economic and political circumstances' (Williams 2011; Davies 2012). Cabinet determined that South Africa's domestic legal structure could sufficiently protect foreign investors. In addition to rights to property and non-discrimination guarantees available in the 1996 constitution, South Africa would 'codify typical BIT provisions into domestic law' so as to ensure compliance with South African basic law (ibid.). South Africa also has been participating, under the auspices of the South African Development Community (SADC), in the development of an alternative model investment treaty (SADC, 2012). Such initiatives, that involve both stopping and doing by reformulating these commitments (Mansbridge, 2012), attest to the fact that capital-importing states of the South continue to have critical choices to make about the future direction transnational legal norms will take.

Global failure

Perhaps it is unremarkable to observe that in both instances – in seeking trade promotion authority and in negotiations with SACU – the US behaved in ways rooted firmly within US traditions and perspectives. The congressional initiative, after all, was aimed at taming the scope of investor rights capable of being claimed against the US. Foreign investors, it is believed, should receive no greater rights than those available to US citizens under the Bill of Rights. This initiative was aimed at ensuring equality of treatment according to national standards while resisting the imposition of foreign or transnational legal norms. The case of SACU negotiations reveals that the standard articulated in Congress has the potential to influence developments far beyond the borders of the US. As Senator Gramm maintained, investment treaty standards are 'modeled' on US law and are 'the standard for protection of private property and investment around the world' (Cong. Rec. S4595). For that reason, investor rights, and the takings rule more particularly, are prime examples of local rules having global impacts. These local constitutional rules, in other words, take on pretensions of universality. In which case, if the congressional modification merely adjusted investor rights to reflect more accurately US constitutional norms, then this adjustment did not expand dramatically the range of social policy options for those countries seeking to diversify state–market relations in ways that test the outer limits of US constitutional doctrine.

The problem, then, is that the authors of this global standard are not exclusively its addressees. Recall that Habermas envisages populations with 'common political cultures' and 'shared conceptions of justice' to be more likely oriented toward a cosmopolitan consciousness rooted within national states (2001a, p. 109). There are, he admits, numerous impediments to achieving this state of 'transnational will-formation'. One is that legislators 'be willing to broaden their perspectives on what counts as the 'national interest' into a viewpoint of 'global governance' (2001a, p. 111) and, another, that populations reward politicians for thinking in this global vein. Congress together with the USTR, on this count, appears blind to the operation of imperial law operating under the guise of the transnational. Or perhaps, more accurately, Congress willingly assumes imperial authority on the assumption that US constitutional standards, as reflected in US Supreme Court jurisprudence, are an apt model for other countries seeking to develop economically. The congressional initiative, from this angle, may be grounded in the 'implicit belief that every human being is a potential American, and that his or her present national or cultural affiliations are an unfortunate but reversible accident' (Prestowitz, 2003, p. 36).

Perhaps it is unreasonable to anticipate an initiative, responsive both to the enhancement of democracy and economy, to emanate from the seat of imperial government. We might look, instead, to other capital-exporting countries for the generation of social norms which, Habermas hopes, carry some weight on a 'cosmopolitan scale' (2001a, p. 112). The problem is that proposals very similar to Washington's are as likely to emerge from London or Berlin or Ottawa. Even before news regarding proposed US treaty modifications was leaked, the government of Canada had been working towards clarifying its version of the takings rule in future investment protection agreements along similar lines (Desrosiers, 2002). As if to underscore the intimate relationship between Canada and the US in the realm of trade and investment policy (Clarkson and Mildenberger, 2011), the Canadian government subsequently issued an annex to its model treaty identical in many respects to proposed new US treaty language. One commentator describes the adoption of US Supreme Court multi-factor balancing in the *Penn Central* case as 'somewhat surprising' (Lévesque, 2006, p. 295). If we understand that Canadian trade and investment policy closely tracks US developments (Schneiderman, 1996; 2008) – if we accept, in other words, that Canada's foreign policy works within an 'ideational hegemony' that is made-in-the-USA (Clarkson and Mildenberger, 2011, p. 186) – this development hardly appears surprising.[13]

European Community leadership in the field offers little more promise. The Lomé Convention (1975) initially guided European-wide trade and aid policy, unilaterally granting preferential access to poorer African, Caribbean and Pacific (ACP) countries on a non-reciprocal basis (as does AGOA in the US). Under pressure from the WTO member countries (Stevens, 2007, p. 223), Lomé was abandoned in 2000 and replaced with the Cotonu Agreement. Non-reciprocal trade preferences were jettisoned in favour of negotiating Economic Partnership Agreements (EPAs) with six different blocs of countries[14] based on an extremely tight timetable. Though Cotonu's declared objectives were about poverty reduction and sustainable development, its principal feature was to phase out preferences for ACP countries by the end of 2007. Only one EPA has been signed to date with the Caribbean (CARIFORUM) region. In addition to the usual provisions on trade, intellectual property and services, the 2008 EPA expands the scope of investor protections by conferring pre-establishment rights (barring, for instance, foreign investment screening), prohibiting capital controls (which could interfere with the repatriation of profits by transnational corporations to shareholders in their home states), and mandating most-favoured nation treatment (which ensures Europeans receive the best treatment available to other foreign investors operating in CARIFORUM countries) (Van Harten, 2008a). Investor disputes with host states, however, proceed only to the more traditional forum of state–state arbitration. Rather than significantly departing from the logic of contemporary transnational legality, the EPA builds on and supplements rights available to European investors under existing BITs that, typically, cover only the post-establishment phase.

The Lisbon Treaty of 2009 (Art. 206), however, enlarges European competence in regard to such matters. Lisbon empowers the EU to reduce restrictions on the movement of foreign direct investment and grants exclusive competence to the EU to implement a unified international investment policy. With this new authority in hand, things appear not to have changed much. Though the European Commission (the EU's inter-state executive authority) proposes that a one-size-fits-all model of investment treaty is 'neither feasible or desirable', it maintains that EU investors 'abroad [should] enjoy a level playing field,

---

13 McIlroy (2004, p. 645) observes that Canada's 2004 model treaty 'clearly signaled that it [Canada] does not wish to sign investment treaties that create investor rights which go beyond those that are recognized by domestic consensus or law'. He does not admit, however, that it turns out that it is US domestic law that is controlling.
14 The Caribbean, the Pacific, southern, central, eastern and western Africa.

which assures both uniform and optimal conditions for investment through the progressive abolition of restrictions on investment' (2010, pp. 6, 4). This entails including all of the 'best available standards' together with 'binding commitments' represented by investor–state dispute settlement. Though without reference to any empirical evidence in this regard (Schneiderman, 2008, pp. 42–3), the European Commission writes that investor–state arbitration 'is such an established feature of investment agreements that its absence would in fact discourage investors and make a host economy less attractive than others' (2010, pp. 5, 10). The European Council (comprising the European heads-of-state) embraced the European Commission's plan of action, agreeing that EU policy 'should increase the current level of protection and legal security for the European investor abroad' (2010, para. 9). New bilateral investment agreements should be as 'equally effective' as existing European BITs with high standards of investor protection acting as the 'main pillars of future EU investment agreements' (2010, para. 14). The European Council subsequently approved a mandate for trade and investment treaty negotiations, ongoing with Canada, India and Singapore, that provides for 'the highest possible level[s] of legal protection and certainty' (Inside US Trade, 2011; Seattle to Brussels Network, 2011). The European Council is the same European body for the promotion of 'executive federalism' that Habermas has rebuked for 'exercising a kind of post-democratic, bureaucratic rule' (Habermas 2012, p. 52; 2011). Though the EU views its development policy as more 'enlightened' than that of the US (Mold, 2007, p. 238), the most recent evidence suggests a fulsome embrace of the disciplining effects of transnational legality over other, seemingly less attractive, alternatives.

It may be more reasonable, then, to expect countries other than the leading OECD states to take this lead. Roberto Unger suggests, for instance, that it is from within large marginalized countries like Brazil, India, Russia and China (the BRICs) where progressive alternatives may credibly be developed. It is only 'through the pressure of rebellion by major countries against the world order' that pluralistic political economies stand a chance of success (Unger, 1998, p. 86). These are some of the leading states in the G20 that successfully scuttled WTO ministerial discussions at Cancun in 2003 (Bello, 2005, pp. 160–4). This is a route that departs significantly from the one charted by Habermas. It is a possibility that I explore in subsequent chapters.

* * *

Habermas correctly diagnoses a need to move beyond contemporary manifestations of global power politics. Yet his proposal for multi-level global governance, even if a 'work in progress' (Cronin, 2011, p. 218), seems unlikely to deviate from the path already laid down by extant transnational legal norms.

Rather than undoing those constraints, his institutional proposal for cosmopolitan government and citizenship is as likely to reinforce those bounds as undo them. It is not merely a matter, then, of having politics catch up with markets in a new post-national constellation, as Habermas describes it, but of making space available for critical resistance that does not take-for-granted the institutional settlement represented by transnational legality.

The path which resistance to investment rules and economic globalization may take admittedly remains opaque. Habermas would have the push for this institutional renovation originate in the powerful liberal democracies of the OECD. The congressional initiative over the scope of investor rights gives us cause for despair. Though the impetus for this reform originated in the peripheral spaces of the public sphere, once manifested in the formal institutions of the public sphere, the initiative turned inward, retrenching investor rights and US constitutional power. As Americans aim to bring investor rights more precisely into line with their own constitutional thinking, they consolidate the supremacy of US law as the global standard of economic success. Though, ultimately, South Africa resisted this specific US-led effort, it still remains mired in the web of transnational legality via numerous treaties signed with European and other states (Schneiderman, 2008, pp. 155–6; South Africa DTI, 2009). The situation of states, like South Africa, otherwise disabled from innovating too much in the realms of economic and social policy, is only marginally improved. Dissonant with the rhetoric of speed and movement (Urry, 2005), the global situation, instead of becoming more fluid, hardens.

4
Santos and the Difficulty of Sustainable Resistance

States play ambivalent roles in contemporary processes associated with economic globalization. On the one hand, they actively participate in the construction of the rules and institutions intended to bind the hands of governments far into the future. In this way, states commit to not act in ways that impede market processes within and across national borders. On the other hand, states are expected to ensure that strategies of self-limitation are complemented by state supports that assist in, and even legitimate, pre-commitments of self-limitation. These supports may take the form of police action to suppress resistance by a mobilized populace or measures for societal self-protection so long as they do not lie beyond the hegemonic norm (Tarullo, 1987, p. 569). As has been noted by others (Weiss, 2005a; Sassen, 2006, p. 229), accompanying processes of deregulation are those of re-regulation. In an age of economic globalization, state functions do not entirely recede into the background, instead, states continue to play critical roles in the structuration of economic globalization.

In Santos' *Toward a New Legal Common Sense* (2002), the state has some prominence in at least three stages of the book's argument. First, the state is critical to the story Santos tells about the rise of modernity. The liberal-capitalist-bureaucratic state is a central figure in this narrative until eclipsed by markets. Second, the post-Westphalian system of states contributes to the unevenness with which globalization is experienced in different parts of the world. This is because particularistic national legal systems, predominantly from the North, compete for hegemony in the modern world system. This leads to Santos' insightful observation that globalization is the product of inter-state competition in which certain local phenomenon are successfully globalized – instances of 'globalized localism' – and in which local conditions correspondingly are restructured in light of transnational hegemonic practices – the phenomenon of 'localized globalism' (2002, p. 179). This puts paid to the claims of universality paraded about by international trade and investment lawyers (Carbonneau, 2002; Ratner, 2008) – claims defending the abstract universalism of international economic law that generally serve to justify the established order of things (Bourdieu, 2000, p. 71). Third, though state authority is diminished in the contemporary period, the task of articulation and coordination of formerly public functions, now sub-contracted to various private actors operating at various scales, remains with the state. Counter-hegemonic movements will want to democratize this 'task of co-ordination', Santos writes (2002, p. 489). Social movements become the key agents for societal transformation, generating pathways away from hegemonic globalization and towards its emancipatory counterpart. As the institutional form the emergent state will take is not yet clear, Santos suggests that, in the interim, we keep open the channels of change – that 'irreversible institutional options' be avoided (ibid.). The state thereby is conceived as the 'newest social movement' (Santos, 2002, p. 492). The focus of this chapter is on Santos' third conception of the state, which suggests an emancipatory pathway out of the persistent problems generated by modernity's fault lines.

Transnational legal norms and forms serve as useful devices for testing hypotheses about the role of the state in the current era. As argued in Chapter 1, it turns out that the investment rules regime disparages state functions beyond those considered normal or dissonant with investment rules strictures. States are considered, for the most part, untrustworthy constituents of social change. This is paradoxical in so far as the regime relies on states to serve certain legitimating functions. Social movement actors and transnational non-governmental organizations (NGOs) are considered non-participants in the investment rules regime. Lastly, those most vulnerable to the machinations of foreign investment activity – the voices of the suffering (Baxi, 2006, p. 6) – are simply excluded from its institutional logic. They are rinsed clean out of the picture. They truly are the subaltern – those who fall outside of capitalism's logic and who have no established agency in the North's culture of consumerism (Spivak, 1999). To the extent that they enter into the picture, they are portrayed as the dupes of rent-seeking competitors or corrupt local actors. Simply put, they are paid to make an appearance. This, for instance, is how the Metalclad Corporation of Newport Beach, California, characterized protests by *campesinos* against Metalclad's hazardous waste facility site in Guadalcazar in 1995 (Schneiderman, 2008, pp. 82–6). It is how those mobilized in opposition to the operation of Spanish-based Técnicas Medioambientales hazardous waste site outside of Hermosillo, Mexico in 1997–1998 were portrayed (discussed next in Chapter 5). It also is how San Francisco-based Bechtel Corporation characterized the mobilization of civil society protests opposed to privatization of local water supplies in Cochabamba, Bolivia, in 2000. All were the subject of investment disputes before international investment tribunals. Metalclad won an award of some US$16 million with the tribunal making little mention of the entirely foreseeable local opposition to the re-opening of a site previously closed down by the Mexican federal government for having leeched hazardous waste into the local water supply. Técnicas Medioambientales, similarly, won an award of US$5.5 million plus compounded interest for Mexico's failure to renew its hazardous waste operating licence. Bechtel sought, in the name of its subsidiary Aguas del Tunari, the sum of US$25–50 million but withdrew its claim after winning an initial award on jurisdiction. I focus on the Cochabamba case in this chapter as it enables us to test the extent to which investment rules 'lock in' states to predetermined policy outcomes and also the capacity of states, civil society groups and transnational NGOs to facilitate meaningful resistance. It turns out that, if states are to become sites of institutional experimentation, this only becomes feasible after loosening up the transnational ties that bind states to market-preferring outcomes discussed in the previous two chapters.

In this chapter, I begin by exploring the role of states in Santos' socio-legal thought and his conception of the state as the newest social movement ('The decomposing state'). In the second part ('Transnational legal fixity'), I illustrate the structural tilt of transnational legality by highlighting the international investment tribunal's decision on jurisdiction in the *Aguas del Tunari* case against Bolivia (*Aguas del Tunari SA v Republic of Bolivia* (2005)). In the last part ('Transnational momentum'), I review the factors giving rise to the withdrawal of the dispute against Bolivia, drawing on the social movement and contentious politics literature. The case study suggests that, though transnational coalitions provide vehicles for disrupting economic globalization's strictures and even transforming local conditions, resistance is episodic. Despite Santos' exhortations, the state remains, under these conditions, the most salient locale with which to resist transnational legality.

The decomposing state

In Santos's view, Western modernity has been an audacious yet contradictory project. If modernity opened up vistas of human possibility previously unforeseen, it also has required the generation of techniques of management with which to control its excesses. Modernity rests, therefore, on the contradictory pillars of emancipation and regulation. The state, in Santos' scheme, is one of the foundational principles, along with the market and community, upon which the dominant pillar of regulation rests. The second chapter of *Toward a New Legal Common Sense* takes up this story of the rise of the liberal-capitalist-bureaucratic state, the fall of its regulatory capacity, the accompanying decline of community, and their eclipse by the market principle (2002, pp. 9, 53).

It follows, Santos argues, that we are in the midst of a paradigmatic transition, where the routine answers associated with modernity are no longer tenable in the current environment. In the face of this 'crisis', a paradigmatic reading provides an opportunity to think beyond modern solutions towards radically new social relations 'that go beyond capitalism' (2002, p. 173). This is in contrast to a sub-paradigmatic reading, which looks for 'structural adjustment' within 'rather than beyond' modernity's framework of possibilities (2002, p. 174).

In the paradigmatic transition, the state plays an increasingly diminished role. Its place as the central unit of analysis is complemented if not overtaken by the activities of non-state actors. Private–public partnerships, privatization and governance are some of the terms we associate with this transfer of authority, oftentimes resulting in outcomes detrimental to those who do not enjoy privileged access to the benefits of globalization. In this age of the 'postinterventionist state' (2002, p. 55), we are pressed to look elsewhere for the means by which communities might be able to countervail markets and open up a range of possible societal futures, a 'non-capitalist, eco-socialist future being one of them' (2002, p. 63). Newer social movements and transnational NGOs provide locales out of which the solidaristic strategies of 'oppositional postmodernism' may be pursued. This version of postmodernism is to be distinguished from what Santos labels 'celebratory postmodernism', a mode of analysis that amounts to nothing more than resignation and reconciliation with that which merely exists (2002, pp. 13–14). Embracing the reality of a paradigmatic transition entails moving beyond an incapacity to 'characterize the transitional moment adequately' and, instead, looks for alternatives that emerge out of the practices of oppressed peoples (2002, p. 14). These will be forms of 'counter-hegemonic globalization', a phrase that gets taken up near the end of Santos' 2002 book and in subsequent work (i.e. Santos and Rodríguez-Garavito, 2005a), that have the potential of generating a 'transnational emancipatory sub-politics' (Santos, 2001, p. 190; cf. Beck, 1992). Replicating Keck and Sikkink's criteria for determining the success of advocacy movements (1998, p. 25), Santos looks to social movements to counter hegemonic globalization by generating discursive shifts in 'agenda setting' and the 'rhetoric of decision makers' and, materially, by generating 'institutional changes' having 'an effective impact on concrete policies' (Santos, 2001, p. 190). These elements were in play in Cochabamba, Bolivia, where privatization of the municipal water supply spawned vociferous local and then transnational opposition generating changes at, arguably, all four of these levels.

In the paradigmatic transition there remain progressive, non-capitalist alternatives and some of these are noted in his discussion of the state as the 'newest social movement' (Santos, 2002, p. 489; Santos and Avritzer, 2005,

p. lxvii). If the functions formerly served by the state have been dispersed, these are 'the object of permanent contention and painstaking negotiation among different social actors' which will take place 'under state coordination' (Santos, 2002, p. 489). Santos here is ambivalent about state capacity in the transition: the state is, on the one hand, an 'imagined', 'partial and fragmented political relation' with seemingly little left to do (ibid.). On the other hand, the state constitutes an 'unregulated political battlefield' which is open to differing agents 'carrying alternative conceptions of the goods to be delivered' (ibid.). Future struggles, he predicts, will be fought over the remains of the state's monopoly over the regulatory pillar (2002, p. 490).

Santos admits that it is difficult to predict precisely the ensuing configuration of new state forms that will emerge. There are an 'unprecedented proliferation of alternatives', Santos claims, which cannot be subsumed under the 'umbrella of a single global alternative' (Santos, 2007, p. 69). What can be predicted is that there will be democratic struggle over 'alternative institutional designs' (Santos, 2002, p. 492) in which preference will be given to experimental forms that guarantee the greatest level of participation to social groupings (Santos, 2007, p. 73). In the interim, therefore, it is preferred that alternatives remain open – that 'irreversible institutional options' be rejected in favour of more fluid outcomes, ones that may result in more egalitarian distribution of global wealth. In this regard, and this is in contrast to Habermas (discussed in Chapter 3), Santos looks to the subaltern 'networks, initiatives, organizations, and movements' of the South rather than the North to play a leadership role in this regard (2007, p. 64; 2002, p. 458).[1] It is in these locales that we can expect a subaltern cosmopolitan consciousness to be articulated and non-capitalistic alternatives devised.

To what extent can the state be re-appropriated for these purposes? To be sure, there remains some room to manoeuvre for states and citizens in the development of elements of social policy. On matters such as welfare reform (Hay, 2005) or industrial and technological subsidies (Weiss, 2005b), for instance, policy differences arise despite globalization's convergence effects. There are thresholds (Coward, 2005, p. 868), however, to what may be permissible in an age of economic globalization – what Santos characterizes as the radically excluded practices that arise on the 'other side of the line' (2007, p. 45; 2006, p. 11) the exclusion of which amounts to the 'waste of

---

1 This prescription of institutional experimentation resembles Unger's in so far as both reject the liberal legal model of institutional design (i.e. Unger, 1996). Unger, Santos argues, continues to work mostly within the modernist paradigm of state forms – the state monopoly over legal production marginalizes existing and emergent pluralist legal forms, including subaltern ones, where hope for democratic consolidation and experimentation may lie. Unger's account, according to Santos, is thereby incompletely radicalized (2002, p. 13).

social experience' (2006, p. 15). Transnational legality operates precisely in this way: by placing substantial limits on the capacity of publics, in both the North and the South, to experiment institutionally and to imagine alternative, democratic and non-capitalistic solutions to problems continuing to be posed by modernity.

Transnational legal fixity

The investment rules regime looks just like the sort of irreversible institutional option that should be eschewed in this period of fluidity and transition. The regime has as its object to limit the imagination of alternative futures whether by state or non-state institutions. As we have seen, the regime is organized around the logic of the market. Priority is placed on the rights of investors rather than the capacity of states to take measures that are considered beyond the norm or out of the ordinary. The investment rules regime, in this way, aims to establish thresholds of tolerable behaviour promoting a culture of markets seemingly freed from the control of politics. All of this is associated with the early twentieth-century idea that there are minimum standards of justice expected of all 'civilized nations' and that departures from these minimum standards are to be discouraged (Schneiderman, 2008, p. 57). In the contemporary world, this is achieved by 'locking' states into these commitments far into the future (Gill, 2003, p. 132), holding in check resistance at local levels. Many small and large acts of resistance to economic globalization are effectively rendered illegal under this new constitutional order.

Local policy initiatives are expected to conform to this culture of limited and constrained government and citizens that rebuff the regime's precepts can anticipate punishment with an award of damages in the range of tens to hundreds of millions of dollars. This is despite the fact that the investment rules regime is critically reliant on stable national legal orders to protect fixed and immovable investment interests. National states are expected to take the difficult and contradictory path, as I argued in Chapter 1, of succumbing to economic globalization's legal edicts while resisting demands for non-market-based solutions to contemporary social problems.

The operational dampening of policy choices on affected citizens is best exemplified by case studies taken up in particular locales, be they national or subnational. It is in these places where resistance to the hegemony of investment rules can be discerned and the capacity to turn things around best evaluated. They also provide us with evidence with which to evaluate Santos' claim about modernity's crisis and the opportunities for paradigmatic readings of the non-capitalist world to emerge. One such instance is the celebrated 'water wars' of Cochabamba, Bolivia. My purpose is not so much to revisit these well-rehearsed events (Olivera and Lewis, 2004; Shultz, 2008) as to take up matters after Bechtel's subsidiaries fled Bolivia.

Under direct pressure from the World Bank, Bolivia introduced new legislation to permit the privatization of water and sanitation services by large municipalities. Public subsidies would cease. This, the World Bank admitted in its Bolivia country report, 'will not be easy to implement' (World Bank, 1999, p. 152). It was expected that privatization in three urban centres would, however, 'liberate' US$13–15 million of public funds (World Bank, 1999, p. 156). Cochabamba, Bolivia's third largest city, embraced the water privatization initiative with gusto leasing its water concession to the Aguas del Tunari consortium, led by subsidiaries of San Francisco-based Bechtel Enterprises. It is important to emphasize that the privatization plan was enthusiastically endorsed not only by national state actors but by the state governor and municipal council until civil society unrest moved the governor, mayor and municipality to withdraw their support (Nickson and Vargas, 2002, p. 113). The state, in this story, was an 'active culprit' and no mere bystander in these events (Santos, 2002, p. 453).

The costs of the privatization plan were enormous. This was, in part, because of a proposal to tunnel water through the Tunari mountains, a plan which the World Bank, to its credit, frowned upon and which Bechtel, according to the company, reluctantly agreed to take on (Quint, 2000). Nevertheless, with a guaranteed annual rate of return of 16 per cent on its investment, price hikes were inevitable if these sorts of profits were to be realized. Cost increases were immediately passed on to the citizens of Cochabamba (at an average of 35 per cent) and without any appreciable improvement in services. Water rates almost doubled. In a city where the minimum wage is less than US$100 per month, many families saw their bills rise by US$20, almost one-fifth of their monthly income. If payment was not made, services were terminated. Traditional forms of water collection were outlawed, irrigation canals threatened and community wells shut down (Finnegan, 2002; Shultz, 2008).

The citizens of Cochabamba took to the streets in protest. Led by the *Coordinadora del Agua y la Vida* (coalition in defence of water and life) – a citizen's movement of consumers, workers, cocoa growers and others, uniting both urban and rural sectors, and led by trade union federation president Oscar Olivera – a general strike shut down the city for four straight days in January 2000. President Hugo Banzer dispatched military troops in February and declared a state of emergency in April. By this time, more than 175 protestors had been injured, two youths blinded and an unarmed 17-year-old, Victor Hugo Daza, killed. After four months of protest, the government of Bolivia relented, advised Aguas del Tunari executives that their safety could not be guaranteed, and the company fled the country. The government declared its concession contract with Aguas del Tunari terminated and the municipality retook control of Cochabamba's water utility (Olivera and Lewis, 2004, pp. 25–49; Finnegan, 2002; Shultz, 2003).

This local story of resistance against a large multinational has inspired a broad spectrum of activists and intellectuals. Anderson mentions it in the closing of his book *Constitutional Rights after Globalization* (Anderson, 2005, p. 150) and, in both the closing parts of the film *The Corporation* (2004) and in the companion book (Bakan, 2004, pp. 164–6), Bakan recounts these events so as to inspire citizens to repatriate power that has been granted to corporations. For Anderson, social movements have shown the capacity to hold corporations to account for exercises of private power. For Bakan, corporations are creatures of public law and so only have power that governments have granted to them which can also be denied to them. But corporate power has established a powerful transnational legal order that can impede local acts of resistance like those in Cochabamba. What is usually recited is only one side of the Cochabamba story – that of a popular movement expelling a rapacious water company from their town.

There is another side to the story and it is the one that interests me here. It concerns a US$25–50 million-dollar claim that Aguas del Tunari launched against the government of Bolivia under a Netherlands–Bolivia bilateral investment treaty (BIT). Originally incorporated in the Cayman Islands, Aguas del Tunari's principal shareholder, International Water, engaged in complex corporate reorganization after the contract with Cochabamba was negotiated. This resulted in the company 'migrating' and re-incorporating in Luxembourg and being subsumed under the ownership structure of two different companies incorporated under the law of the Netherlands, of which Bechtel remained a principal shareholder (de Gramont, 2006, pp. 12–13). This, purportedly, was done for tax reasons but undoubtedly also to take advantage of investor rights available under the investment treaty, including rights entitling investors to sue should they be substantially deprived of their investment interests (de Gramont, 2006, p. 25).[2]

These proceedings were treated as confidential by the International Centre for the Settlement of Investment Disputes (ICSID), the World Bank arbitration facility which administered the arbitration proceedings. It was in late 2005, after the arbitration tribunal established to resolve this investment dispute released its preliminary ruling on jurisdiction, that we learnt conclusively

---

2 As de Gramont, who appeared for Bolivia advises, the claimant 'argued vigorously that the changes to its intermediate ownership structure were for tax reasons and had been planned (though not implemented) long before any problems with the investment were apparent. However, AdT [Aguas del Tunari] did not present any evidence to support that assertion and the majority decision rejected Bolivia's request for the production of any such evidence.' (2006, p. 25)

that the company was arguing that there was a 'taking' of its investment interest. There were other disciplines in the investment treaty available to the investor, including those prohibiting denials of 'fair and equitable treatment' and 'full security and protection' of its investment (Schneiderman, 2004b, p. 79). That is, the company could have claimed that the government of Bolivia did not make sufficient effort to secure and protect the viability of the consortium's investment. The state's brutal response to the *Coordinadora's* campaign, in other words, was not only warranted by the regime but may not have gone far enough as far as the company is concerned. So while there was much to celebrate in the streets of Cochabamba, analysts have failed to take into account the corporate response. For these reasons, one cannot but agree with Shamir who writes that 'any effort to explore and to theorize counter-hegemonic practices must also deal with corporate responses to such threats' (2005, p. 94).

Here, I review briefly the tribunal's decision on jurisdiction so as to explicate the structural tilt of the investment rules regime, one that decidedly favours investors over state and non-state actors. There are four principal lessons to be drawn from the tribunal's ruling.

First, local and transnational NGOs are relegated to the sidelines in this model of dispute resolution. In August 2002, one year after proceedings were initiated by Aguas del Tunari, the US-based environmental NGO, Earth Justice, filed a petition on behalf of the *Coordinadora*, Friends of the Earth-Netherlands, Oscar Olivera and others to intervene in the arbitration (the petition, coordinated by the Institute for Policy Studies, is discussed below under 'Transnational momentum'). The petition to intervene was denied by the tribunal. Though politely acknowledging their concerns, the tribunal unanimously concluded that the NGOs' request was not within the competence of the tribunal to grant. Control over the proceedings rested with the parties, not the tribunal and, absent the consent of both sides, the tribunal could not 'join a non-party to the proceedings; to provide access to hearings to non-parties and, a fortiori, to the public generally; or to make the documents of the proceedings public' (*Aguas del Tunari* (2005), para. 17).

This is not an unsurprising result as international arbitration of investment disputes is structured on the private law model of commercial arbitration. This is a model intended to resolve disputes rather limited in scope, in camera and in an ad hoc fashion, with no oversight by non-parties. This is in contrast to the ideal public law model which insists on the principles of openness, transparency and oversight, even participation, by non-parties (Van Harten, 2007, ch. 7). This is somewhat ironic, given that investors insist that investment rules require state parties to adhere to the principles of openness, transparency and procedural fairness. They will have none of this when they seek claims for damages that would bankrupt the economies of many states in the world. Investors do not have it entirely their way, however (Stern, 2007). Recent changes to ICSID rules permit the submission of third-party briefs (ICSID, 2006, rule 37(2)) at the discretion of the tribunal, applying a multi-factor analysis, and permit the attendance of non-parties to proceedings if all of the parties provide their consent (ICSID, 2006, rule 32(2)).

Second, it is difficult for states to avoid investment rules disciplines. Bolivia argued that the tribunal was without jurisdiction in the dispute by reason of the choice-of-forum clause in the concession contract (de Gramont, 2006, pp. 16–17). The contract granted exclusive jurisdiction to settle disputes as between Aguas del Tunari and Bolivia to Bolivian courts applying only Bolivian law (Art. 41.2). This clause, however, did not preclude access to international arbitration by the concessionaires' shareholders (Art. 41.3). The tribunal would not accept that it was intended by the parties that exclusive jurisdiction be granted to Bolivian courts in the former case. Aguas del Tunari's claim, after all, was not about an alleged breach of contract but an alleged violation of an international investment treaty (*Aguas del Tunari* (2005), para. 114). If a waiver of ICSID jurisdiction was intended, the tribunal surmised, this would have required a specific and clear expression of the parties' intent, which was not evident in this case (para. 118). This is a typical response to choice-of-forum clauses in investment arbitration (*Compañía de Aguas del Aconquija SA and Vivendi Universal SA v Argentina* (2002), para. 202).

Bolivia also claimed that it had not contemplated that the Netherlands–Bolivia BIT would govern relations between itself and Aguas del Tunari. For this reason, Bolivia effectively had not granted consent to arbitration, a fundamental prerequisite to ICSID jurisdiction. The concession was structured specifically so that it would not fall under a BIT. They argued, in other words, that the contract was awarded to Aguas del Tunari so that no foreign investor could take advantage of commitments to investor protection beyond those available in the concession contract (*Aguas del Tunari* (2005), para. 195). Professor Rudolf Dolzer, a well-recognized authority in the area and a champion of the investment rules regime, backed up the Bolivian case with his expert evidence. Dolzer opined that the 'circle of beneficiaries' was carefully circumscribed. Each investment operates within a specific legal setting and the Bolivians were under the impression that the specific setting would be within the framework of Bolivia's law and regulations (*Aguas del Tunari* (2005), para. 199).

The tribunal preferred the position taken· by the investor which accepts the BIT as general written consent to authorize arbitration (Arbitrator Alberro-Semerena dissented on this point). This is how other tribunals have resolved similar claims. In cases against Argentina, for instance, ICSID panels have found the consent requirement satisfied as soon as the state, via a BIT, extends a 'generic invitation' to all investors from the other contracting state

(*Lanco International Inc. v Argentina* (2001), para. 43) Investors are entitled to accept this offer which, when accepted, cannot be withdrawn unilaterally; nor is that consent vitiated by a clause in a concession contract entitling investors to pursue their claims in local courts (*Lanco International* (2001), para. 40).

Third, despite its foundation in a series of bilateral treaties, the nationality of the foreign investor is of less consequence than would appear in taking advantage of investment disciplines. Investment rules, in other words, will catch states in its web regardless of an investor's national origins. Bolivia argued that Aguas del Tunari's principle shareholder, International Water, could not invoke the Dutch–Bolivia BIT as the company was not 'controlled' by a Dutch national. International Water was merely a corporate shell, incorporated under Dutch law but under the control of US-based Bechtel Corporation. No investment treaty existed between the US and Bolivia upon which Bechtel could rely. Aguas del Tunari admittedly was under the control of foreigners but not those of the correct nationality. The tribunal rejected this argument too, preferring to adopt a formalistic definition of control, that is, one requiring only a 'legal capacity to control' to be 'ascertained with reference to the percentage of shares held' rather than an 'actual day-to-day or ultimate control' (*Aguas del Tunari* (2005), para. 264) (Arbitrator Alberro-Semerena also dissented on this point.) It was sufficient that International Water was incorporated in the Netherlands though decisions may actually have been made back at Bechtel headquarters in San Francisco.[3] This, too, is consistent with arbitral trends: all that is required is that the company be formally incorporated in accordance with the laws of the home state (*Mobil Corporation Venezuela Holdings BV and Others v Venezuela* (2010)).

The Dutch government expressed some ambivalence about whether Aguas del Tunari and International Water should be entitled to take advantage of these treaty commitments. Responding to questions put to the government of the Netherlands in 2002, the State Secretary for Economic Affairs twice replied that it was up to the discretion of the tribunal to determine jurisdiction (*Aguas del Tunari* (2005), paras 253–54). On a third occasion, when five Dutch MPs put the question to the government, the Minister for Housing, Spatial Planning and Environment responded on behalf of his ministry and two others (the Minister for Development Cooperation and State Secretary for Economic Affairs) that, as noted in the previous responses, 'the Government is of the view that the investment treaty is not applicable to this particular case' (*Aguas del Tunari* (2005), para. 255). The government, in fact, had not

---

3 The tribunal relied, in a footnote, on the ruling of another tribunal in *Aucoven* which found that this 'formality' of corporate control 'is the fundamental building block of the global economy' (*Autopista Concesionada de Venezuela CA ('Aucoven') v Bolivarian Republic of Venezuela* (2001), para. 67).

responded in this way on the two previous occasions. This caused the tribunal rightly to observe that the third response was 'inconsistent' with the previous two (*Aguas del Tunari* (2005), para. 258). The tribunal took the extraordinary step of seeking clarification directly from the government of the Netherlands. The tribunal sought to elicit from the government documentary evidence upon which it may have relied when responding to parliamentary questions, which could constitute evidence of 'subsequent practice ... which establishes the agreement of the parties' pursuant to the Vienna Convention of the Law of Treaties (Art. 31[3]) (para. 251). The tribunal's inquiry prompted a reply letter from the legal advisor to the Dutch Ministry of Foreign Affairs with little more than a recital of the Vienna Convention (*Aguas del Tunari* (2005), para. 260). According to the tribunal, the Netherlands government failed to 'express with any clarity the position that the BIT does not apply in this case'. In any event, the tribunal concluded, the government was correct to say on the two prior occasions that this remained a matter for the tribunal alone to decide (*Aguas del Tunari* (2005), para. 263). If we understand that the state has little substantive unity (Jessop, 1990, p. 9; Santos, 2006, p. 174;), this kind of fragmented response from the Dutch government might have been anticipated. Ultimately, it was the legal advisor directing the right hand of the state – the one handling the investment treaty dossier – who delivered the muted response of the Dutch government to the tribunal.

In its concluding observations, the tribunal resisted finding any bad faith on the part of the company in shifting its corporate nationality. International Water of the Cayman Islands would not have moved corporate headquarters first to Luxembourg so as to be under the subsequent control of a Netherlands holding company in anticipation of an investment dispute, the tribunal generously finds, as the record shows that the 'severity' of resistance was not 'foreseeable' (*Aguas del Tunari* (2005), para. 329). Yet, as the dissenting reasons show, opposition to the concession was foreseeable even on the eve of the signing of the contract. According to de Gramont (co-lead counsel for Bolivia before ICSID), 'the Dutch holding companies were inserted into AdT's intermediate ownership structure after the street protests and negative press reports had begun, and after public calls to cancel the Concession Agreement had been made' (de Gramont, 2006, p. 24). Instead, the tribunal was satisfied that the company had changed corporate nationality for tax reasons, though:

> it is not uncommon in practice, and – absent a particular limitation – not illegal to locate one's operations in a jurisdiction perceived to provide a beneficial regulatory and legal environment in terms, for examples [sic], of taxation or the substantive law of the jurisdiction, including the availability of a BIT (*Aguas del Tunari* (2005), para. 330).

So there was no fraud being perpetrated on the ICSID tribunal by the claimant company. Instead, the tribunal declared that, though considered primarily as bilateral treaties, 'such treaties serve in many cases more broadly as portals' (*Aguas del Tunari* (2005), para. 332) – entry points for footloose capital caught between the contradiction of having the ability to move capital easily across borders while relying on fixed and immobile capital investments that require security and stability (also *Tokios Tokelès* v *Ukraine*, (2004), para. 80). This truly is a worldwide network of investment disciplines, with over 2700 BITs in place, from which most states will find it difficult to hide.

Despite the compelling nature of the facts on the ground at Cochabamba, the logic of international investment law, and the primacy it places on the security of investment interests, led not only to the finding of jurisdiction but, as I have suggested elsewhere, may very well have resulted in a successful claim for damages (Schneiderman, 2004b). Admittedly, there were many outstanding questions of fact and law yet to be settled. Additionally, Bolivia planned to file its own counter-claim against Aguas del Tunari and this may have also have precipitated a negotiated outcome. Nevertheless, exceptions to investment disciplines are read narrowly (*CMS Gas Transmission Company v República Argentina* (2005), paras 316–17, 355) and the takings standard will more easily be satisfied in the case of a total loss of an investment. If Aguas del Tunari had succeeded in its multi-million-dollar claim, small victories like the one in Cochabamba simply would not be economically sustainable. Worse yet, they would provide warrant for even more brutal responses to local resistance against global economic actors. As it turns out, the company withdrew its claim and aborted the process in return for the payment of a few Bolivian cents. So although the investment rules regime signals a loss in the capacity to reorder and redistribute public functions in progressive ways, the regime has its weak links. In the next part, I examine the features of the resistance that precipitated this withdrawal. Is this a form of oppositional postmodernism, as Santos describes it, that seeks solutions beyond modernity? Or is this achievement more simply a return to local standards of normalcy staged in accordance with modernity's traditional repertoires and along its familiar fault lines? Moreover, are there lessons to be learned about the capacity of states together with social movements from the South coordinating with NGOS from the North to resist the regime's disciplinary effects?

Transnational momentum

In this part, I examine strategies taken up by the coalition of local social movement actors, the Bolivian state and NGOs operating in the global North that precipitated the withdrawal of Aguas del Tunari's investment dispute. It is true that parties occasionally settle foreign investment disputes. What was largely unprecedented was the counter-hegemonic campaign waged at multiple scales that convinced Bechtel Corporation (the controlling shareholder in the investment consortium) that it was best to withdraw from the dispute instead of pursuing it to its logical conclusion. In this way, the Bolivian state could recapture the water assets of Cochabamba (meagre as they were) and pursue alternative strategies by which the state could experiment with more socially sustainable and progressive outcomes. Are there features of this campaign that are generalizable to other investment disputes in other locales around the world which could re-energize state capacity in similar ways? Does this case generate resources of hope for those wishing to roll back or extinguish these constitution-like commitments that inhibit state action and guarantee rates of return for foreign investors? Are these resources nothing more than the familiar ones of economic coercion based on calculations of profit and loss, claim-making strategies familiar to those who have been operating under the paradigm of modernity? In this part, I move beyond describing hegemonic constraints and take up the task of analysing these spaces for and strategies of counter hegemony (Santos and Rodríguez-Garavito, 2005a, p. 11). I do so by utilizing the literature on social mobilization together with a small sample of interviews I conducted with activists and lawyers who were involved in the dispute.[4] I conclude that movements for the advancement of transnational social justice are likely to be mired in the goals and tactics associated with 'sub-paradigmatic' modernity.

I am aware of only one other instance where an investor abandoned a pending claim in response to bad publicity precipitated by a social movement campaign.[5] It concerns a dispute brought by Big Food Group in the UK, formerly Iceland, one of the UK's largest supermarket chains headquartered in Wales (*Booker plc v Co-operative Republic of Guyana* (2001)). Big Food acquired Booker plc, the sugar conglomerate, in 2000. It also acquired debt owed to Booker as a result of the nationalization of its partly owned Guyanese sugar subsidiary, Guyusco, in 1975. Guyana dutifully made payments to Booker until 1989, when the President of Guyana began seeking debt relief under the Paris Club rules developed by Organization for Economic Co-operation and Development (OECD) state creditors and, later, under the joint World Bank and IMF Heavily Indebted Poor Countries Initiative (HIPC). Guyana could not even voluntarily agree to Booker's compensation demands without jeopardizing its application for debt relief under the HIPC (Saxegaard, 2004, p. 729). Having gone without payment for almost a decade, in September

---

4 I recognize that Santos dismisses this literature as exhibiting the 'poverty – conceptual hubris coupled with bloodless narrow positivism – of the mainstream US sociology of social movements' (Santos, 2006, p. 9, fn. 2). I am of the view that this literature generates useful tools of analysis that help us understand the strategic and multi-level nature of social activism in the contemporary world.

5 I am grateful to Luke Peterson for bringing this dispute to my attention.

2001, Booker launched its investment claim against Guyana under a UK–Guyanese BIT. Slated to be heard before a single arbitrator (Brigitte Stern) in London commencing on 31 March 2003, the investor sought £12 million in compensation (Mathiason, 2003a). The UK Jubilee Debt Campaign, collaborating with the World Development Movement, mobilized only a few weeks before the scheduled hearing was to commence. It was perverse, argued Ashok Sinha of the Jubilee Debt Campaign, to allow an investor to recover damages when Guyana qualified for debt relief. Otherwise, the benefits of debt relief would flow not toward poverty reduction but to the coffers of a multinational conglomerate (Gibbs, 2003; Mathiason, 2003a).

In the lead-up to the hearing of the dispute, unfavourable reports began appearing in the pages of *The Guardian* and *Observer* newspapers with headlines such as 'UK Food group Squeez[ing] Poverty-Stricken Guyana for £12 million' (Mathiason, 2003a). Jubilee Debt threatened protests outside Iceland's South London store dressed in penguin costumes (appropriating the supermarket chain's corporate mascot) with banners declaring 'Penguins Against Third World Debt' (Bowers, 2003; Mathiason, 2003b). The day before the scheduled protest, Big Food dropped the claim, alleging that it had taken 'some months' of consideration to arrive at this position (Bowers, 2003). The incredulous Sunday *Observer* described the reversal as a 'spectacular climb-down', occurring merely one day after a negative front-page story appeared in that paper's business section (Mathiason, 2003b; 2003c). The paper reported, instead, that 'BFG is angry...it believes that it was bullied into capitulation and that an important property rights principle was at stake' (Mathiason, 2003c).[6] Whatever the impetus for Big Food's capitulation, it was clearly concerned about the loss of reputation resulting from its investor-claim strategy of 'squeezing poverty-stricken Guyana'. Better to abandon the dispute, the company must have surmised, than risk the rebuke of UK consumers. The Bechtel Corporation would undertake a similar sort of calculation a few years later.

As the Big Food Group case suggests, the current global scene provides new opportunities to engage in the politics of contention.[7] Though ordinarily undertaken at the local and national levels (Tilly and Tarrow, 2007, p. 22), the rules and institutions of globalization provide 'political opportunity

---

6 President Bharrat Jagdeo of Guyana subsequently expressed his gratitude to the *Guardian* and *Observer* journalists and to the work of the Jubilee Debt Campaign and the World Development Movement in 'securing cancellation of the debt' (Stabroek News, 2003).

7 Contentious politics are defined as 'interactions in which actors make claims bearing on someone else's interests, leading to coordinated efforts on behalf of shared interests or programs, in which governments are involved as targets, initiators of claims or third parties. Contentious politics thus brings together three familiar features of social life: contention, collective action, and politics.' (Tilly and Tarrow, 2007, p. 4).

structures' to engage in new practices of transnational activism (Soule, 2009, p. 44; Tarrow, 2005, p. 8). Political opportunity structures can both facilitate and inhibit collective action (Tilly and Tarrow, 2007, pp. 49, 176) – they are, one might say, strategically selective (Jessop, 1990, pp. 9–10). If the ICSID proceedings at the World Bank closed their doors to social movement actors deeply implicated in the dispute, such as the *Coordinadora*, other opportunities opened up for contentious politics (though this was not inevitable). Even if they had been welcomed to participate in the legal proceedings, this was not a locale that movement actors would have wanted to end up in, according to Jim Shultz of the Democracy Center. That was a forum of Bechtel's own choosing where social movements could exercise little influence or exhibit real strength. Rather than being confined to monolingual-legalistic argumentation in World Bank arbitration facilities, social movements would want to raise the level of discourse from a legal to a moral one.[8]

It is appropriate to begin this discussion by introducing Jim Shultz, who probably had the greatest hand in facilitating the transnational network of social activists. If in its first phase, the struggle in Cochabamba largely was a domesticated one, the subsequent scale shift, from the domestic to the transnational plane, can largely be attributed to the efforts of Jim Shultz. Shultz is executive director and founder of the Democracy Center, an organization that educates and empowers people by reporting, training and organizing movements for human rights and social justice. Originally based in San Francisco, the Democracy Center moved its offices to Cochabamba in 1998 where Shultz has established an impressive network over the internet to publicize its work. Shultz capitalized on this network and contacts in San Francisco when he made public, in the midst of the 2000 water wars, the role of San Francisco-based Bechtel Corporation as the parent company with control over the consortium. Activists in the Bay area occupied Bechtel corporate headquarters. Protestors as far away as Auckland hosed down the Bolivian embassy with high-pressure water hoses from a borrowed fire truck in protest against both the state's brutal response and Bechtel's involvement (Shultz, 2003, p. 274). Shultz disseminated the email of its president and chief executive officer (CEO), Riley Bechtel, and activists bombarded him with e-mails. Shultz exploited Bay-area media connections. Democracy Center reports were syndicated by the Pacific News Service and then picked up in the US and Canada, generating a spiral of interest in national US media outlets like *The New Yorker* (Finnegan, 2002) and PBS (Moyers, 2001; Shultz, 2003, p. 274).

Once Aguas del Tunari was forced out, the second phase of the campaign kicked into gear that would pressure the company to withdraw its claim for

---

8   Personal interview with Jim Shultz (13 July 2007).

US$25–50 million in damages. Bechtel offices were again occupied and protestors chained together in Bechtel's lobby (Harris, 2006). Municipal allies were conscripted. The San Francisco Board of Supervisors approved a resolution calling on Bechtel to withdraw its claim (Harris, 2006). Shultz happened to be visiting family in the Bay area at the time and so was able to appear in person before the municipal council.[9] Abengoa SA of Spain, a minority shareholder in International Water of the Netherlands, helped direct the legal proceedings along with Bechtel and so this prompted civil society action in Spain, resulting in hundreds of further e-mails to Bechtel. King Juan Carlos and Spanish Prime Minister Zapatero called on Abengoa to drop its claim against Bolivia (Harris, 2006). Dutch parliamentarians and NGOs were conscripted (as discussed above), calling on the government of the Netherlands to denounce corporate forum shopping which entitled International Water to sue under a Dutch–Bolivia BIT.

Oscar Olivera became an international celebrity. The Washington DC-based Institute for Policy Studies (IPS) awarded Olivero the Letelier-Moffit award for human rights in 2000. It was on meeting Olivero that IPS began to participate in this global campaign. The IPS's global economy project, under the direction of Sarah Anderson, took a lead role in soliciting support from over 300 civil society organizations across five different continents seeking to make the ICSID proceedings public and allowing for participation by Olivera and others in the dispute. Anderson organized protests outside the Virginia home of Bechtel's Washington lobbyist. All of this was done, she advises, in consultation with the *Coordinadora* and the government of Bolivia. She admitted to me that there was a 'good flow of information' between the government and IPS; meetings were held directly with the Bolivian government and its DC lawyers.[10] They were 'happy to have the activists back them', she said. The network of activists in Bolivia (Shultz, Olivera) and in the US (EarthJustice, IPS), together with their personal ties (Olivera's sister, Marcela, worked for Ralph Nader's Public Citizen in DC) helped to ensure that there were 'strong bridges' of solidarity across national frontiers. There was at least one idea, she advises, 'that we thought a real winner' but it was later dropped 'because people in Cochabamba disagreed with that approach' (Anderson, 2006).

In the social movement and contentious politics literature, this was an instance of transnational contention whereby transnational activists were linked to one another, to states and to international fora (Tarrow, 2005, p. 25). This transnational advocacy network (Keck and Sikkink, 1998, p. 16), though rooted in specific national and subnational contexts, engaged in contentious political activities that linked it with activists in other national contexts, shifting its activities from the local to the transnational, and then

---

9   Personal interview with Jim Shultz (13 July 2007).
10   Personal interview with Sarah Anderson (26 October 2006).

back again to the local (Tarrow, 2005, p. 29; Soule, 2009, p. 51). It is not that some transnational global civil society emerged out of this activity, rather, activists remain rooted largely in the local, exploiting local contacts and institutions (Johnston and Laxer, 2003; Tarrow, 2005, p. 43).

What were some of the reasons that Bechtel dropped the case, even though, after winning the decision on jurisdiction, it might also have won on the merits? Bechtel, after all, was a 'tough adversary'.[11] It was unlike Gap Inc. – without storefronts and not vulnerable to consumer activism. Nor was Bechtel a publicly traded company, which would have provided outlets for contention through shareholder activism. In these ways, the company truly was a 'global abstraction' (Dirlik, 1994). So the company presumably could have held out. In an email, Anderson identified a number of factors that helped to contribute to this 'rare' victory (Anderson, 2006). They mostly appear to be associated with worries about bad publicity that would imperil company profits. For instance, Bechtel received one of the first and largest contracts for Iraq's reconstruction (worth up to US$680 million) (CorpWatch et al., 2003, p. 4). With subsequent work to be done, Bechtel was awarded the staggering sum of US$2.8 billion in Iraqi reconstruction contracts (Juhasz, 2006, pp. 229–30). Bechtel also secured a large contract to help rebuild New Orleans after Hurricane Katrina. The bad publicity associated with Aguas del Tunari, according to Anderson, may have jeopardized future, similarly lucrative, contracts. It was significant that San Francisco's Board of Supervisors issued a resolution calling on Bechtel to withdraw from the suit. This threatened future municipal water contracts with the city of San Francisco and elsewhere. Lastly, the protest appears to have got 'under the skin' of CEO Riley Bechtel. He was flooded with e-mails and portrayed as the lord of darkness in a fight over something as necessary and basic to human existence as water. According to Bolivia's lead negotiator, Eduardo Valdivia, Bechtel 'personally intervened' to ensure the case was settled. It was not 'worth the damage to the company's reputation', he had concluded (Shultz, 2008, p. 32). In an interview with me, Jim Shultz emphasized the significance of social movement corporate campaigns that rely on repertoires associated with reputation. If social movements can't take the fight to the mall or to shareholder meetings, movements can always go after the CEO.[12] Shultz likened this to throwing rocks over a brick wall – you are never sure if you are hitting your corporate targets but, given their thin skins, you are sure to find out if you do.[13]

Ultimately, Shultz described the corporation as akin to a mathematician – the strategy is to change its understanding of the math. The math,

---

11   Personal interview with Sarah Anderson (26 October 2006).
12   Shultz, in *The Democracy Owners' Manual: A Practical Guide to Changing the World*, admonishes activists to 'make it personal, name names, and bring it close to home' (Shultz, 2002, p. 117).
13   Personal interview with Jim Shultz (13 July 2007).

ultimately, proved to be decisive. For the most part, it appears that this transnational movement campaign was effective to the extent that it could undermine Bechtel's potential future profits. In other words, it was the threat of economic loss, greater than the sunk costs and lost profits in Cochabamba, which precipitated the withdrawal of the company claim. This was a calculation based, perhaps, on nothing more than the bottom line of company balance sheets.

What I have been describing is a claim-making strategy familiar to those who have been operating under the paradigm of modernity. The labour movement, for instance, was best able to secure collective bargaining rights and the improvement of working conditions and wages based on the threat of withdrawal of labour power. These were conflicts over 'the power to inflict costs' (Biggs, 2002, pp. 589, 611) – workers, by withdrawing their labour power, and employers, by locking out or replacing those workers. If class has declined as a salient marker for collective action, other solidaristic movements have been able to effect change using nothing more than their economic power. Ethical consumer activists and anti-sweatshop activists have been able to use the 'power of the purse' to sway corporate production practices somewhat (Klein, 1999). This is not to say that, in this period of transition, hegemonic tools might not be used to achieve non-hegemonic purposes. Nor do I mean to suggest that there is nothing outside of or beyond modernity (Aparicio and Blaser, 2009, p. 73) – as Santos argues, the subaltern produces knowledge that is unacknowledged by modernity as it originates on the 'other side of the line' (2007, p. 45). Rather, it is to say that there is still much work to be done under the paradigm of modernity using modernity's tools, particularly through the aegis of the state – the most proper agent with which to unlock the ball and chain of transnational legality (Tarrow, 2003, p. 36).

What appears to be most effective, then, are claim-making strategies of economic coercion. It may be that similarly bad publicity will work against other large transnational enterprises. It may not work as well, however, against small to medium-size operations that rely more heavily on expected returns from an investment dispute. I am thinking here of the Metalclad Corporation, Marvin Feldman, Thunderbird Gaming Corporation and numerous other claimants who have invoked the North American Free Trade Agreement's investment chapter and for whom a large damage award based on future lost profits would have provided salvation to company ownership (Wälde, 2007, p. 62).[14]

---

14 As Thomas Wälde observes: 'Investment arbitration is not an instrument of particular preference or suitability for large multinational companies – except as a bargaining card that should not be played; it is mainly for smaller players with an exit and never-come-back strategy.' (Wälde, 2007, p. 62) On voice over exit as a strategy for larger investors, see Wells and Ahmed (2007).

There is the associated problem of organizing global campaigns of this sort. The singular circumstances giving rise to the Cochabamba water wars will not be easy to replicate. The *Coordinadora* – a non-hierarchical umbrella organization giving voice to interests both modern and traditional (Linera, 2004, p. 76) – linked arms with the Democracy Center, headquartered in Cochabamba, an intermediary that could share a base of information with activists in the global North in real time over the internet. Jim Shultz and the Democracy Center, in this way, acted as a 'transnational hinge' or broker for activists working across borders (Tarrow, 2005, p. 190). In their discussion of scale shift, Tarrow and McAdam suggest that communication through 'brokerage' – where a broker links previously unconnected social sites – is less durable and more short-lived than communication through 'relational diffusion' – conveying information along previously established lines of communication (2005, pp. 127–30). Though there were elements of diffusion once the campaign entered into its second phase, brokerage was a key to its success. As predicted, the movement quickly disassembled once short-term victory was secured. In this second phase (after company executives fled the country), the campaign's sole objective was to have Bechtel (and Abengoa) withdraw its investment dispute against Bolivia. This was, in Tarrow's lexicon, a short-term 'instrumental' or 'event coalition', exhibiting an intensity of participant involvement and the potential for future collaboration, but of limited duration (Tarrow, 2005, p. 168). It was not a long-term 'campaign coalition', which is less thrilling than short-term coalitions but 'may be the wave of the transnational future' (Tarrow, 2005, p. 179). While the Democracy Center has been actively generating resources for activists in campaigns to resist corporate power and is one of the co-founders of the Network for Justice in Global Investment ('Just Investment'),[15] significantly, there appear to be no plans to initiate another direct campaign of this sort in the near future.[16]

This was a strategy that also relied on traditional legal forms. The frustrated intervention in the ICSID dispute at the World Bank and its supporting petition sought to invoke conventional principles of procedural justice. Bolivian constitutional principles were conscripted into the campaign: water is a national resource available for public use rather than for private gain, the Bolivian Constitution provides. So law and legal forms played an ambiguous role in this struggle – a discourse to be embraced and resisted, underscoring the 'complexities, contingencies, and ironies at stake in legal mobilization' (McCann, 2006, p. 19). To the extent the *Coordinadora* and its allies were

---

15 I sit on the Advisory Committee for the Network for Justice in Global Investment.
16 The episodic nature of transnational coalitions is observed by Rodríguez-Garavito and Arenas in the case of the struggle of the U'wa people of Colombia (2005, p. 259).

successful, water resources would revert back to the public regulator and, indirectly, to the state.

This modernist result left open the possibility of pursuing alternative, more democratic and participatory institutional designs, as Santos hopefully suggests. Regrettably, the local water authority (SEMAPA) resumed control and revived its tradition of cronyism and corruption. Its operations are described as 'a mess' (Shultz, 2008, p. 39). There are other, more helpful, indicators. The establishment of a national Inter-Institutional Water Council (CONIAG) in 2002, drawing representation from government, civil society groups and the business sector, precipitated a 2004 law recognizing local and customary laws regarding access to water (de Vos et al., 2006, p. 44). At the same time, local water committees in southern Cochabamba, in districts that have not been serviced by SEMAPA continue to proliferate. Their answer to the question 'After the water war, what?' are new models of co-management which do not surrender to state sectors' control over local water supplies but maintain an 'equal footing in the community water systems and perhaps...their own power base' (Zibechi, 2009). The story so far suggests that the political opportunity structures generated by economic globalization, in this instance repelling World Bank-induced modes of privatization, can be exploited for the purposes of generating new modes of institutional design at local levels, but this continues to be dependent on domestic and local opportunity structures.

There is also the no small matter of the impact of the *Coordinadora's* success on the local Bolivian oppositional movement, helping to mobilize support for Evo Morales' presidential bid in 2000, ultimately winning the presidency in 2005 (Linera, 2006). In addition to 'nationalising' gas and oil markets in Bolivia, Morales has vowed to remove water from the table of any future international trade negotiations. Moreover, Bolivia has withdrawn its consent from the ICSID Convention (though it may still be party to investment disputes under ICSID's Additional Facility Rules) (ICSID, 2007; Gaillard, 2007). This, of course, is part of a wider trend of resistance to neoliberal rules and institutions in Latin America (Lomnitz, 2006). In its *World Investment Report* 2006, the United Nations Commission on Trade and Development (UNCTAD) reported that, in the year 2005, there were an unprecedented number of regulatory changes making host countries 'less welcome' to foreign investment (the highest ever recorded by UNCTAD). Two-thirds of these changes issued out of Latin American states (UNCTAD, 2006, p. 25).[17] The trend identified in 2006 continues (UNCTAD, 2009a, p. 70)

---

17 There is a debate brewing amongst investment lawyers about whether Carlos Calvo is having a revival in Latin America. See, for instance, Cremades (2005) and Shan (2007).

There remained a residual controversy over whether the settlement of the *Aguas del Tunari* claim was on terms that were beneficial to Bolivians. The state paid the sum of 2 bolivianos (about 30 US cents) in exchange for an 80 per cent interest in the company (the remaining shareholders, all local Bolivian nationals, were not party to the settlement). Legal fees in the amount of US$1.6 million were also paid by Bolivia (Harris, 2006). Oscar Olivera, on behalf of the *Coordinadora*, worried that Bolivia had assumed the company's debt of some €7 million (about US$8.2 million). Olivera, however, had seen only 18 pages of a 25-page English document (*La Razón,* 2006). The Bolivian Vice Minister of Public Utilities, Eduardo Rojas, denied that the state had taken up company debt of this enormity. Warranties were made, he claims, that there were no debts or liabilities exceeding US$100. As if underscoring the non-transparent nature of the investment dispute process, he admitted that the agreement was executed in English and was not yet translated into Spanish (*La Prensa,* 2006). The Bolivian–Bechtel/Abengoa settlement hung in the balance following these allegations by Olivera. The settlement documents confirm, however, that Aguas del Tunari's debt of some €5 million was cancelled. Other debts, associated with Aguas del Tunari's short-lived operations in Bolivia, including social security contributions, health care contributions and value added tax, were assumed by the state as principal shareholder.

*   *   *

Victory in social justice struggles is rare. In so far as the citizens of Cochabamba won the water wars, in both of its phases, they have generated fertile ground for oppositional politics in many places around the world. After all, as Shultz aptly put it, the 'revolt over water was a revolt against everything' (Shultz, 2003, p. 273). People in many places in the world are fed up. Polanyian measures for societal self-protection drawing on market models, to the extent they are fiscally available to states and citizens, may no longer be sufficient (Patel and McMichael, 2004). Santos' hopeful account of the paradigmatic transition suggests there are struggles yet to be won, alternative futures to be imagined, their specificities to be worked out in a spirit of democratic contestation and pluralism. In the meanwhile, there are more mundane but no less difficult things to be achieved which require toiling in the mines of the sub-paradigm, such as abolishing those binding legal constraints on the capacity of publics so that they may go about doing this sort of work.

5
Wolin and Democracy's Debasement

One would expect critical resistance to be facilitated by inclusive democratic practices and responsive democratic institutions. Just how open is contemporary democratic practice to facilitating and encouraging resistance to transnational legality? For political theorist Sheldon Wolin, democracy today as practised in 'advanced' democracies is significantly dampened by the institutionalization of barriers to imagining both old and new commonalities. The privatization of public authority, the reduction of citizenship to consumer citizenship and democracy to shareholder democracy are just some of the features that have contributed to the debasement of democratic practice. The potential for ordinary people to become 'political beings through the self-discovery of common concerns', Wolin writes, is sublimated in contemporary democratic practice (1994, p. 11; 2008, p. 260). As a consequence of these features, contemporary democracy works to suppress the emergence of new forms to mediate common concerns. If it is correct to claim that there is a correlation between economic inequality and politics (Bartels, 2008, p. 3), then democracy's shrinking space signals a chastened ability to disturb wealth and power distribution beyond the prevailing status quo.

Transnational legal norms have contributed somewhat to this debasement of democracy. Marks notes, for instance, international law's penchant for promoting 'low-intensity democracy' (Gills and Rocamora, 1993), requiring only episodic elections that leave 'established centres of power essentially intact' (Marks, 2000, p. 53). The priority in democracy promotion under the supervision of international institutions is given to that, she observes, 'which can most readily be monitored by international observers' (Marks, 2000, p. 63). This is in contrast to more participatory or popular forms of democracy that conjoin politics with socioeconomic justice.

Investment treaties and international investment tribunals charged with interpreting these treaties have not had much to say about the operation of democratic processes. The regime has been described, on occasion, as promoting democratic values by contributing to 'good governance', transparency and respect for due process (Newcombe, 2007, p. 403).[1] It is significant, then, that an investment tribunal conscripted democratic theory into its ruling, arguing that the interests of foreign investors ordinarily will not be represented within a host state's political processes (*Técnicas Medioambientales Tecmed SA v Mexico* (2003)). Laying claim to democratic theory in this context – in addition to its surfacing in other arbitral awards (*Loewen Group Inc. and Loewen v United States* (2003), para. 224) and in the work of some scholars (Alvarez and Khamsi, 2009, p. 446) – paradoxically is premised on a model of democratic passivity and elides the role of transnational legality in suppressing democratic alternatives.

This resort by an investment tribunal to the 'high ground of democratic theory', for this reason, is revealing (Ackerman, 1985, p. 715). The tribunal invoked justifications that, as in national constitutional settings, tend to legitimate judicial power to negative governmental decision-making. Symbolically, this suggests that investment tribunals stand in a situation similar to national high courts. Substantively, it underscores the degree to which investment rules mimic the constitutional constraints of particularistic national legal systems (Schneiderman, 2008).

In this chapter I inquire into this smuggling of democratic theory and constitutional postulates into international investment law. By looking to the US origins of political process doctrine (or representation-reinforcement review), I argue that its invocation by the *Tecmed* tribunal is inapposite given the doctrine's concern with relegating ordinary economic regulation to relaxed scrutiny. Reference to the European experience in this context is not all that helpful – representation-reinforcement review has not been a hallmark of European jurisprudence. Nor has the European Court of Human Rights (ECtHR) been all that interested in deprivations of foreign wealth (Kriebaum, 2008; 2009). As I have argued in Chapter 1, investment law's operative rules and structure reveal a great deal of ambivalence, if not outright disdain, for the product of democratic processes beyond those considered 'normal'. Democratic processes are considered, for the most part, to be untrustworthy constituents of social change. Rather than reinforcing norms of good governance, I argue that this worry over democratic processes masks an attempt at legitimating controversial review by investment tribunals of high public policy matters. Furthermore, this solicitude offered to investors by political process review is mostly unwarranted. The corporate political activity and business risk literature, which I canvass below, suggests that foreign corporate actors

---

1 Others have made claims that the General Agreement on Tariffs and Trade–World Trade Organization agreements (Farber and Hudec, 1994, p. 1405; McGinnis and Movsevian, 2000, p. 515) and international law, more generally, reinforce the operation of domestic political processes (Chander, 2005, p. 1234).

can and do shape host domestic policy. Indeed, not only is corporate political power present and pervasive in almost every part of the world (Sklair, 2002), corporate power distorts political processes in ways that undermine democracy's rationales.

Wolin proves to be an interesting guide through these turbulent waters. First, he traces the malaise in contemporary democratic practice to the sorts of 'constitutional' constraints that I have been discussing in this book that liberate private power, privatize previously public domains and discourage the possibility of arriving at public solutions to collective problems. Second, Wolin's theoretical trajectory is instructive in so far as he has given up on states as a source of authority to countervail these developments. While the *Tecmed* case study, on the one hand, provides fodder for Wolin's despondency about democracy's prospects in the age of transnational legality, on the other hand, the case suggests that tiers of government within national states continue to provide salient sites for critical resistance. This is a source of jurisdiction that Wolin abandons at our peril.

The chapter proceeds as follows. First, I look to Wolin's critique of contemporary democratic practice and his movement away from states as the primary vehicle for the identification of political commonality in the direction of embracing what he calls 'archaic' local movements. I then move to a fuller discussion of the *Tecmed* tribunal decision, its resort to political process doctrine and the place of European law in the tribunal's formulation. I then turn to a discussion of political process doctrine as it is understood in US constitutional law. These constitutional presuppositions help to elucidate the motivation for the tribunal's conscription of democratic theory in *Tecmed*, namely, as a legitimating device while eliding the role this form of transnational legality plays in dampening policy options and political opportunities. The empirical evidence shores up the chapter by revealing the degree to which business political activity can be expected to play a role within the processes of operative democracies all over the world, underscoring worrying trends that have led Wolin to throw up his hands in despair.

I should acknowledge that there is a superficial appeal to *Tecmed*'s embrace of political process formulations. In a highly integrated world, it seems beneficial to improve democratic processes so that the interests of those affected by decision-making within national borders are taken into account. It is especially appealing for those who are rendered vulnerable by national and transnational processes of economic integration that further the advantage of economically advanced states. I argue, however, that this is a harder case to make for foreign investors who can in no way be considered equivalent to the vulnerable persons unaccounted for in contemporary democratic processes.

Dispiriting democracy

Constitutional democracy, for Wolin, is 'democracy fitted to a constitution'. Constitutionalism, following the tradition of Hobbes, Madison and Tocqueville, is about laying down boundaries and regulating the amount of politics that gets let in. In constitutional democracies, 'curatorship of the simulacra of democracy' resides with dominant elites, legitimating their continuing stranglehold over the reins of power. For these elites, Wolin writes, 'elections are investment opportunities from which they hope to reap a return' (1994, pp. 13–14).

With the hope of refurbishing our democratic potential, Wolin distinguishes between the 'political' and 'politics'. He associates the political with the pursuit of collective projects that promote common well-being. Politics, by contrast, concerns public contestation for access to institutions that promote an individual's or a group's competitive advantage. The political, according to Wolin, is episodic and fugitive; politics, by contrast, is never ending (Wolin, 1994, p. 11; 2004, p. 11).[2] With democracy colonized by markets and the ascendance of unaccountable corporate power, Wolin describes contemporary democratic experience as giving rise to an 'inverted totalitarianism' where political leadership is modelled on a corporate 'head', democracy is 'managed' without it appearing to be suppressed, and citizens are demobilized and educated in the art of political futility (Wolin, 2004, p. 592; 2008, pp. 44, 47, 65). This is a regime of

> politics all of the time but a politics untempered by the political...[namely] the commitment to finding where the common good lies amidst the welter of well-financed, highly organized, single-minded interests rabidly seeking governmental favors and overwhelming the practices of representative government and public administration by a sea of cash (Wolin, 2008, p. 66).

Transnational legality's conception of democracy, I want to suggest, infuses democratic practice with these sorts of characteristics, failing to account for the ways in which economic power overwhelms politics.

Though its prospects remain dim, Wolin admits that democracy remains a recurrent possibility, principally at local levels (2004, pp. 587, 603). As do many of the theorists we have encountered in this book, he eschews the state as a locale of viable resistance. Wolin, however, has not always exhibited this preference for the local over the national. In the first edition of

---

2 Wolin's distinction between the political and politics mirrors, to some degree, Rancière's distinction between police or policing (the limiting and legitimizing features of government) and politics (whatever breaks free of the constraints of policing). See Rancière (1999, pp. 28–9).

his contemporary classic, *Politics and Vision* (1960), Wolin considered local associational life too disassociated from the political, resulting in the 'chopping-up of political man' (Wolin, 1960, p. 430). Political 'responsibility has meaning only in terms of a general constituency', Wolin wrote, 'and no multiplication of fragmentary constituencies will provide a substitute' (1960, p. 433). Disparaging the 'fetish of groupism' (1960, p. 434), he preferred to keep his focus, in this early work, on the state as the 'central referent of the political' (1960, p. 417). In light of the experience of managed democracy in the US, and taking cues, perhaps, from his more recent studies of Tocqueville (Wolin, 2001, p. 240) and Dewey (Wolin, 2004, p. 514), Wolin became estranged from the state and so turned to those lesser associations that politicize public aspects of our daily lives (Wolin, 1989, p. 81; 2008, p. 291). Individuals who work for

> low income housing, worker ownership of factories, better schools, better health care, safer water, controls over toxic waste disposals, and a thousand other common concerns of ordinary lives are experiencing a democratic moment and contributing to the discovery, care, and tending of a commonality of shared concerns (Wolin, 1994, p. 24).

This is the politics of those who are the 'leisureless' (2008, p. 277), those who have withdrawn from traditional politics of citizenship and have rejected the state as 'primary structure' (Wolin, 1982, p. 251). These are movements that can trace their origins to the rejectionism of the 1960s (as in 'turn on, tune in, drop out') (Wolin, 1982, p. 251). The task now is to nurture 'grassroots movements' that have 'grown up outside of the state-corporate structure and have flourished despite repeated efforts to discredit them' (Wolin, 1982, p. 252; cf. Zibechi, 2005). This is a 'contemporary version' of an 'old struggle', writes Wolin. It is not about bringing 'new powers' into the world, but about 'hard-won struggles we can prevent from disappearing' (Wolin, 2008, p. 292). It is reminiscent of Santos' argument against 'lazy reason' and the 'waste of social experience' (Santos, 2004).

There remains a real concern, acknowledged by Wolin, about the capacity of local movements to check power exercised at local levels and beyond (1994, p. 24). If we understand institutionalized globalization as multi-scalar and multi-form (Jessop, 2002, p. 113) then power that is 'agile, restless, [and] contemptuous of national boundaries' (Wolin, 2004, p. 563) likely will escape the clutches of episodic non-state resistance. If local political movements narrow the distance between ruler and ruled, their externalities, except in rare cases, are unlikely to extend beyond their immediate confines (Hobsbawm, 1996, pp. 63–5). Local acts of resistance, conversely, likely cannot escape globalization's disciplinary reach. Indeed, local political movements are as likely to adopt political orientations amenable to dominant power relations as opposed to them. Wolin even admits that such movements are unreliable conduits for resistance: they draw on an 'archaic political culture' and remain a 'negligible' factor in national politics (Wolin, 1989, p. 81). Archaic oppositional movements, nevertheless, represent 'the main, perhaps the only, democratic counterthrust to statism' (ibid.). Wolin holds out hope that these 'champions of the archaic' will act as 'provocateurs whose passionate commitments can arouse self-consciousness in the public, stimulating the latter to become aware of what they believe and of the mixed legacies that compose a collective inheritance' (Wolin, 2004, p. 604).

Wolin remains casual about precisely under what conditions and in what forms democracy can rebuild its legitimacy and then take on power at local, national and levels beyond.[3] After all, inverted totalitarian power appears to maintain a death grip on transformation in a democratic direction. This looks very much like the regime without exit for which he, early on, scolded Foucault. Foucault produced, charged Wolin, an 'insurrectionary gesture against a corporatized world with no exits' (Wolin, 1988, p. 179; Kateb, 2001, p. 42; Wiley, 2006, p. 228).

Even if there remain good reasons to be sceptical about the prospects of harnessing state power in the pursuit of the common good, we might also want to be sceptical about Wolin's description of the state as being hopelessly immovable. If we understand the state not as irreducibly unified but as multifarious and divided (Poulantzas, 1978, p. 132) – a 'complex social relation that reflects the changing balance of social forces in a determinate conjuncture' (Jessop, 1982, p. 221) – then we might expect to see state apparatuses function in unexpected, even contradictory, ways. Rejecting a view of the state as homogenous and reducible to the interest of capital, Jessop describes state power as 'strategically selective' (1990, p. 256) – providing opportunity for some actors and constraint for others – and dependent for its effectiveness on forces and powers within and beyond the state (2002, pp. 40–1). The state, in other words, is treated as a social relation, an institutional ensemble embedded within specific spatio-temporal locations with its own tensions and contradictions. Perhaps, even if the state is understood in this way, Wolin is right to be despondent about the capacity to reroute dominant trends over the last half century. In doing so, however, Wolin disregards an important lesson that Tocqueville draws from his mid-nineteenth-century American tour: the capacity to change one's mind. Democracies are agitated

---

3 Wolin describes Dewey's conception of the reconceived state as 'casual about the precise form' the new state would take (Wolin, 2004, p. 510) and 'vague' about disentangling democracy from capitalism (2004, p. 512). Turning the tables, Kateb writes that his own 'complaint [about Wolin] is that fugitive democracy is underdescribed, barely sketched' (Kateb, 2001, p. 44).

by a 'permanent fever that is turned to innovation of all kinds', some of which turn out to be costly. One of the chief advantages of democracy in America, wrote Tocqueville, is the ability to respond to these sorts of 'repairable mistakes' (Tocqueville, 2000, p. 216). Wolin, however, disparages this aspect of Tocquevillian thought, associating it with an administrative logic in which 'all mistakes are remediable' and in which there are 'endless opportunities for new beginnings' in America's 'utopia' (Wolin, 2001, p. 363). Rather than exhibiting a celebration of pragmatism or of scientific–technological expertise in the administration of societal problems, we feasibly can read Tocqueville otherwise, as describing energetic law-making processes that can keep open the channels of change (Hurst, 1956, p. 27; Lefort, 1988, p. 169; Keane, 1991, p. 176). This is a version of democratic constitutionalism that is open, writes the Tocquevillian Lefort, to 'the *gestation* of new social relationships, new ways of thinking, new representations of what is good or evil, of what is just or unjust, right or wrong, also real or imaginary, possible or impossible: a gestation that operates in the thickness of the social under the juridico-political surface' (2002, p. 456).

International investment law does not conceive of democratic practice as so wide open. Its proponents instead have devised a constitution-like structure that dampens democratic initiative, whether issuing from spaces national or subnational, rendering politics closed to almost everything but to the logic of markets. The *Tecmed* case, I suggest in the next part, exhibits this dispiriting feature symptomatic of transnational legality. The investor–state dispute also suggests, contra Wolin, that national states can give effect to manifestations of the 'political' at local levels and beyond.

No voice, costly exit?

The *Tecmed* dispute arose under a Spain–Mexico bilateral investment treaty (BIT) and concerned failure to renew a permit to operate the Cytrar hazardous waste facility site at Los Víboras, 8 km from Hermosillo, the Sonora state capital. The Madrid-based company Técnicas Medioambientales SA (Tecmed) purchased the site at auction from the municipality in the expectation that it would continue to operate the facility for years to come under a newly formed Mexican subsidiary (also named Cytrar) (*Tecmed* (2003), para. 88). The facility operated for two years (from 1996–1998) mostly without incident. Civil society opposition began to mobilize against Cytrar, however, once reports began circulating that a truck driver had developed a burn on his leg after coming into contact with soil contaminated with toxic waste destined for the site. Subsequent surveillance at the site revealed an open toxic dump with waste lying exposed and uncontained (O'Leary, 2002, p. 1, 4). It was also revealed that Cytrar had accepted landfill and contaminated soil from the Alco Pacifico plant near Tijuana. Alco Pacifico was a US-owned facility that had previously been shut down by federal authorities for violating Mexican federal environmental law (Boren, 1998a; 1998b). Prompted by growing community outrage, subsequent investigation of Cytrar by the Federal Environmental Protection Attorney's Office (PROFEPA) revealed that trucks carried hazardous waste from Alco Pacifico in exposed, open sacks (ibid.). It was later learned that Cytrar had been authorized to transport and store Alco Pacifico waste pursuant to an agreement with Mexican federal authorities (*Tecmed* (2003), para. 107). Other PROFEPA investigations found 'irregularities' in the disposal of Alco Pacifica waste, resulting in fines and findings that 'there are circumstances that pose or may pose a risk to the environment or to health'. This gave rise to the imposition of further urgent measures (ibid.) and to fines for exceeding landfill limits, though these latter offences, PROFEPA later admitted, 'did not have a significant effect on public health' (*Tecmed* (2003), para. 100).

Hermosillo-based activists first obtained a court ruling to prohibit the importation of waste from outside of the state of Sonora. As the order remained unenforced, a coalition of civil society forces took direct action and blocked the entrance to the Cytrar site for 37 days in January and February 1998. The numbers blockading the site rose to approximately 300 persons, until forcibly dislocated by over 100 police officers (Boren, 1998a). This precipitated the filing of human rights commission complaints and a further blockade, thwarted by the police, in April 1998 (Boren, 1998b). Setting up their headquarters in the main square in Hermosillo, over the course of 192 days activists secured over 30,000 signatures to a petition opposing the operation of the site. Hundreds also attended rallies and marches (Boren, 1998b; *Tecmed* (2003), para. 108).

Activists initially targeted municipal authorities, aiming to 'work the system from the bottom up' (Mumme, 2000, p. 119). Under civil society pressure, the newly elected municipal president engaged in direct negotiations with Tecmed securing a commitment from the company to relocate the hazardous waste facility to another site within the state (ibid.). Activists opposed the behind-closed-door negotiations and insisted on consultations about relocation and guarantees that waste not be imported from out-of-state sources. These demands were joined with a 'right to know campaign', seeking access to information and co-decision-making in the environmental review process (Mehranvar, 2009, p. 68). The municipality rebuffed these demands. With relations between civil society and local government severed, activists expanded their repertoires of contention, moving from conventional to more radical and non-institutional forms of resistance and taking their complaints up to state and federal levels (O'Leary, 2002, pp. 4–5). There was even a modest attempt at transcending the national scale by joining with other activists in the Sonoroa–Texas border region, submitting complaints (unsuccessfully) to the North American Free Trade Agreement Commission for Environmental Cooperation and another submission to the non-governmental International Court of Environmental Arbitration and Conciliation (Mehranvar, 2009, pp. 51, 60). In contrast to the successful transnational campaign led by the Cochabamba-based Democracy Center, in conjunction with the *Coordinadora*, Hermosillan efforts at transcending the national scale never really took flight.

Civil society opposition was fuelled by a Mexican federal regulation requiring that hazardous waste dumps be located at least 25 km distance from any municipality with a population of more than 10,000.[4] The Cytrar site, 8 km from Hermosillo, appeared to be in violation of the federal requirement. The measure was promulgated, however, after Tecmed purchased the site and obtained its initial licence. The law was in full force, however, when Cytrar's annual application for renewal came before Mexican federal authority. Having forestalled succumbing to the demands of local activists for a couple of years, the relevant federal authority decided to reject Cytrar's request for renewal (Orellana, 2007, p. 775).

As Wolin would have it, local social movement actors aroused public consciousness within Hermosillo and neighbouring municipalities, politicizing the public aspects of their daily lives. Yet it is inescapable that this local success (such as it is) could only be secured via the aegis of the state. Ultimately, it was the federal body with jurisdiction – the National Ecology Institute of Mexico (INE) – that took the decisive step of denying Cytrar's annual application for renewal. This, naturally, precipitated a corporate response from Tecmed. Investment disciplines reliably could render the Mexican federal government responsible for sunk costs and future lost profits. Given the suspicion and disdain with which transnational legality holds democratic processes, it would not be unexpected to see these small acts of resistance disparaged by an investment tribunal and decisively checked. The investor's assessment of transnational legality's structural tilt proved to be correct.

The investment tribunal hearing the dispute acknowledged that opposition to the landfill was 'widespread and aggressive' (*Tecmed* (2003), para. 108). Yet, the tribunal continued, 'however intense, aggressive and sustained', it was not 'in any way massive or went any further than the positions assumed by some individuals or the members of some groups that were opposed to the landfill' (*Tecmed* (2003), para. 144). '[O]nly two hundred to four hundred people', the tribunal observed, out of a population of almost 1 million, participated in the demonstrations (ibid.). In which case, the intensity of local opposition to the site could be disregarded by the tribunal – not only was the rationale

---

4 Official Mexican Regulations NOM-055–ECOL-1993, point 5.15.1 issued by INE (Ojeda-Mestre, 2007, p. 153).

for their opposition suspect, it could provide no excuse for the government's actions.

Nor were there legitimate environmental or public health concerns that could buttress the government's refusal to renew the operating permit. Yet the grounds for refusal precisely addressed such concerns: Cytrar had exceeded landfill limits, temporarily stored hazardous waste outside of the landfill, and received 'liquid and biological-infectious waste' that was not authorized by its permit (*Tecmed* (2003), para. 99). Even if Cytrar had been guilty of a number of environmental transgressions, ruled the tribunal, these did not 'compromise public health, impair ecological balance or protection of the environment, or... [were] the reason for a genuine social crisis' (*Tecmed* (2003), para. 124). Remarkably, the tribunal concluded that the resolution 'does not specify any reasons of public interest' that could justify it (*Tecmed* (2003), para. 125). In which case, there had to be some other reason for the failure to renew.

One is left wondering, however, what otherwise would have precipitated vociferous local opposition to the site. It is important to note that that the tribunal found there was no discriminatory intent behind the Mexican federal government's decision. The decision was not intended to target foreign-owned wealth and so should not have given rise to any concerns that the measures were intended to penalize non-nationals (Franck, 1995, p. 470). It could only be viewed, then, as arbitrary or irrational or, worse yet, political. The resolution 'was mainly driven by socio-political factors' the tribunal surmises (*Tecmed* (2003), para. 130). These were 'social or political circumstances', reasons having to do with the proximity of the site to the local municipality (*Tecmed* (2003), para. 132).[5] By separating out public health concerns from socio-political motivations, the tribunal could shield itself from accusations that it had thwarted legitimate environmental or public health regulation.

The investor principally claimed that this was a compensable event tantamount to expropriation and that there was a denial of fair and equitable treatment. For our purposes, we need only focus on the first claim (though the second claim also was successful[6]). Regulatory takings fall within the terms of the Spain–Mexico investment treaty as a sub-set of indirect expropriations. These will be measures which are 'irreversible and permanent, and if the asset or rights subject to such measures have been affected in such a way

---

5   The tribunal reports that the company was prepared to relocate to another part of the state in order to placate community objections – an offer that apparently was never taken up by Sonora or federal state officials (*Tecmed* (2003), para. 148).

6   The tribunal also found that there was a denial of fair and equitable treatment due to the 'lack of transparency' and 'ambiguity and uncertainty' about the future of the investment. This was conduct which upset the investor's legitimate expectations and so amounted to another ground for compensation (*Tecmed* (2003), paras 164, 172).

that "any form of exploitation thereof..." has disappeared; i.e. the economic value of the use, enjoyment or disposition of the assets or rights affected by the administrative action or decision have been neutralized or destroyed', then there will have been a taking requiring the payment of compensation (*Tecmed* (2003), para. 116). Even where measures are 'beneficial to society as a whole – such as environmental protection'. the obligation to pay compensation remains (*Tecmed* (2003), para. 121; *Compañía del Desarrollo de Santa Elena SA v Republic of Costa Rica* (2000), paras 72, 76). The 'government's intention', the tribunal wrote, 'is less important than the effects of the measure' on the investor (*Tecmed* (2003), para. 116). In this instance, the government's actions 'fully and irrevocably destroyed' the investment and so amounted to an expropriation (*Tecmed* (2003), para. 117).

The tribunal was not content with examining only the effects of a measure on an investor or investment, however. In order to determine whether the government's action was expropriatory, and not merely an innocent exercise of the regulatory capacity of the state, the tribunal sought to determine whether such a measure was proportionate in its effects in light of the government's objective. This should have the effect of mitigating an emphasis solely on the impact of a measure on an investor. Even here, the tribunal admitted, 'the significance of such [an] impact has a key role' in determining whether there has been proportionality (*Tecmed* (2003), para. 122).

The question, as framed by the tribunal, was 'whether such measures are reasonable with respect to their goals, the deprivation of economic rights and the legitimate expectations of [those] who suffered such deprivation' (*Tecmed* (2003), para. 122). Though having already found the measure to rise to the level of a compensable taking, the analysis began with the 'due deference' that is owed to the state when it takes measures in the public interest. Among the factors to be considered in assessing proportionality, the tribunal added, was the 'size of the ownership deprivation' and whether compensation was offered (ibid.). Also weighing into the proportionality analysis, added the tribunal, is 'that the foreign investor has a reduced or nil participation in the taking of the decisions that affect it, partly because investors are not entitle[d] to exercise political rights reserved to the nationals of the state, such as voting for the authorities that will issue the decisions that affect such investors' (ibid.). Defects in the political process, in other words, gave support to the investor's sense of being wronged. In support of this political process rationale, the tribunal drew not on US constitutional law, where political process doctrine is a dominant trope, but on a ruling of the ECtHR in *James and Others v United Kingdom* (1986). The tribunal noted that the Strasbourg court also considers the extent to which foreign investors are disenfranchised from participating in decisions that give rise to such measures by public authority, 'partly because the investors are not entitled to exercise political rights reserved to the nationals of the State' (*Tecmed* (2003), para. 122). It turns out that this is not a very nuanced representation of the ECtHR's work.[7]

James concerned leasehold reform legislation in the UK requiring the owners of some 2000 homes in the districts of Belgravia and Mayfair in central London, including the Duke of Westminster, to sell their leased property at significantly reduced rates to lessees. The forced sale resulted in massive windfalls for some tenants. In dispute was the amount of compensation owed to James, which was substantially less than full value. The court, applying its 'margin of appreciation' doctrine, required the state only to show some 'reasonable relationship of proportionality' between means (compensation provided) and ends (the promotion of social justice) (*James* (1986), paras 46, 50; Allen, 2005, p. 133). It was appropriate, the court observed, that nationals bear this kind of burden in contrast to non-nationals who will have 'played no part in the election or designation of its authors nor have been consulted on its adoption' (*James* (1986), para. 63).[8] For this reason, the 'general principles of international law' mentioned in Art. 1 of Protocol I of the European Convention on Human Rights, which may have required compliance with a strict standard of prompt, adequate and effective compensation, did not apply to the taking of property owned by nationals of the state doing the taking. The state legitimately could provide compensation at rates less than the strict standard. The court used similar reasoning in *Lithgow*, decided later that same year. This second case concerned the nationalization, with compensation at less than full value, of the British aircraft and shipbuilding industry (*Lithgow and Others v United Kingdom* (1986), para. 116). On these two occasions where the court seemed to embrace the political process rationale, it did so not to strike at discriminatory economic legislation, rather, it did so to shield national state measures from any greater scrutiny than was required under its loose margin of appreciation doctrine. This is consistent with the ECtHR's overall stance as regards economic matters, one in which 'acceptance of the member States' entitlement to regulate their respective economies is embedded in the Convention's structure' (Emberland, 2006, p. 192; Becker, 2007, p. 282).

---

7 Coe Jr and Rubins (2005, p. 625) and Hirsch (2008, p. 172) similarly fail to catch the nuances in the ECtHR jurisprudence.

8 The ECtHR opinion states: 'Especially as regards a taking of property effected in the context of a social reform, there may well be good grounds for drawing a distinction between nationals and non-nationals as far as compensation is concerned. To begin with, non-nationals are more vulnerable to domestic legislation: unlike nationals, they will generally have played no part in the election or designation of its authors nor have been consulted on its adoption. Secondly, although a taking of property must always be effected in the public interest, different considerations may apply to nationals and non-nationals and there may well be legitimate reason for requiring nationals to bear a greater burden in the public interest than non-nationals.' (*James* (1986), para. 63)

Might the same hold true in the case of alien-owned property? It is important to underscore that the ECtHR, in both *James* and *Lithgow*, invoked understandings of the way political processes operate in the context of deciding whether to apply stricter standards associated with general principles of international law. The ECtHR not only rejected the application of strict standards in these two cases, it has otherwise not seen fit to strictly scrutinize takings of alien property. *Beyeler v Italy* (2001) seems representative of these developments. There, the court seemed disinterested in the fact that the claimant was a non-national contesting Italian law. The law vested a historic work of art by Van Gogh in the state by reason of the Swiss owner failing to adequately declare his interest in the painting. Rather than preferring a strict test of compensation under the expropriation provisions of Protocol I, the ECtHR applied a loose balancing test (Rudolf, 2000, p. 739). In *Iran Shipping Lines v Turkey* (2007), by contrast, the court found that compensation was due to an Iranian company once Turkey interfered unjustifiably with the use of its Cypriot-owned chartered vessel. The court came to this conclusion, however, after applying its usual standard of proportionality, keeping in mind the wide margin of appreciation owed to signatory states (*Iran Shipping Lines*, 2007, para. 94). No special consideration was owed to the applicant due to its foreignness or that the property at issue was foreign-owned. Even if these cases might be characterized as ones 'with an extra-national flavour', for example (Tomuschat, 2009, p. 645), in almost every instance where non-nationals have invoked their property rights under the European Convention the ECtHR has shown little or no heightened interest in interferences with foreign-owned wealth. Consequently, it never has applied the strict criteria that may be mandated by general principles of international law under Art. 1, Protocol I (Kriebaum, 2008, p. 657; Kriebaum, 2009, p. 242). It can be fairly said that democratic theory in general and political process doctrine in particular has not played a significant role in European human rights jurisprudence.[9] This is not to say that such concerns have not animated intellectual contributions to understanding the European project (Joerges, 2006, p. 22), only that these concerns have not taken hold in European judicial institutions (Somek, 2010, p. 344).

There is another source to consider for *Tecmed*'s formulation of political process doctrine, aside from US constitutional law, and that is customary international law. The political process rationale appears in early

---

9 Representation-reinforcement functions generally have not been served by European courts outside of the European Court of Justice doctrine of 'institutional balance' (Lenaerts and Verhooeven, 2002, p. 37; Harlow and Rawlings, 2007, p. 547). The doctrine purports to ensure that each institution within the European Community, in the exercise of its authority, respects the competences granted to other institutions (Lenaerts and Verhoeven, 2002, p. 44). Harlow likens it to the doctrine of the separation of powers (Harlow, 2002, p. 44).

twentieth-century articulations of the international minimum standard of treatment rule. One reason that non-nationals – alien investors, to be exact – are entitled to better treatment than the crudest standard applied to nationals, Edwin Borchard wrote in 1916, is because nationals are 'presumed to have a political remedy, whereas the alien's inability to exercise political rights deprives him of one of the principal safeguards of the rights of the citizen' (Borchard, 1915, pp. 43, 106; 1939, p. 57; 1940, p. 453).[10] In support of this proposition, Borchard refers repeatedly to a brief by Columbia law professor John Bassett Moore in the *Constancia Sugar Refining* case before the Spanish Treaty Claims Commission *(Constancia Sugar Refining Co. v United States* (1909)).[11] Borchard appears to have been mistaken as the argument makes no appearance in Moore's brief[12] (nor does it seem to appear anywhere else, which is curious, as Borchard was employed at this very time in the Library of Congress law library at the US Supreme Court). Indeed, Borchard would have had little basis to cite Moore in support of a proposition entitling aliens to rights greater than those available to nationals. Moore described this purported principle, in correspondence with Borchard, as an 'exorbitant claim' – it 'invest[s] with the character of a rule of law what should be regarded as an exception based upon no definite principle'.[13] Borchard continued to misrepresent Moore's views by citing him in support of a proposition that Moore thought confusing and extravagant. Borchard, we can surmise,

---

10 The claim was repeated by T R Armstrong of Standard Oil in response to expropriation of foreign-owned oil properties in Mexico. See Gordon (1976, p. 167).

11 In Borchard's 1915 book, he also makes reference to Pinheiro-Ferreira's comments on G F de Martens in Praider Fodéré (1885, para. 405, fn. 3). These comments do not appear to rest on arguments about voice and representation but, instead, are premised on aliens' ability to seek the authority of home state in the case of host state wrongdoing. Moreover, Pinheiro-Ferreira appears somewhat ambivalent about the controversy. He notes that foreigners would not have granted their 'consent' to an injustice, like being 'stripped' of property – they are 'not placed on the same line' as nationals – yet acknowledges that foreigners must respect local law even if 'hard, and onerous, unfair even' (ibid.). It is noteworthy that the Pinheiro-Ferreira reference does not appear again in Borchard's later work, though the Moore reference does appear repeatedly. Also, note that Fachiri (1925) quotes from 'observactions generales' presented by the British government to an arbitration tribunal concerning Portuguese religious properties. The UK document makes an identical political process argument to Borchard's and quotes from a 'celebrated Portuguese jurist', presumably Pinheiro-Ferreira, to the effect that 'a foreigner who had no part therein [in the country's public affairs] cannot be placed upon the same footing' (Fachiri, 1925, p. 168). As mentioned, this is not an entirely accurate representation of the Portuguese jurist's position.

12 See 'Reply Brief for Claimant' (*The Constancia Sugar Refining Co. v United States*, No 196), The Spanish Treaty Claims Commission, vol. 19, No 4 in the Library of Congress.

13 Letter from Moore to Borchard dated 26 April 1915, in John Bassett Moore Papers, Library of Congress, Box 29, file 'General Correspondence 1915'.

preferred to anchor support for this doctrinal innovation in Moore's reputation rather than in US constitutional law, to which I turn next (Borchard, 1915, p. 107; 1939, p. 57; 1940, p. 453).

A constitutional revolution

Whatever the genealogy of Borchard's or the *Tecmed* tribunal's formulations, they are undeniably related to constitutional principles foundational to US constitutional law. I have in mind the decision of the US Supreme Court in *United States* v *Carolene Products Co.* (1937) and its reformulation by John Hart Ely in *Democracy and Distrust* (1980) (though the idea is traceable to earlier periods of constitutional time, see Schneiderman 2010b, pp. 928–31). The brief ruling in *Carolene Products* reads mostly as an addendum to what has been described as the 'constitutional revolution' of 1937 (Balkin, 1989, p. 294). Up until this time, post-civil-war era courts had scrutinized legislative measures with a view to determining whether the scheme advanced particular 'private' over more generalized 'public interests' – what lawyers and judges in this period would characterize as 'class' legislation (Gillman, 1993, p. 62). The tendency to strike down class legislation was typified by the decision in *Lochner v New York* (1905) where the Supreme Court struck down a limitation on the hours of bakery workers in New York State (hence, the period is now known as the 'Lochner era'). Not all such legislative interventions were struck down, but government regulation of markets by both federal and state governments was presumptively suspect in this period. *Carolene Products* reversed this order of constitutional priority – the status quo would no longer prevail over innovative policy measures, even those loosely associated with advancing the public welfare. If constitutional presumptions had favoured freedom of liberty and of contract in contrast to measures intended to improve the working conditions of labourers, the new presumption post-1937 favoured legislative measures adopted to prevent the 'exploitation of a class of workers who are…relatively defenceless against the denial of a living wage' (*West Coast Hotel v Parrish* (1937), para. 399).

In ten short pages of the Supreme Court Reports, Justice Stone for the court upheld the congressional Filled Milk Act of 1923 as a valid enactment under the federal commerce clause and, furthermore, not in violation of the equal protection and takings clauses of the US Constitution. That the congressional enactment was upheld is remarkable considering that, only two years earlier, its constitutional validity would have been in some doubt. Indeed, Miller describes the statute upheld in the case as 'an utterly unprincipled example of special interest legislation' and Justice Stone's justifications as 'patently bogus' (Miller, 1987, pp. 398–9). The presumption of constitutionality now turned in the other direction. Even in the absence of affirmative evidence to sustain the legislation, Justice Stone wrote:

> the existence of facts supporting the legislative judgment is to be presumed, for regulatory legislation affecting ordinary commercial transactions is not to be pronounced unconstitutional unless in the light of the facts made known or generally assumed it is of such a character as to preclude the assumption that it rests upon some rational basis within the knowledge and experience of the legislators (*Carolene Products* (1938), p. 152).

Carolene Products represents, then, the effective withdrawal of run-of-the-mill economic regulation from the purview of constitutional review so long as a rational basis exists for the legislative measure. The political process will be presumed to be operating fairly, in other words, in the case of market regulation. In which case, Congress could rely on commerce clause authority to justify all variety of economic regulation and would have the endorsement of the Supreme Court to do so, for the next half-century.

There will be exceptions to the presumption of constitutionality, and these are described in footnote four to the case. First, Justice Stone admits there 'may be a narrower scope for the operation of the presumption in cases when legislation appears on its face to be within a specific prohibition of the Constitution', such as in the first ten amendments (*Carolene Products* (1938), p. 152, fn. 4). Nor was it necessary to consider whether legislation 'which restricts those political processes which can ordinarily be expected to bring about repeal of undesirable legislation' – such as measures restricting the right to vote or choking off political opposition – would also be immune to the presumption and would call for more 'exacting judicial scrutiny' under the 14th Amendment. Lastly, stated in the negative, the court need not inquire into whether statutes directed at religious, national or racial minorities – what is described as 'prejudice against discrete and insular minorities' – call for a 'correspondingly more searching judicial inquiry' (1938, p. 153, fn. 4).

The second and third paragraphs of footnote four represent a tentatively stated theory justifying the rigour with which the court would review legislative initiatives that block access to the political process or evince a prejudice toward vulnerable minorities. In his elegantly framed argument in *Democracy and Distrust*, John Hart Ely developed Justice Stone's footnote four into a full-blown theoretical justification for mid-century-Warren-court era case law. According to Ely, the US Constitution is concerned almost exclusively with political process in the broad sense – 'with clearing the channels of political change, on the one hand, and with correcting certain kinds of discrimination against minorities, on the other' (1980, pp. 74, 103). Substantive questions,

Ely maintained, were left 'almost entirely to the political process' and so were not an appropriate subject for judicial review.

Reviving the discredited idea of 'virtual representation' (Greene, 2011, pp. 71–2), Ely argued that the interests of those without political power – political outsiders – should, in some instances, be tied constitutionally to those with power (1980, p. 83). Treatment of non-residents under the 'dormant' commerce clause (the implied limitation on state power that protects out-of state citizens), Ely suggested, is a paradigmatic instance of the 'literally voteless' being entitled to virtual representation. Even the 'technically represented' might find themselves 'functionally powerless' and so in need of virtual representation (1980, pp. 84, 98). The question for Ely was whether it was 'appropriate constitutionally to bind the interests of the majority to those of some minority with which no felt community of interests has naturally developed' (ibid.).

As Tribe noted in an early review of Ely's book, the process–substance distinction is hard to manage in this context. Determining those groups whose stereotyping is worthy of constitutional protection is, itself, a substantive question of constitutional law (1980, p. 1075). By this reason alone (in addition to other elements in the text of the US Constitution), there will be no escape from substance (Klarman, 1991, p. 785). Having reasoned through some of these questions in his book, Ely admitted that distinctions on the basis of alienage (or citizenship) were 'a relatively easy case' for, without voting rights, representation could only be 'virtual' (1980, p. 161).[14] Corporate actors, however, would not qualify under Ely's formulation. Firms, local or foreign, do not have the right to vote in state or congressional elections (per Stevens J in *Citizens United v Federal Election Commission* (2010)). Their interests, Ely observed, 'generally have to be protected by persons whose interests are tied up with theirs – officers, employees, stockholders' (1980, p. 85). Consumers and allied producers can also represent foreign corporate interests (Korobkin, 1995, pp. 751–2) effectively reducing the 'deficit in participatory lawmaking' (Gerhart and Baron, 2004, pp. 519–20). If consumer interests are considered too diffuse to countervail well-organized peak organizations (Olson, 1965; Tushnet, 1979, p. 133), then others, such as sources of capital and businesses with common interests, suppliers and state agencies promoting inward investment, can also speak on behalf of investors. There is also

---

14 There are numerous instances in US history, however, where discrimination against foreign business actors has occurred at the federal and state levels and has even been upheld by courts. See discussion in Wilkins (1989, pp. at 580–1) and Vagts (1961, pp. 1494– 5). There are, in addition, national security exceptions, which are found in most BITs and monitored in the US by the Committee on Foreign Investment in the United States. See Economist Intelligence Unit ViewsWire (2007b, pp. 74–5).

the likelihood that foreign subsidiaries themselves will participate, directly or indirectly, in host state deliberations that affect future profitability. The empirical evidence in support of this proposition, to which I turn next, points precisely in this direction. In which case, a major problem with the *Tecmed* ruling is the naïve way in which the tribunal invokes political process doctrine without any inquiry into how investors may be implicated in local or national political decision-making.

The more obvious difficulty is that the Tecmed tribunal invokes the political process rationale for purposes at odds with its rationale in the post-1937 universe. If its impetus was to shield regulation of markets from judicial review and to reserve strict scrutiny for measures impacting negatively on discrete and insular groups, then the tribunal's approach appears to be the mirror opposite. Unless, that is, transnational business organizations can be likened to groups discriminated against on the grounds of religion, nationality, or race. Writing in the context of 1938, the minorities that Justice Stone had in mind were those, according to Cover, that were 'isolated in the social structure', occupying positions 'relatively resistant to change' and 'vulnerable to attack by others' (Cover, 1982, p. 1299). Rather than bearing any resemblance to the concerns motivating Justice Stone, the *Tecmed* formulation looks more like a version of what Baxi calls 'trade-related market friendly human rights' that serve as a checking mechanism on exercises of democratic authority that do not advance the interests of economically powerful foreign firms (2006, p. 234).

Unjustifiable solicitude

In his penetrating critique of *Carolene Products*, Ackerman upsets a number of assumptions associated with political process theory. His objective is to reconstruct US constitutional doctrine by merging it with a 'well-developed body of pluralist political science' (1985, p. 729). He pointedly remarks that Justice Stone got it wrong: the judiciary should be moved to protect 'anonymous and diffuse' groups, rather than those who are discrete and insular, for it is 'these groups that both political science and American history indicate are systematically disadvantaged in pluralist democracy' (1985, p. 724). Rather than racial or religious minorities, Ackerman writes, 'victims of sexual discrimination or poverty' are the groups having the 'greatest claim on *Carolene*'s concern with the fairness of the pluralist process' (1985, p. 718). Reversing the order of priority established by *Lochner*, Ackerman suggests that it is those without property rights who lack 'ample opportunity to safeguard their own interests through the political process' (1985, p. 715).

By engaging with a well-developed body of empirical literature, the aim in this part is to unsettle understandings about those interests entitled to similar solicitude. The object is to document how corporate influence may come to bear on legislators and regulators, not to celebrate business's ability to sway democratically elected governments. As the pattern of experience in the US and other mature democracies establishes, the pathologies associated with the influence of money on politics significantly disturb the possibilities for democratic practice and reform (Habermas, 2001c, p. 153). Wolin, for this reason, likens unaccountable influence peddling in the US (unaccountable, that is, except to shareholders) to a form of corruption which, when normalized, 'is so widely pervasive as to be functional to the operation of a system and, at the same time, so deeply embedded as to incapacitate the system from reforming itself' (Wolin, 2004, p. 600; 2008, p. 287). For my purposes, it is sufficient to show (if evidence is needed) that solicitude directed toward foreign investors by investment tribunals seems ill considered.

This is an era in which states compete aggressively for scarce foreign capital (Stopford and Strange, 1991; Elkins et al., 2004). Desirous of signalling to investors that they will be accorded the highest priority within the policy-making apparatus of the state, state actors have adopted a variety of devices for this purpose: abandoning foreign investment screening mechanisms and regulatory measures or executing concession contracts with guaranteed rates of return, among others. In this pre-establishment phase, conditions for wealthy corporate actors typically are favourable. According to the theory of the obsolescing bargain, emerging out of studies of natural resources nationalization (Vernon, 1971, p. 47), it is in the post-establishment phase that investments are most vulnerable to political risk (Fagre and Wells Jr, 1982). Almost 'from the moment that the signatures have dried on the document', observes Vernon, 'powerful forces go to work that quickly render the agreements obsolete in the eyes of the government' (Vernon, 1971, p. 47). Foreign investors are vulnerable to all sorts of bad behaviour that is discriminatory, even retaliatory, on the ground of national origin. Chua, for instance, has documented how cycles of renationalization are often driven by ethnically charged targeting of foreign economic actors residing within (1995, p. 226).

Political actors, nevertheless, continue to be dependent upon the success of private markets (Thacker, 2000, pp. 74–5). The generation of private wealth through markets helps to generate resources for the state both to tax and to borrow, resources which partly determine political success. These are some of the 'structural mechanisms' that help to explain the continuing influence of capital on state managers despite the 'relative autonomy' of states (Block, 1987). Even in the age of lobbyists like Jack Abramoff (the K Street lobbyist convicted for bribing public officials, including fellow convicted felon Congressman Bob Ney), there is something going on other than a simple one-to-one correspondence between the desires of capital and the actions of politicians (Jessop, 1990, p. 99). It is precisely in that space – between the exercise of the franchise and the vote on the legislative floor – that representative democracy offers opportunities for well-organized interests to have their voices heard (Lindblom, 1977; Vogel, 1989). Lessig labels this opportunity structure, whereby powerful corporate interests get to have their way with the US Congress, 'dependence corruption' (2011, pp. 230ff). Because of a heavy dependence on access to campaign cash, Congress gets diverted from serving constituents' needs in favour of the needs of those who can supply the requisite funds to ensure electoral success. For these reasons, it can be said that 'the best-represented interests on Capitol Hill and in state capitals are surely the interests of corporations and businesses that are not even eligible to vote' (Gardner, 1997, p. 951).

The empirical evidence within the US unsurprisingly indicates that corporate actors will endeavour to effect political change (Hillman, 2003, p. 458). Adopting the premise of profit maximization as an explanation for corporate political activity (Grier et al., 1994), studies reveal that corporations making their home within the US will use political activity to modify costly regulations or to secure government contracts (Hansen and Mitchell, 2000, p. 892). Businesses are likely to use a variety of means to achieve these political ends, including contributing to political action committees (PACS), lobbying and charitable giving. Foreign firms operating within the US, however, are less likely to engage in visible political activity, will have fewer PACS[15] and also give less to charity (Hansen and Mitchell, 2000, p. 895). Though they are likely to lobby less than home firms, lobbying is more common among foreign firms than other political activities due to its low levels of visibility (Hansen and Mitchell, 2000, p. 898). Foreign firms, in other words, do not want to appear to be participating or interfering in democratic processes within host states (Hansen et al., 2004, p. 422). This is even the case for Canadian-owned foreign firms, those who might be considered the 'least foreign' of foreign firms (Hansen and Mitchell, 2001, pp. 14, 17).

Other factors, coming out of the political risk literature, help to explain business success and failure in shaping host state domestic policy. There are factors, many of them internal to foreign subsidiaries, which help to mitigate investor vulnerability to political risk. Data drawn from the experience of managers of foreign multinationals in Tanzania, Zambia, Indonesia and Kenya in the 1970s suggests that the more complex the managerial and operational tasks undertaken by the foreign firm, the larger the volume of sales to associated firms, the more intense the volume of exports, and the greater the proportion

---

15 PAC activity is permissible for US-based affiliates of foreign firms so long as committees are run by US citizens and financed by US citizens or resident aliens (Hansen and Mitchell, 2001, p. 9).

of foreigners in managerial and technical positions, the greater foreign firm bargaining power vis-à-vis the host government (Poynter, 1982, p. 21). Poynter adds that, according to his data set, the more 'politically aggressive firms' experienced significantly less governmental intervention in their operations. The more frequent the contacts between the subsidiary and government, in other words, the less likely government would intervene negatively in the firm's operations (Poynter, 1982, pp. 19, 20). Determinative of firm bargaining power, according to other studies, is the intensity of competition faced by a foreign subsidiary (Kim, 1988) and the number of 'firm-specific resources that are hard to copy' (Moon and Lado, 2000, p. 110). Bargaining power will likely erode over time to the extent that firm-specific resources can be 'easily imitated' or for which there are 'strategically equivalent substitutes' (Moon and Lado, 2000, p. 111; Wells and Ahmed, 2007, p. 68).

How well does this experience translate to emerging or new democracies in the global South? Extrapolating from the work of Hansen and her colleagues, it is reasonable to assume that foreign corporate actors will also engage in political activity within these states. Premised upon the standard model of corporate profit maximization, the incentives to participate will be the same for both domestic and foreign corporations (Hansen and Mitchell, 2001, p. 6). Foreign firms can also be expected to adopt political practices viewed as legitimate within the host country political context. Japanese and British firms, according to a small sample of 1988 US data, were likely to spread political contributions to incumbents in both parties in much less partisan ways than they might have done at home (Stopford and Strange, 1991, pp. 224–5; Hansen and Mitchell, 2001, p. 15). The point is that 'corporate political strategies converge' around practices common within the host-state context – that foreign entities do not 'carry their home practices abroad' (Hansen and Mitchell, 2001, p. 17).

Despite the rhetoric about obsolescing bargains, the data reveal that foreign investors have a wide variety of mechanisms available to ameliorate political risk and engage in extensive lobbying, either alone or in coalitions. Resisting the notion that investors have only one shot at bargaining with host states, in a study testing investor influence in 25 transition states, Malesky found that 'coalitions of investors do indeed lobby for political change and often have significant impact on the economic trajectory of their host countries' (Malesky, 2005, p. 26). In a 1999–2000 survey using a sample of 4085 US and foreign firms operating in 48 developing countries, Desbordes and Vauday test the hypothesis represented by the 'national preference model' – that foreign firms will be discriminated against in favour of domestic firms (2007, p. 429). The 'foreign privilege hypothesis finds more empirical ground than the national preference' one, they conclude (2007, p. 432). Foreign and domestic firms, they find, have equivalent degrees of political influence and hybrid firms (those with both foreign and domestic nationality) are more influential. Foreign firms, it also turns out, 'enjoy a better business climate' than other less influential firms by 'benefiting from lower fiscal and regulatory constraints'. Typically, they will have extracted favourable concessions upon entry into the host state and have the capacity, and this is particularly true for hybrid enterprises, to maintain that political influence over time (2007, p. 424). In which case, the premise of the obsolescing bargain – that investment conditions are favourable upon entry but decline 'from the moment the signatures have dried' and so render investments vulnerable to political risk (Vernon, 1971, p. 47) – does not hold up, according to their results (Desbordes and Vauday, 2007, p. 446). We can provisionally conclude that foreign corporate actors within host states with operative representative democracies would not be voiceless and would even be 'represented' in ways similar to nationally based corporate actors. They might elect, however, to engage in less visible forms of political action for fear of being seen as illegitimately influencing national or local politics.

Yet the *Tecmed* tribunal was content to conclude, on the basis of no empirical data whatever and with the superficial backing of the ECtHR, which has declined to scrutinize closely measures that deprive foreign wealth, that Mexico was so unfaithful to democratic principles that it should give rise to a heightened suspicion that something was amiss in the decision not to renew. There is more than a little irony at work here. Reports from Hermosillo suggest that collusion between the investor and various levels of government early on tarnished state–civil society relations (O'Leary, 2002, p. 4). Permits were issued and renewed, orders unenforced, fines slapped, but no decisive action taken despite the repeated violations of the permit and related authorizations (*Tecmed* (2003), para. 107). In response to social movement complaints about the treatment of Alco Pacifico waste, PROFEPA declared that it would not even take into account those violations in determining whether to renew the landfill's permit (*Tecmed* (2003), para. 123). Ultimately, the INE listened to the community, local authority and the voices of environmentalists and human rights activists, denying renewal of the permit on public health grounds. A moment of Wolin's 'commonality' arose. Yet this is precisely why, according to *Tecmed*, the decision was defective. In political process terms, because foreign investors are not represented in Mexican institutions of government they are denied a voice. This gives rise to the spectre of discrimination against non-nationals, yet events on the ground confirm conclusively that this was not the case.

Transnational legal rules facilitate the checking of democratic institutions so as to control the unanticipated adventure that is democratic life (Rancière, 2006, p. 7). This is the message that is buried in the conscription of political process doctrine in the *Tecmed* case. From this 'democratic' point of view, perhaps no decision adverse to the investor could have been free of defects – surely a perverse outcome that debases democratic principle and justifies Wolin's dispiriting outlook.

* * *

The object of this chapter has been to show how investment rules do not promote but, instead, undermine democratic progress. Despite resort to the high ground of democratic theory in international investment arbitration, it turns out that international investment law looks disparagingly on popular initiatives that have a substantial negative impact on investment interests. By focusing on episodic national elections, rather than voting as part of a much larger set of ongoing political practices (Marks, 2000, pp. 58–9; Rosanvallon, 2008), transnational legal institutions deploy anxieties about political processes in ways that impede the performance of democratic institutions both inside and outside of official channels; this, despite the continuing prevalence of foreign business firms operating in the subterranean channels of political systems abroad.

Treating foreign corporate actors as if they were enfranchised citizens turns out to be the wrong analogy. As empirical evidence reveals, foreign corporate actors instead should be likened to host state corporate actors in operative democracies who do not have the right to vote but who nevertheless participate, and aim to influence, political processes. If only we were able to redirect the political process concerns of international investment tribunals to those more worthy of their solicitude – to the propertyless rather than the propertied (Ackerman, 1985) – the regime might begin to serve democracy's cause.

6
Foucault, Ecuador and On Being 'Freer Than They Feel'

I asked at the beginning of this volume whether the legal mechanisms associated with economic globalization were too deeply entrenched to be the subject of critical revision and resistance.[1] Are they irresistible or, alternatively, is it possible to generate practices that enable us to adjust, even diminish, transnational legality's forms of domination? If the material conditions under which those marginalized by globalization's processes were determinative, resistance would be more widespread than it is at present. One of the stumbling blocks undoubtedly is the difficulty of channelling this contention into an effective politics of resistance. Understanding that alternative possibilities exist runs up against a powerful network of actors and institutions – operating in the realms of politics, economic and culture and at various levels – touting globalization's benefits, insisting that global well-being has improved and that, if they only wait their turn, redemption is just around the corner. In the meanwhile, political solutions to pressing social questions facing marginalized citizens effectively are ruled out of bounds.

In order to help navigate through this ensuing despair, I turn to Michel Foucault's later work, principally his lectures at the Collège de France recently translated into English. Foucault admonishes us, though constrained by techniques of government that structure 'the possible field of action of others' (what he calls 'governmentality') (Foucault, 1982, p. 138), to interrogate the presuppositions of the commonplace – to explore the ground beneath our feet (1979, p. 448). As resistance is adumbrated with power relations, occasions to reconsider taken-for-granted truths are persistent for Foucault. In addition to forging subjectivities, power is productive in precisely this way, in giving rise to opportunities for resistance (Foucault, 1984a, p. 34). Near the

---

1   The phrase 'freer than they feel' in the chapter title is from Foucault's interview in Martin (1988, p. 10).

end of his life, Foucault suggestively resurrected the classical Greco-Roman idea of 'care of the self' (Foucault, 1984a; 1988; 2005), emphasizing its social dimensions, and hinting at possible routes through which modern governmental power might be resisted (Veyne, 1986, p. 230). Foucault was motivated to do so not because he thought these specific practices were a route beyond specific predicaments but, rather, 'by a passion to understand how our present came to be what it is and...why things did not turn out differently' (Valverde, 2010, para. 3.13). In this chapter, I draw on this aspect of Foucault as a means of awakening practices of democratic citizenship that call for innovation and reinvention (Flax, 2007, p. 95), all the while attending to the danger of encountering setbacks – of having to begin over again (Foucault, 1984b, p. 54).

Citizens, social movements and states are tallying up the costs and benefits of embracing globalization's strictures in various locales. Notably in Latin America, they are discarding some of its constituent elements including aspects of the investment rules regime. In the second part of the chapter, I take up Ecuador's muscular discourse in response to investment rule disciplines. The government of Ecuador has withdrawn from the convention that grants jurisdiction to the International Center for the Settlement of Investment Disputes (ICSID) (ICSID, 2009), has denounced nine bilateral investment treaties (BITs) that have proven less than fruitful to the Ecuadorian economy (UNCTAD, 2009a) and has considered denouncing a variety of BITs with capital-exporting states such as Germany, the UK and Finland (Alvaro, 2009). This response, though garnering condemnation from expected quarters (Schnabl and Bédard, 2007), is instructive in so far as it explicates the possibilities for undoing the disciplines associated with transnational legality. The Ecuadorean case also exhibits some of the real limits – the 'field of sparse available possibilities' (Foucault, 1982, p. 137) – to realizing change under conditions of hegemonic neoliberalism. My object is to instil a 'pessimistic activism' (Foucault, 1983, p. 104) that can generate new and unexpected forms of resistance in response to recurring patterns of domination while reminding ourselves that danger lurks everywhere.

I turn, first, to a reading of Foucault's later work. I consider his methodology as generating resources for helping us to develop the critical ethos necessary to confront the challenges of resistance in the contemporary world. Because it is not sufficient merely to imagine such possibilities, in the subsequent part, I turn to strategies for dealing with transnational legality's techniques of domination by investigating recent developments in Ecuador. This is an inquiry into how very specific and partial resistance via national states runs up against the contemporary transnational legal constraints. By taking up the relationship between Ecuador and China as revealed in the legal framework for the treatment of foreign investment, we learn that citizens and states remain 'deeply constrained' by transnational legal norms (Butler, 2004, p. 193) – that there is always the danger of having to begin again.

Before beginning, I should say a few words about utilizing Foucault's 'analytical grids' (Foucault, 2008, p. 186) and methods in this context, that is, as a resource for thinking our way through patterns of domination associated with transnational legality. Foucault ordinarily is not associated with thinking about neoliberal rationality and modes of legal governance in this age of networks and global interconnectedness. Fraser, for instance, reads Foucault as having drawn the perimeters of power firmly within a national frame and so considers him somewhat anachronistic. Locating Foucault within the then dominant frame of the Keynesian welfare state, Fraser writes, he 'mapped the contours of the disciplinary society just as the ground was being cut out from under it' (Fraser, 2003, p. 160). Fraser, however, unduly historicizes Foucault. In recently translated lectures, Foucault reveals a great deal about Europe as a global economic unit with the world as its market (Foucault, 2008, p. 54) and about the origins of neoliberal thought (ibid.). It might be said that Foucault anticipated new forms of government by decentring the national frame and emphasizing other mechanisms of power that today are associated with the term 'governance' (Donzelot and Gordon, 2008, p. 58).

Having rendered Foucault outdated, Fraser nevertheless advocates taking a 'quasi-Foucauldian point of view' in the study of globalization (Fraser, 2003, p. 167). If social regulation is now untethered from the national state (a familiar trope of hyperglobalization theorists – see Held et al., 1999, pp. 3–5), Fraser calls for further study in Foucauldian style of the 'new vehicles of postfordist governmentality' (Fraser, 2003, p. 169). Others have been working precisely with this frame of analysis in mind. Hardt and Negri acknowledge that Foucault 'prepared the terrain' for their diagnosis of the 'globalized biopolitical machine' they designate as empire, discussed in Chapter 1, which becomes a site of resistance and usurpation by the global multitude (Hardt and Negri, 2000, pp. 22, 40; Hardt and Negri, 2009, pp. 56–61). Gill fruitfully exploits Foucault's historical work on disciplinary mechanisms (Foucault, 1977a) by connecting these up with a historical–materialist understanding of contemporary power (Gill, 1995a). Gill argues that the institutions associated with economic globalization perform a panoptic function (drawing on Foucault's reading of Bentham's work on prisons) (Foucault, 1977a, pp. 200–8) by imposing discipline on political actors and institutions which he likens to a 'new constitutionalism' (ibid.; Gill, 2003, p. 132).

Nor does Foucault seem like an ideal interlocutor for discussions about critical resistance to economic globalization and the role of national states in facilitating that sort of resistance. If Foucault regretted that political theory was obsessed with exercises of sovereignty at its apex – in 'political thought and analysis', he wrote, 'we still have not cut off the head of the king' (1990, pp. 88–9) – framing modalities of resistance via extant national political systems seems unsympathetic to a Foucauldian analytic. Foucault's lectures again disclose, however, that states are implicated in techniques of 'government' (in the enlarged sense of the term). Though the state remains a contingent formation – the 'mobile effect of a regime of multiple governmentalities' – the state provides for Foucault a bridging device across scales and levels for the governing of subjects (Jessop, 2008, p. 153; 2011, p. 68).[2] Indeed, one might say the state continues to provide a terrain over which are played out a variety of rationalities that are in conflict (Santos, 2002, p. 489; Cerny, 2009, p. 14), including those associated with neoliberalism and Polanyian movements for societal self-protection.

Lastly, there is the danger of misreading or (perhaps worse) misappropriating Foucault in ways that are at odds with his own methods. Both Dean (1999, pp. 36–8) and Brown (1995, pp. 22, 64), for instance, deny that Foucault's methods permit the endorsement of any particular normative stance against domination (also Gordon, 1980, p. 256). They maintain that his mode of critique opens space in no particular direction – it does not, more specifically, point us in the direction of how to think about governing ourselves or others differently. Dean acknowledges Foucault's statements about politics to the opposite effect while Brown distinguishes between his analytic strategy and his political commitments (Dean, 1999, p. 35; Brown, 1995, p. 22). Neither faithfully captures Foucault's orientation. He reveals ambivalence about this question in his first lecture in 1978 at the Collège de France: 'an imperative discourse that consists in saying "strike against this and do so in this way"', he declares, 'seems to me to be very flimsy when delivered from a teaching institution' (Foucault, 2007, p. 3). He prefers, instead, that a 'conditional imperative' underpins his lectures: 'If you want to struggle, here are some key points, here are some lines of force, here are some constrictions and blockages... these imperatives [are] no more than tactical pointers.' (2007, p. 3) So Foucault anticipated that his methods could encourage movement in certain normative directions. In his *hommage* to Foucault, Veyne (2010) captures well Foucault's thinking in this regard. Critique might equally awaken an activist orientation as it might induce further slumber:

> To do so...must be a personal decision, for the new system of government will be just as arbitrary as the last one – not that this is a consideration that has ever stopped anyone from going ahead (2010, p. 39).

---

2 Foucault rejected the idea of the state as a political universal or as having any 'universal essence' (Foucault, 1978, p. 93; 2008, p. 77). In which case, the complexity of state formations belies any attempt at discovering an essence, underscoring its character as an essentially contested concept (Cerny, 2009, p. 6).

Veyne observes that 'the very spirit of Foucauldism lies in not closing our eyes' (2010, p. 75).[3] This book is premised upon moving ahead and, following the lead of other neo-Foucauldians who, with eyes wide open, drag Foucauldian analytics onto a more normative terrain (Connolly, 1993; Dumm, 2000; Hoy, 2004), so shall I.

Thinking differently

Managing possibilities

In contrast to the historical genealogies that preoccupied Foucault throughout much of his career, the notion of 'governmentality', introduced abruptly in the fourth in a series of lectures at the Collège de France in 1978, provides an opportunity to think in the present and beyond. Governmentality concerns the various practices and techniques by which we are ruled and rule ourselves. This is no command and control structure, rather, it is 'a set of actions on possible actions' (Foucault, 1982, p. 138). Nor is it confined to state action, instead, the state is enabled to survive by the various practices associated with government and is rendered effective in so far as it relies on 'an elaborate network of relations', both public and private (2008, p. 109; Rose and Miller, 1992, p. 55). Government in this enlarged sense, then, is the contact point where techniques of power interact with techniques of the self (Burchell, 1996, p. 20; Foucault, 2005, p. 252). If power is productive in this way, by bringing into being new subject populations (Foucault, 2003b, p. 50), it also provides an opening for the reawakening of political opportunities (Foucault, 1982, p. 143). Foucault wonders whether we might take this opportunity to productively imagine modes of 'acting and behaving that at one and the same time marks a relation of belonging and presents itself as a task' (1984b, p. 84) – belonging in the present, that is, with the task of locating the contingent and arbitrary (Rabinow, 1997, p. xxxi). The directing of conduct presupposes, then, a 'semblance of freedom' (Brown, 2006, p. 73).

In its early formulations in political thought, governmental reason is theorized as *raison d'état* (literally, reason of state) and enforced via techniques associated with the 'police' (involving potentially the regulation of

---

3 Veyne (2010, p. 116) elaborates further: 'his readers and audience could find in [his genealogical histories] plenty of reasons to militate against the established order, on any point they wished to. It may be that Foucault, the scholar, silently derived a certain satisfaction from this.' Further: 'Foucauldism is a critique of actuality that is careful not to dictate prescriptions for action, but does provide a degree of understanding.' (ibid., also p. 119)

everything) (Foucault, 1979b, pp. 193–5; 2007, pp. 312, 326).[4] Dominated by mercantilist thought, all economic production upon which the success of the prince relied was subject to government rationality (though there was more economic liberty than Foucault surmised; Harcourt, 2011, p.153).[5] The *économistes* presaged a new form of governmentality, one of unencumbered competition between individuals and their states. The state was now viewed as the 'regulator of interests', not the guarantor of the happiness of all (Foucault, 2007, p. 346). The success of the state was calculated by the extent to which it respected and facilitated natural processes associated with markets. Civil society emerged as a body independent of the state with its own natural processes of which the state also must take account (2007, p. 352). Foucault traces here the rise of the facilitative state whose 'essential function [is that] of ensuring the security of the natural phenomena of economic processes or processes intrinsic to the population' (2007, p. 353). Moving from reason of state to 'reason of the least state' (2008, p. 43), the marketization of all relations emerges as the pre-eminent technique of government associated with neoliberalism, a subject Foucault took up in detail in his 1979 lectures (2008). On the eve of Prime Minister Margaret Thatcher's election in the UK, Foucault traced the origins of political economy as an internal limit on governmental reason. Foucault draws out fine distinctions between the German post-war variant of neoliberal thought (*ordoliberalism*) and neoliberal workings of political reason in the US (associated with University of Chicago economists Gary Becker and Milton Friedman) (Burchell, 1996; Foucault, 2008). Whereas, for German ordoliberals, the state was legitimate to the extent it actively created space for market freedoms (Foucault, 2008, pp. 84–5) (via the idea of *Rechstaat*, for example), for American neoliberals associated with the Chicago school, the state and most everything else was subsumed under the rubric of economic rationality (Lemke, 2001). This retreat of the state – the inversion of rule by 'reason of state' – is felicitously described by neo-Foucauldians as the imperative of *raison du monde* (Cerny, 2009; Dardot and Laval, 2009).

Foucault does not unquestioningly succumb to the neoliberal edict that all state functions are diminished when at the mercy of markets (Harcourt, 2011). After all, Foucault understands that new forms of governmentality require the production of realms of freedom (Foucault, 2008, p. 63). With its dissembling

---

4 'Generally speaking, what police has to govern, its fundamental object, is all the forms of, let's say, men's coexistence with each other.' (Foucault, 2007, p. 326) These are associated with the 'problem of the town' (Foucault, 2007, p. 335).

5 Modes of police regulation are not confined solely to the level of the state. Foucault describes the Treaty of Westphalia, for instance, as a site for the maintenance of equilibrium and good order. In this way, Europe operates 'as a sort of interstate police or interstate law' (2007, p. 322; Valverde, 2007, p. 171).

of reason of state into the reason of the least state, contemporary governmental rationality gives rise to a contradiction: 'Liberalism must produce freedom, but this very act entails the establishment of limitations, controls, forms of coercion and obligations relying on threats, etcetera.' (Foucault, 2008, p. 64) Foucault asks, for instance, how might free trade be instituted 'if we do not control and limit a number of things' including the establishment of barriers to trade in order to protect nascent industry or, in the case of internal trade, establishing mechanisms to block anti-competitive behaviour (ibid.)? This is a version of 'the game of freedom and security' at the heart of contemporary liberalism which calls for the constant production of freedom (Foucault, 2008, p. 65) – a contradiction that was identified by Polanyi some time earlier in his formulation that '[l]aissez faire was planned' (Polanyi, 2001/1944, p. 147). So it is not the case that Foucault misses the myriad ways in which the state is implicated in the production of 'free markets'.

Power is productive in yet another sense. The logic of liberalism, like other forms of power, produces realms of freedom – 'power relations are possible only insofar as the subjects are free' – giving rise to the formulation that there is no power without resistance (Foucault, 1984a, p. 34). Governmentality encompasses a range of practices and techniques which 'individuals in their freedom can use in dealing with each other' (Foucault, 1984a, p. 41). It is here, in these interstices, that freedom is 'born in the margins of order' (Dumm, 2000, p. 42). If techniques of self-governance give space to freedom, how might 'those who seek to govern imagine their world and seek to fashion it anew?' (Rose et al., 2006, p. 100; Butler, 2002, p. 218).

Practices of freedom

The ethical idea of the 'care of the self' (*epimeleia heautou*) a classical notion taken up by Foucault in his 1981–1982 lectures at the Collège de France (2005), partly answers this question by suggesting routes through modern forms of power. The care of the self refers to an ethical injunction regarding the government of self and others traceable to the Socratic dialogue in Plato's *Alcibiades*.[6] The notion of taking care of oneself was linked to the moment at which one enters into a position of political power – those who governed the city had to be instructed first in how to govern themselves. As Foucault puts it: 'One cannot govern others well, one cannot transform one's privileges into political action on others, into rational action, if one is not concerned about oneself.' (Foucault, 2005, p. 36) In its later stages in Roman thought

---

6　Alcibiades, descended from a politically prominent and wealthy family, has political aspirations. Socrates asks him the proverbial question of the time: will he go on as before or will he care for himself (Plato, 2003, p. 38)?

there is a generalization of the principle to all ages and a universalization of the message 'addressed to and laid down for everyone' (2005, pp. 111–13).

The ethical notion of caring for the self calls not for relaxation, but for 'practical tasks, various activities' such as reflection on one's day, finding inspiration through reading and talking with others, or exercises in abstinence. 'Taking care of oneself is not a rest cure', writes Foucault (1988, pp. 50–1). Nor is it an opportunity for self-absorbed solitude, rather, it is an opportunity to contemplate the self in relation 'to others and the world' (Foucault, 2005, p. 10).[7] This was a set of practices, Rabinow emphasizes, 'that prepared one for a lifelong battle against external events' (Rabinow, 2003, p. 9). The move from 'care' of the self and of others to 'government' of one's self and of others underscores the element of power relations that renders power productive in critical and unanticipated ways.

Foucault sought to awaken the possibility of generating techniques and practices – laborious work, as mentioned – that facilitate resistance and an openness to change. He described three elements to his moral outlook: 'refusal, curiosity and innovation' (1980b). It was this second element that was critical to developing one's capacity to imagine alternatives 'since we can accomplish nothing without reflection and understanding' (ibid.). In one of his last pieces of writing, he described his own philosophical activity as engaging in curiosity, 'not the curiosity that seeks to assimilate what is proper for one to know but that which enables one to get free of oneself' (Foucault, 1985, p. 8).

We might understand, then, the practices of governmental power as linked to care of the self in this way: in passing through the subject, such practices invite the subject to reflect on the relationship of self to self and to others and to, thereby, transform oneself in light of possibilities previously unrecognized (Foucault, 2005, p. 252). Conjoined here are both ethics and politics; thinking about the government of oneself as well as the government of others. This is no flight from politics, but a re-engagement with its tactics and strategies (Dumm, 2000, pp. 2–3). This presents an opportunity for us to learn for ourselves how, under present conditions, power is made through the actions of each and that 'faced with a relationship of power, a whole

---

7   Taking care of the self is not conducted in solitude but is a 'real social practice' (Foucault, 1988, p. 51) and an 'intensifier of social relations' (quoted in Gros, 2005, p. 537) premised upon 'a deep engagement with others' (Dumm, 2000, p. 153). In his lecture notes, Foucault identifies the sort of work expected of the Stoics in Roman times. Rather than being the subject of right and law which creates distance and differentiation, care requires 'questioning yourself about what you are in order to infer from this what it is fitting to do ... not so as to turn away from active life, but so as to give a rule of conduct to someone who is an inhabitant of the world and a citizen of his town' (Gros, 2005, quoting Foucault at p. 540).

field of responses, reactions, results and possible inventions may open up'
(Foucault, 1982, p. 138).

How then to imagine politics beyond the force of normalcy which renders
the contemporary as common sense? Building on Foucault's project, Connolly
emphasizes the notions of contingency, care and curiosity – evoking the care
of what exists, what might exist and a sharpened but not immobilized sense
of reality (Foucault, 1980a, p. 177; Connolly, 1993, p. 379). It entails an
agonistic respect for the plurality of political affiliations and constituencies:
a 'care for the strife and interdependence of contingent identities' together
with a 'willingness to act in such ambiguous circumstances' (Connolly, 1993,
pp. 381, 384).

By situating such conduct within contemporary democratic practice,
Connolly emphasizes a politics of resistance that 'exceeds' the boundaries
of national states. Boundary crossing contributes to 'the democratic drive to
participate in the events that define our lives and ventilate dead pockets of air
within contemporary states' (Connolly, 1993, p. 381). Care of the self emerges,
in its post-Foucauldian version, not as a practice for self-improvement but
as an element 'in a series of resistances' to the dominance of normalizing
discourse (Dumm, 2000, p. 137). Flax finds in Foucault's turn to ethics a
means of developing and sustaining 'a more egalitarian democratic politics' –
a valuable resource for 'analyzing dysfunctional habits and imagining less
oppressive ones' (Flax, 2007, p. 82). She connects the insights offered by these
ancient practices to contemporary experience and the possibility of 'what we
could do otherwise', which she associates with resistance (Flax, 2007, p. 90).
'If they could be otherwise', she observes, then 'other practices are equally
possible.' (Flax, 2007, p. 94) Contemporary ethical practices of democratic
citizenship, Flax insists, like the ancient ones that Foucault takes up, require
constant work and endless reinvention. They require 'the willing by unstable
subjects in concert with others, equally tenuously situated, of imperfect and
uncertain alternatives' (Flax, 2007, p. 95).

Achieving these sorts of levels of self and mutual understanding will not
be easy. Inquiries of the sort that Foucault envisages will be local and partial.
Ensuing transformations will be 'very specific' rather than 'programs for a
new man' (1984b, p. 54). There is the possibility that dominating structures
of normalization will determine outcomes. The ability to move beyond theoretical and practical knowledge 'is always limited'. In which case, there is the
danger of being in the 'position of beginning again' (ibid.). It is a matter,
then, of working within the interstices of contemporary possibility: 'to grasp
the points where change is possible and desirable and to determine the
precise form this change should take' (ibid.).

There are some limiting features associated with strategizing resistance
via technologies of the self. There is, first, the question of whether Foucault

confined this notion to its merely individualistic and aesthetic dimensions. Almost the whole of the interview entitled 'On the Geneaology of Ethics' is seemingly devoted to emphasizing this aesthetic element: why 'couldn't everyone's life become a work of art'? Foucault asks (Foucault, 1983, p. 109) In his 'Preface' to *The History of Sexuality* vol. 2, he described his efforts as concerning the 'arts of existence' by which subjects are enabled to 'transform themselves ... and to make their life into an *oeuvre* that carries certain aesthetic values' (1985, pp. 10–11). Foucault did little to dispel this limiting feature of care of the self, yet, Rabinow insists, he refused this artistic restriction. Instead, he sought to offer a 'practice of thought formed in direct contact with social and political realities' (Rabinow, 1997, p. xxxii). Veyne agrees that this is not 'some aestheticism for dandies' but the initiative of a 'transformation of oneself by oneself', an aestheticization that is 'initiated by freedom' (Veyne, 2010, pp. 104–5). This is made apparent by Foucault's last lectures at the Collège de France (2010) and at Berkeley (2001) on truth-telling (or *parrhesia*) in the ancient world. Foucault describes the problemitization of the duty to tell the truth to political rulers and to others as being associated with the theme of care of the self (2001, p. 24). Both *parrhesia* and *epimeleia heautou* concern the government of all: persuading rulers and subjects, via acts of truth-telling, to care for themselves and for others (Foucault, 2001, p. 106; Gros, 2010, p. 378).

Second, this appears a rather modest means of upstaging the technologies of modern power that Foucault fruitfully described in his earlier work (Harvey, 1990, p. 46; Brown, 2007). As the mechanisms of discipline and bio-power operate on individuals as members of collectivities, Ella Myers observes, 'the techniques of self-care are inadequate instruments for confronting the specifically depoliticizing effects of discipline and biopower, which concern the configuration of plurality' (Myers, 2008, p. 135). Myers takes note here of the problem of levels. Foucault writes about both individual subjects and collectivities, and even regional areas like Europe (Foucault, 2007, p. 322; Valverde, 2007, p. 171), perhaps carelessly, without distinguishing too carefully between modes of power and capacity for resistance at each level. Foucault describes governmentality, for instance, as not being confined 'to a precise domain determined by a sector of the scale, but should be considered simply as a point of view, a method of decipherment which may be valid for the whole scale, whatever its size' (Foucault, 2008, p. 187). Methodologically speaking, Foucault deliberately sought to draw together micro and macro levels of power (Gordon, 2000, p. xxv), adopting a 'scalable' approach that can be applied equally to individuals as to institutions (Jessop, 2011, p. 63). We might understand the distinction between 'tactics' and 'strategies' – tactics operating at micro (Foucault, 1978, p. 100) and strategies at meso and macro levels (Foucault, 1982, pp. 142–3) – as yet another means of conceptualizing power relations that enables fluid analytical movement between levels (Lynch, 2011, p. 25). Foucault, nevertheless, did not adequately (and deliberately did not) relate resistance via care of the self to power operating at particular levels. When asked whether the care of the self could contribute to a new way of thinking about politics, Foucault responded that he had 'not got very far in this direction...I don't like to reply to questions I haven't studied' (1984a, p. 36).

There is also the minor problem of the fullness of Foucault's historical account. Foucault's colleague Pierre Hadot, on whose account of the ancient world he relied in part, accuses him of misreading the ancients on the practices of the self by failing to appreciate how these practices were meant to connect oneself to a cosmic whole outside of the self – to a universalization, rather than a seeming interiorization, of the self (Hadot, 1995, p. 211; 2009, p. 136). Foucault may have been at fault for having failed to connect practices of the self to Greco-Roman cosmology, but it is clear that Foucault did not consider revival of ancient practices as a 'real option' (Williams, 1975, p. 222; Lukes, 2003, p. 105). They only are 'notional' in the sense that they do not present themselves as socially viable – they are experiences too distant for moderns truly to experience (ibid.). Foucault's methods, after all, were not about mapping out paths for useful resistance drawing on the logic of ancient practices. Rather than taking direction from Foucault's genealogical exercises, we might think of his work merely as suggestive of new horizons for political possibility (Hoy, 2004, p. 66). The work calls on us to be attentive to the fact that resistance opens up only a limited range of options; that often there is only a 'field of sparse available possibilities' (Foucault, 1982, p. 137).

Foucault suggests that we look to the periphery – at the margins of authority – for potentialities in this field of scarcity. It is not power in its 'central locations' that should preoccupy us but 'power at its extremities, in its ultimate destinations...[at] those points where it becomes capillary, that is, in its more regional and local forms and institutions' (Foucault, 1976, p. 96). It is in these locales that we might envisage practices of resistance that will serve 'as a chemical catalyst so as to bring to light power relations, locate their position, find out their point of application and methods used' (Foucault, 1982, p. 128). I propose doing so in the next section.

Acting differently

An end to the long neoliberal night?

By any number of indicators, Latin America has become the principal site of resistance to the rules and institutions of international investment law. The United Nations Commission on Trade and Development (UNCTAD) reports that among the national regulatory changes in 2006 and 2007 affecting inward investment, 20 to 24 per cent of those changes were in an unfavourable direction (rendering host country climates less favourable to foreign direct investment (FDI)) (UNCTAD, 2007, p.14; 2008, p. 11). Latin America and the Caribbean had the highest proportion of these unfriendly changes, most of them concerning extractive industries (UNCTAD, 2007, p. 15; 2008, pp. 12–13). Each of Venezuela, Bolivia and Ecuador, for instance, introduced legal changes drastically increasing their share of revenue from oil and gas projects (UNCTAD, 2007, p. 163; 2008, pp. 63–4). Though the incidence of restrictive measures globally had fallen off by 2011 (UNCTAD, 2012, p. 76), a variety of Latin American states continue to impose more restrictive regulatory environments in their natural resource sectors (UNCTAD, 2012, p. 79).

On the front lines of experimentalism associated with neoliberalism – what Grandin calls 'empire's workshop' (2006, p. 210) – it comes as little surprise that citizens and political leadership in Latin America are rejecting the shrinking state associated with the Washington Consensus. We might look here for refusals of the present state of affairs that generate space for resistant practices and techniques that enhance the prospects for self-government. The case of Ecuador provides revealing evidence of the productive ways of neoliberal governmentality: redirecting the orientation of state so that it is compliant with transnational legal effects while generating a lexicon of resistance precipitating the possibility of thinking differently. Ecuador is now on a path seemingly of rejecting these strictures but, as I argue below, there is the danger of mistaking opportunity for a period of yet further domination.

Neoliberalism's ascendance in Ecuador, as elsewhere, required the active complicity of the state to such a degree that the social and political unrest precipitated by its advance facilitated its ultimate demise (Zamosc, 2004, p. 143). Rather than generating peace and stability – the soft virtues of commerce (Hirschman, 1977) – 'legislative reforms seeking to modernize and normalize the Ecuadorian populace ironically helped produce transgressive subaltern subjects' (Sawyer, 2004, p. 93). When, at its origins, Ecuador embraced neoliberal governmental reason, it is not apparent that the administration of President Febres Cordero (1984–1988) simply followed the edicts of international financial institutions. Rather, Conaghan et al. conjecture that 'neoliberalism was consciously chosen by policymakers [in the Central Andes] with an eye toward specific power relations in their respective societies' (Conaghan et al., 1990, p. 4). According to their account, emergent political leadership worked in tandem with powerful local business interests which had become disenchanted with military authority. As civilian rule became entrenched and economic crisis deepened, political leaders could exploit powerful presidential offices without the checking mechanisms of the legislature (Nino, 1996, pp. 176–9). Exercising solely executive authority, President Cordero reversed campaign policy and opportunistically embraced the new global orthodoxy, revitalizing the economy on the basis of 'work, production and foreign investment' (Conaghan et al., 1990, p. 13). Though more gradualist than others in the region, the administration eschewed import substitution – as international financial institutions had insisted (Amsden, 2007, pp. 128–9) – and issued 26 'urgent' economic decrees between 1984–1985 lowering the minimum wage, encouraging foreign investment and deregulating exchange and interest rates (Conaghan et al., 1990, p. 21). Similar shifts in course were taken up by subsequent administrations, raising gas prices and electricity rates and devaluing the sucre (Stokes, 2001, pp. 43–4). The Ecuadorean economy quickly became integrated into global markets with FDI tripling (UNCTAD, 2001, p. 8) and exports doubling in the 1990s (Robinson, 2008, p. 66). Still the country faced severe economic crises, resulting in popular mobilization and default on debt, culminating in the March 2000 Economic Transformation Law. The executive on this occasion again introduced a variety of significant social and economic reforms including the abandonment of the sucre and adoption of the US dollar as Ecuador's currency (UNCTAD, 2001, p. 7). Political turmoil continued unabated until 2006, with the election of University of Illinois-educated economist and reform-minded Rafael Correa. His election, he later proclaimed, would put an end to the 'long and sad night of neoliberalism' and usher in 'socialism of the 21st century' (Conaghan, 2008, p. 46).

Much of the foregoing history is linked to the rise of a militant Ecuadorean indigenous political movement. No other Indian organization, observes Zamosc, 'has demonstrated the power to paralyze a country again and again', as is the case with Ecuador's Confederation of Indigenous Nationalities (CONAIE) (Zamosc, 2004, p. 134). Under the auspices of CONAIE, the social protection of ethnic communities was conjoined with the recognition of Ecuador as a 'plurinational' state. This was initially to advance agrarian reform and later to buffer some of the deleterious effects of neoliberal policy, particularly as oil and gas development took off in the 1980s (Korovkin, 2007). Sawyer describes 'unimaginable' interethnic political coalitions – between indigenous and agrarian peasant subjects – having been 'unwittingly produced' by the turning of the screws of the neoliberal state (2004, p. 180). The political left joined hands in this struggle to promote indigeneity and indigenous rights. Both 'class and ethnicity', Becker observes, 'have been critical to the success of an indigenous movement: the two cannot easily be separated' (2008, pp. 14–15). After some success toppling successive administrations, CONAIE's political party wing, Pachakutik, discredited for having participated in a failed alliance with the neoliberal administration of President Lucio Guttierez, attracted only a small percentage of the vote in 2006 (Schaefer, 2009, pp. 400, 410). Instead, Correa's new Movimento Alianza Pais (MAP) managed to garner much of the indigenous vote, the left and the disenchanted middle in a convincing electoral victory (Burbach, 2007).

Correa immediately put an end to US–Ecuador negotiations toward a new free trade agreement (stalled under the previous Palacio regime) though a BIT signed in August 1993 continues in force (US State Department, 2009). The previous administration of President Alfredo Palacio already had amended the Arbitration and Mediation Law barring international arbitration if contrary to the 'national interest' and, in its Hydrocarbons Law of 2006, demanded 50 per cent of earnings deemed to be 'excess' windfall profit (Economist Intelligence Unit ViewsWire, 2007a).[8] Under Correa, things heated up. As the US Department of State put it, 'Ecuador can be a difficult place to do business.' (US State Department, 2009) In December 2007, Correa's government demanded an increased share in excess oil and gas revenues (from 50 to 99 per cent) and up to 70 per cent of royalties for new petroleum contracts (giving rise to the renegotiation of contracts and new investment disputes filed with ICSID) (Vincentelli, 2008, p. 46; Zaldumbide-Serrano, 2008). Following a similar action by Bolivia (Vis-Dunbar et al., 2007), Ecuador also tendered notice that it would withdraw consent to ICSID, housed at the World Bank, having jurisdiction over investment disputes arising from oil and gas exploitation (Gardiner et al., 2008; ICSID, 2009). The state also gave notice that it would terminate at least nine BITs that it considers oppressive in their terms and with little return, so to speak, in attracting new inward investment, to which I turn next (Peterson, 2008; UNCTAD, 2009a). The following year, Ecuador defaulted on US$30.6 million in interest payments on its foreign debt.

The last gesture to take note of here was the new text of the Ecuadorian Constitution. Averaging constitutional reform every 10 years since 1830 (*The Economist*, 2008), a new constitution drafted by an elected constituent assembly was approved in a national referendum in September 2008. Signalling a departure from reforms of the past, indigenous communities must be consulted in respect of mining ventures that may affect their collective rights (Art. 57(17)). Throwing a wrench into the investment rules works, the constitution also provides that no jurisdiction will be ceded to international arbitration concerning commercial and contractual disputes (Art. 422).[9] It turns out that the potential for the constitutional clause to bar access to international arbitration may be narrower in scope than appears

---

8 Most companies complied with the 2006 law, except for City Oriente, which filed an investment dispute under the US–Ecuador BIT with ICSID (Zaldumbide-Serrano, 2008). The Palacio administration also terminated Occidental Petroleum's oil concessions in the state, giving rise to one of the largest and ongoing investment disputes with the US-based company.

9 The one exception is to disputes between Latin American states which would be resolved before regional tribunals. The text reads: 'Art. 422.- No se podrá celebrar tratados o instrumentos internacionales en los que el Estado ecuatoriano ceda jurisdicción soberana a instancias de arbitraje internacional, en controversias contractuales o de índole comercial, entre el Estado y personas naturales o jurídicas privadas.

at first glance (Gómez, 2012, p. 455).[10] Indeed, the Correa administration appears to be relaxing its opposition to arbitration. Despite constitutional plans for revitalizing the Ecuadorean economy based on the principles of solidarity, reciprocity and communalism, there are few indications that Ecuador will be departing significantly from the economic trajectory associated with dominant orthodoxy (with its post-financial crisis Keynesian variant in some cases). This will necessitate deeper integration into global export markets based on the extraction of resources such as oil, bananas and cut flowers.

Freer than they feel?

Ecuador has signed or ratified some 25 BITs, 13 of them with other Latin American states, and others with capital-exporting states such as the US, Canada and China. It also has faced the greatest number of investor disputes in the region (an estimated 15) (Van Harten, 2008b), some of which have given rise to latitudinarian interpretation by investment tribunals (Sornarajah, 2008). In the *Occidental* case (*Occidental Exploration and Production Company* v *Ecuador*(2004)), for instance, Ecuador was held liable for denying to the petroleum sector value added tax (VAT) refunds that were available to other sectors of the economy (e.g. exporters of cut flowers). Both foreign-owned and nationally owned petroleum operators, however, were treated identically. This resulted in a US$75 million award against Ecuador, even though the VAT decision, according to the tribunal, was not motivated by 'prejudice' but was based, instead, on the exercise of 'good faith' determinations of 'reason and fact' by a 'very professional' state agency (*Occidental* (2004), paras 186, 163, 177). The *Occidental* decision has been described as 'disconcerting' and 'troubling', even by supporters of the regime (Franck, 2005, pp. 678, 680). At present, Chevron is seeking an order from an investment tribunal to forestall enforcement of an Ecuadorean court's US$18 billion award for environmental degradation in the Ecuadorian Amazon (Crooks and Mapstone, 2012). Chevron alleges,

---

[n 9 continued] Se exceptúan los tratados e instrumentos internacionales que establezcan la solución de controversias entre Estados y ciudadanos en Latinoamérica por instancias arbitrales regionales o porórganos jurisdiccionales de designación de los países signatarios. No podrán intervenir jueces de los Estados que como tales o sus nacionales sean parte de la controversia.

En el caso de controversias relacionadas con la deuda externa, el Estado ecuatoriano promoverá soluciones arbitrales en función del origen de la deuda y con sujeción a los principios de transparencia, equidad y justicia internacional.'

10 The government of Ecuador's subsequent behaviour, including the execution of loan agreements and of mining and oil concessions, suggests that the government does not intend to have the constitutional prohibition restrict entirely its ability to provide a measure of comfort to investors in terms of dispute resolution processes (Gómez, 2012, pp. 482).

based on out-takes from the award-winning documentary film *Crude* (2009) (Chevron, 2011), that Ecuador colluded with the plaintiffs to secure a sham judgment from Ecuadorian courts (Keefe, 2012). The tribunal has ordered, by way of interim measures, that Ecuador suspend enforcement of the award (*Chevron Corporation and Texaco Petroleum Corporation v the Republic of Ecuador* (2012a), para. 3). It also has determined that it has jurisdiction to adjudicate the merits of the dispute. The tribunal's future work, it has declared, will be to consider some of the 'gravest accusations which can be advanced by a claimant against a modern State subject to the rule of law' (*Chevron Corporation and Texaco Petroleum Corporation v the Republic of Ecuador* (2012b), para. 4.57).

The Consulting Committee on Investment of the Ecuadorean National Assembly initially was tasked with the responsibility of assessing the utility of Ecuador's BIT programme and came to the conclusion that it had not been productive in attracting new inward investment (Ecuador, 2007). At the same time, Ecuador faced claims (decided or pending) valuing more than US$12 billion before international investment tribunals (Ecuador, 2004). Though more work needed to be done in this regard, the Consulting Committee was prepared to advise the denunciation of several BITs with other developing states, including those in Central America (Honduras, El Salvador, Guatemala and Nicaragua) together with the Dominican Republic, Cuba, Paraguay, Uruguay and Romania – states, it should be observed, with whom Ecuador is unlikely to face any investment disputes. The Consulting Committee was not prepared to recommend the denunciation of BITs with many developed states as, in some instances, investment was 'significant' or because these BITs 'were important for social and political reasons'. The Consulting Committee, instead, recommended their renegotiation. Indications were that a revised text would require the specific consent of states before matters could proceed to international arbitration.[11] It was expected that treaties with South American states, such as Bolivia, Peru, Argentina and Chile, would also be renegotiated as economic integration deepened in the Andean region. Lastly, the Consulting Committee noted that China was one of the main investors in Ecuador and it was 'hoped that Chinese–Ecuadorian relations continue to increase in the short term' (Ecuador, 2007).

In the face of the Consulting Committee's cautious advice, President Correa recommended to the National Assembly that it denounce a further 13 BITs with capital-exporting states such as the US, Germany, France, the UK and even China (Alvaro, 2009). The President's communication to the Assembly cited Article 422 of the new Ecuadorean Constitution (*El Comercio*, 2009) and

---

11 Ecuadorian Attorney General Xavier Garaicoa suggested that, in the case of the US, this could be done by issuing an 'interpretation' requiring the consent of Ecuador to proceed to international arbitration. See BBC (2007).

also that BITs violated tax sovereignty (a likely reference to the *Occidental* (2004) decision) (Asamblea Nacional del Ecuador, 2009a). In his appearance before the Assembly committee charged with developing recommendations, Deputy Trade Minister Julio Oleas explained that a strategy of denunciation was preferable and more expeditious than renegotiating each of these BITS. Bilateral reform, he explained, would take five to eight years, doubling the life of these investment obligations to almost 20 years. There is some urgency, he explained, in defending national interests and in rebalancing arbitration with human rights obligations (Asamblea Nacional del Ecuador, 2009b).

At the behest of the National Assembly, President Correa in January 2010 referred to Ecuador's Constitutional Court the question of whether the terms of these various BITs were consistent with the constitution. The Constitutional Court replied in the negative. In a sequence of 13 separate decisions, the court ruled that these BITs mostly were inconsistent with the aforementioned Article 422 of the 2008 constitution that barred 'treaties and international instruments' ceding 'sovereign jurisdiction to international arbitration entities' (Gómez, 2012, p. 467). This was so even in the case of the modest arbitral mechanism available under the Ecuador–China BIT (the details of which I next turn to) authorizing investor-initiated arbitration only in those cases where the amount of compensation due as a result of expro-priation is in dispute (Ecuador–China BIT, Art. 9.3) (Ecuador, 2010a).

The question of denunciation returned to the National Assembly for its consideration and approved requests to terminate BITs with the UK, Germany and Finland. Requests to terminate BITs with France, Sweden and the Netherlands remain outstanding. The National Assembly, however, chose not to approve the President's request to terminate Ecuador's BIT with China (US Department of State, 2011). The hope undoubtedly is that Chinese investment will be a principal source of fresh capital. The question, however, remains: can Ecuador relax the legal conditions attached to investment rules disciplines? That seems unlikely – indeed, everywhere Ecuador will turn, these strictures loom large.

The new normal?

Given a global recession and state oil revenues at rock bottom, Correa has called for foreign investment in new mining concessions (Mance, 2009). This has precipitated vocal opposition from indigenous constituencies that helped bring him to power (i.e. CONAIE). The President labelled as 'childish' those environmentalists, leftists and indigenous groups who reject massive devel-opment projects of this sort. 'Those who say no to oil, to the mines, and to not using our renewable energy', he is reported to have said, are 'like a beggar sitting on top of a sack of gold.' (Zibechi, 2011) Over their objections, Correa has signed the country's first large-scale mining project with Chinese-owned

Ecuaorriente (Reuters, 2012), agreed to the construction of a hydropower project with China's Harbin Electric International (China Business Newswire, 2012), and signed contracts with US-based Schlumberger and Argentina's Tecpetrol worth US$1.7 billion to develop mature oil reserves (Economist Intelligence Unit ViewsWire, 2012).

Correa was reported to have even been quietly 'rekindling ties to the International Monetary Fund' (IMF) in order to gain quick access to its vast cash reserves (Forero and Partlow, 2009; Romero, 2009). It turned out that Ecuador could avoid IMF conditionalities by looking instead to China's vast foreign currency reserves, capitalizing on the Chinese thirst for oil.[12] Ecuador has negotiated three 'loan for oil' packages worth US$4 billion secured by oil exports to China paid for at market value. While these loans avoid the conditionalities typically associated with international financial institutions (like the IMF) they are not entirely untied. The loan-for-oil contracts require continual oil shipments to China in excess of that required to repay Ecuadorean loans and are tied partly to the purchase of Chinese goods (Gallagher et al., 2012, pp. 14, 19).

Revealing of the ruling state of mind is the Consulting Committee's hope that bilateral relations with China will deepen – that increasingly it will be a site for new FDI. This hope, too, is implied in the National Assembly's decision not to denounce the Ecuador–China BIT notwithstanding the Constitutional Court's finding of constitutional inconsistency. Indeed, China has been flexing its new economic might in a variety of places around the globe including in Latin America. Having invested in places like Africa and South America as part of its 'Going Abroad' strategy (Gallagher and Shan, 2009, pp. 12–13), China has been energetically signing BITs – it is the second highest signatory of BITs – with other developing countries. UNCTAD reports that about 60 per cent of the Chinese BITs concluded between 2002–2007 'were with other developing countries, mainly in Africa' (UNCTAD, 2008, p. 15). This can be explained, in part, by China's heavy investment in the African natural resource sector that will help to fuel its economic boom (UNCTAD, 2004, pp. 25–7). China has also been actively renegotiating BITs based on a new model represented by a 1998 BIT with Barbados. The change in policy appears

---

12 Having defaulted on sovereign debt, Chinese lending 'is filling in for the sovereign debt market' which effectively is unavailable to it (Gallagher et al., 2012, p. 8). Ecuador is one of four Latin American countries (along with Venezuela, Brazil and Argentina) to have benefited from 91 per cent of Chinese lending in Latin America since 2005, most of it to encourage oil production. Lending from the Chinese Development Bank and the China-Export-Import Bank to the region far exceeds that provided by the World Bank and the Inter-American Development Bank (Gallagher et al., 2007, pp. 5–7).

to be motivated by concerns about protecting Chinese investments abroad from political risk (Congyan, 2006, p. 638).

Schill describes the new standard Chinese BIT (the third-generation model according to Gallagher and Shan, 2009, p 320) as 'in all major aspects what can be considered standard treaty practice in approximately 2,500 BITs world-wide' (Schill, 2007, p. 76). The main innovation of the new Chinese model is that it provides consent to investor–state dispute mechanisms subject to only prior administrative review. The 2005 Germany–China BIT, for instance, calls for the passage of three months' time since the investor submitted the dispute to a Chinese administrative court. This can be described as a requirement to exhaust local remedies (Gallager and Shan, 2009, p. 365) but it may also be correct to characterize this as an attempt to govern at a distance by root-ing out corruption at local levels and departure from Chinese national laws (Peerenboom, 2002, pp. 398, 429; Moustafa, 2007, pp. 28–20). The minimal experience to date, as related by Gallagher and Shan, suggests that adminis-trative review can have the effect of sniffing out local protectionism but that a change in the legal regime upsetting investor expectations may not attract much solicitude from Chinese administrative courts (Gallager and Shan, 2009, pp. 371–6). Among other deviations from standard investment treaty norms are exemptions from national treatment for existing non-conforming meas-ures. Amendments of those measures are permitted so long as amendment does not increase non-conformity (what is called standstill). China under-takes in these agreements also to progressively remove all non-conforming measures (what is called rollback) (see agreements with Germany (2005) and Finland (2006)).[13]

The Ecuador–China BIT of 1996 predates the 1998 change in policy and so is based on China's earlier model treaty (corresponding to the second model Chinese BIT formulated in the late 1980s) (Gallagher and Shan, 2009, p. 37). Containing more limited protections for investors, this may be a further reason Ecuador prefers dealing with inward Chinese investment. In these earlier models, state sovereignty was repeatedly underscored (ibid.) with investor–state arbitration available only in the case of a failure to agree on 'the amount of compensation for expropriation within six months after resort to negotiations' (Art. 9.3). Investors otherwise are entitled only to 'submit the dispute to the competent court of the Contracting Party accepting the invest-ment' (Art. 9.2). This limited consent to investment arbitration, Schill argues,

---

13 The 2005 Germany–China BIT is unusual for having exempted from national and most-favoured nation treatment measures 'taken for reasons of public security and order, public health or morality' (2005, para. 4(a)). But for recent attempts to carve out bona fide public health, safety and environmental measures in the case of expropriation or nation-alization in US and Canadian investment agreements, exceptions such as these are not usually available.

was 'hardly a sufficient bulwark against governmental interferences' (Schill, 2007, p. 91). Yet this limited consent to investor–state disputes appears to be Ecuador's preferred policy, confining ICSID jurisdiction to specific case-by-case consent.

China has been aggressively pursuing an investment protection strategy that replicates the high standards touted by most countries in the developed world as representing international law. China has already renegotiated 15 of its old BITs (UNCTAD, 2008, p. 15), with undoubtedly more to come. Though China holds itself out as a model for economic progress that is more developmentally friendly than the American model (Wong, 2008; Jacques, 2009, p. 397),[14] that Ecuador will be entitled to entertain inward Chinese investment on these old terms seems unlikely going forward. Rather, it would appear that the legal framework for the promotion and protection of foreign investment will be framed in terms no different than those previously encountered by states of the global South.[15] It turns out, then, that there is no escape from globalization's disciplines taking up this particular path of resistance.

Some voices within China have expressed dismay with this change in the course of Chinese foreign investment policy. Such concerns are precipitated by the new ability of foreign investors to initiate claims against Chinese authorities. Chen describes the abandonment of protections shielding Chinese sovereignty as opening 'the door without any defence...the consequences may be ghastly and endless troubles once the unpredictable and unavoidable crises occur under the attack of international capital or speculative "giant crocodiles"' (Chen, 2006, pp. 912–13). Others, outside of China, are encouraged by these developments. They point to China's embrace of standard model treaty protections as evidence that these are not 'tools of hegemonic empire' or 'one-sided tools for the imposition of western power' (Alvarez, 2010, p. 626). Instead, Alvarez argues, it affirms the proposition that states all over the world, including non-Western states like China, are 'evolving toward common positions on a number of crucial [investment treaty] provisions' (Alvarez, 2010, p. 634). Alvarez goes so far as to claim that recent modifications to investment strictures, such as those narrowing the scope of expropriations in the 2005 US model treaty (discussed in Chapter 3), can be interpreted as measures for societal self-protection – part of the 'countermovement' – contemplated by Polanyi in *The Great Transformation* (1944/2001) (Alvarez, 2010, p. 640). What goes

---

14 Arrighi is more ambivalent about the prospects of China offering a more progressive alternative to the dominant capital-exporting model (2008, p. 389). Also see Supiot (2012).
15 Schill writes that 'in relation to these countries the PRC behaves like a traditional-capital exporting country that attempts to secure its investment abroad without much probability of being involved as a respondent in any investor–State dispute' (2007, p. 93).

unacknowledged by Alvarez, and the real achievement secured by investment law's norm entrepreneurs, is that China now takes as given capital-exporting state norms long claimed to have risen to the level of customary international law, including an idealized version of the metropole's conception of property rights that bears little resemblance to China's distinctive national property rules (Lee, 2010). Whereas previously Alvarez acknowledged that investment treaty relationships hardly reflect 'a voluntary, uncoerced transaction' (Alvarez, 1992, p. 552), today Alvarez prefers to elide the fact that powerful capital-exporting states continue to call the tune for those in need of inward investment – a signal achievement by any measure.

The sparse field of available possibilities

The Ecuadorean case suggests that Foucauldian analytics might prove fruitful in understanding transnational legal effects and pathways leading away from them. If neoliberal governmentality posed an internal and permanent check on national political action, the phenomenon Foucault described has gone global (Dardot and Laval, 2009). Cerny attributes the global spread of governmentality to the successful 'expansion of the hegemony of practices learned from the domestic sphere' such as state-supervised competition (Cerny, 2009). Yet he maintains that these hegemonic practices are not embodied in 'institutions as such' (Cerny, 2008, pp. 224–5). The hypothesis that practices learned at the domestic level are now expanding to global environs complements well the processes I have been describing. Contra Cerny, however, we can say with confidence that transnational legality institutionalizes neoliberal discourse thereby making it even more difficult to resist.

We are urged by Foucauldian analytics, moreover, to examine power operating outside of traditional centres of authority. This should lead researchers to consider the application of transnational authority in the periphery, at the margins of imperial authority. This has the potential benefit of resurrecting subjugated knowledges, offering insurgent and locally informed accounts that help to comprehend exercises of contemporary power (Santos, 2004). It is in these heterogeneous locales, as many of the theorists examined in this book suggest, that strategies rejecting the false necessity of economic globalization can be devised and tested. These are places where 'practical critique that takes the form of a possible crossing-over' can be developed (Foucault, 1984b, p. 53). But critical resistance is not sustainable at local levels alone, certainly not in the realm of investment rules.

We are prompted, then, to turn back toward the state as the salient locale with which to engage in critical resistance. It could be said that the 'privatization' of authority conceals the persistent role of states in managing and maintaining transnational legal forms and norms. The abstraction of privately governed economic spaces elides the agency of states and the ambivalent relationship states have with the citizenry that they are deemed to represent. In which case, citizens should want to have recourse, at least in the interim, to states as a means of engaging in critical, non-retrograde resistance.

The Ecuadorean case also invites a reconceptualization of the ethical edict to care for the self and for others. Such a reconceptualization would take us beyond the individual subject to the level of collective action, even to the level of states, premised on an appreciation that states remain 'a unique and uniquely vulnerable object of political accountability' (Brown, 2006, p. 78). We then are in a position to appreciate the turn in Ecuador away from globalization's disciplines, at least initially, as being the product of collective learning undertaken over the previous period of neoliberal rule. Even if such practices of 'taking care' do not have the character of classical Greek or Roman modes, the Ecuadorean case suggests a parallel of a sort: having lived under forms of neoliberal governmentality for some time, citizens began to undertake the hard work – or 'state work' (Sassen, 2006, p. 232) – of responding to the dele- terious effects of economic globalization. This work can take different forms as, in Ecuador, electing a social democratic president, engaging in legislative or constitutional, reform, rescinding investment treaties, and denouncing international conventions. Other states, similarly, are undertaking this sort of work. In South Africa, for instance, the African National Congress govern- ment has chosen to abandon an oft-utilized UK investment treaty model in favour of a newer one better suited to South Africa's developmental needs (South Africa DTI, 2009; Williams, 2011). Even middle power countries, like Australia, have indicated that they will no longer adhere to commitments to resolve disputes between investors and host states through the aegis of investment arbitration. Previously, such commitments were included at the behest of Australian business, the Gillard government acknowledges. Going forward,'[i]f Australian businesses are concerned about sovereign risk in Australian trading partner countries, they will need to make their own assess- ments about whether they want to commit to investing in those countries' (Australia, Department of Foreign Affairs and Trade, 2011, p. 14).

The sort of work described here is partial, specific and decidedly not univer- salist. Rather than contemplating a global programme of renewal, the work envisaged here is attuned to the trajectories of specified forms of transnational legality (Foucault, 1984b, p. 54). There will be no general formula 'for all peoples at all times', rather, solutions will be 'contextual, historically specific, and, inevitably, provisional' (Chatterjee, 2004, p. 22). This complements well the role Foucault envisaged for theory: 'not to formulate the global system- atic theory which holds everything in place, but to analyse the specificity of mechanisms of power, to locate the connections and extensions and to build little by little strategic knowledge' (Foucault, 1977b, p. 145). Rather than dissolving projects of resistance into utopian formulations, this pathway has the more modest objective of producing less, perhaps only more tolerable, forms of domination (Foucault, 1984a, p. 40).

Which brings us, lastly, to the Ecuadorian strategy of rejecting the transnational legal commitments on offer from Organization for Economic Co-operation and Development states in favour of strictures associated with new inward Chinese investment. Unlike the gringo states of the global North, the Ecuadorians appear to be saying, 'The Chinese are our friends.' (Moyo, 2009, p. 98) Chinese modalities for exercising authority are to be preferred as they make fewer demands on subject populations. As we have seen in the realm of investment rules, the prognosis seems overly optimistic. By insisting on the highest standards of investor protection, Chinese investment disciplines mostly mirror those of other powerful capital-exporting entities, like the US and the EU. As they concern Ecuador's turn away from the 'long and sad night of neoliberalism' (Conaghan, 2008, p. 46), developments in this domain, as in others, remain ambivalent at best (Sawyer, 2004, p. 207). Foucault's cautious optimism about choosing pathways away from contemporary domination is apposite here. Acknowledging that a 'historico-critical attitude' requires experimentation, we must consistently put such attitudes 'to the test of reality', he warns (1984b, p. 55). Such an attitude requires that we both 'grasp the points where change is possible and desirable, and...determine the precise form this change should take' (ibid.). This entails both the possibility of reversing relationships of domination but also avoiding mistaking conditions of 'free play' and possibilities of reversal for fixed and 'stable mechanisms' of authority (Foucault, 1982, p. 142). Such pathways away from domination always run the risk, then, of running into roadblocks (Sawyer, 2004, p. 219) – that 'we are always in the position of having to begin again' (Foucault, 1984b, p. 54).

*   *   *

Foucault admonishes us to understand that power can be both positive and productive, opening up new opportunities for action and resistance. Power also constrains the horizon of possibilities, perhaps leaving few options open. In such circumstances, it is imperative not to misrecognize openness for domination (Hoy, 2004, p. 92). In the case of Ecuador, there seems to be little remove from the constraints of the past, indeed, Ecuador seems to be moving from one form of domination to another. Despite taking bold action in the realms of legislative and constitutional reform, and rethinking its investment treaty policy, there seems otherwise little experimentation going beyond the constraints imposed by transnational legality's strictures. The practices of transformation must call for something more than merely taking note of the shrinking horizon of possibilities.

Conclusion: Resistance's Prospects

I asked at the beginning of this book whether economic globalization is irresistible. It turns out that transnational legality's version of economic globalization is hard to resist. This is not, of course, because neoliberal globalization is so utterly desirable, rather, it is because it constitutes our 'present history' – we are enmired within its web. Instances of critical resistance – those pathways away from transnational legal disciplines that do not merely reinforce existing relations of domination – appear episodic, if not futile.

Transnational legal ties are intended to bind states far into the future. Alternative paths are difficult to imagine when the weight of that legal order comes to bear down on those who dare to think and act differently. Many of the theoretical resources available, though provocative, seem inadequate to the task of strategizing beyond maintaining constituent elements of the status quo. Though the conjuncture of a global financial crisis together with increasing disenchantment with economic globalization's legal strictures invite multiple opportunities to imagine the world anew, it turns out that exit strategies are few. By way of conclusion, I review the circumstances giving rise to this limited horizon of possibility.

This book's argument is premised upon the central role of states both in binding governments and citizens to transnational legal strictures and in the unique legal capacity of states to undo those constraints. The state is the 'singularly accountable object in the field of political power' that has the jurisdiction to both knit and to unravel technologies of contemporary global governance (Brown, 2006, p. 79). When the 2008 global recession hit and financial markets were in free fall, we learned that only states were capable of responding and that they chose to do so by collectivizing the private risks of some of the wealthiest individuals and institutions in the world (Judt, 2010, p. 195).

As this episode suggests, state authority is ambivalent, even untrustworthy. State power, after all, has been conscripted to lend its support to

neoliberalism's discursive strategies of comparative advantage, consumer freedom and the rule of law, each of which cumulatively contributes to the spread
and maintenance of transnational legal norms and forms. Yet transnational
legal rules exhibit a great deal of disdain for states and the publics that states
are intended to serve, rendering unstable the scaffolding provided by states
to transnational legality's edifice. This is well exhibited by international
investment law's response to measures taken by Argentina in reaction to its
economic meltdown of 2000–2001. Not only are investment rules intended
to place limits on the redistributive capacity of states, they are intended to
dampen citizen expectations – to spread a new 'common sense', one that
places limits on the capacity of government to take Polanyian measures for
societal self-protection. This is a cultural achievement of no small measure.
It is this same power of states that I call upon in this book. Yet this means of
resistance will be denied by many of the theorists under discussion. Hardt
and Negri, for instance, deny the capacity of states to alter globalization's
trajectory. The multitude, they predict, is better served by taking control of
the constitutional order of an extant universal republic they call empire. This
sort of theorizing, I have argued, unilaterally disarms publics from having
recourse to an effective and powerful resource for change.

Though heavily reliant on state functions to secure their ongoing legitimacy, transnational legal norms aim not only to institutionalize the ideology of limited government by calling on states to denationalize critical
public functions (such as public pensions) or privatize aspects of the national
patrimony (such as oil and gas resources). The logic of such disciplines is
to punish deviant governments and to cabin policy options that deviate
from the best advice of international financial institutions like the World
Bank and International Monetary Fund. These disciplines, moreover, insist
that states model their behaviour on private commercial actors. Should
states act in ways that deviate from the standard rational actor model – the
self-maximizing business enterprise that is expected to secure the highest
returns possible – then states are vulnerable to being penalized with large
damage awards. Behaving politically is considered deviant and beyond the
pale. States, instead, are expected to engage only in 'normal' commercial
behaviour. Having contracted out water and sewerage services to an incom-
petent British service provider, Tanzania could not deviate from the expected
norms of private contractual behaviour. On this basis, an investment tribunal could hold Tanzania liable for exercising what remained of its sovereign
authority when it summarily cancelled the contract on behalf of its vulnerable citizens. Systems-inspired accounts, such as Teubner's societal constitutionalism, disentitle states from responding to the normative edicts of these
'autonomous' legal orders. These systems mostly are left intact, free to maximize the logic of their own normative tilt. As transnational legal norms take

hold, states and citizens can be expected to do no more than make 'noise' in the hope that these autonomous legal orders listen and respond accordingly. Critical resistance calls for something more than the dynamic equilibrium contemplated by the legal autopoietic account.

In what locales might resistance be generated? The countries of the global North typically are expected to generate the cosmopolitan consciousness that will help tame the deleterious effects of unconstrained market power. Our discussion pointed, however, in another direction. Two episodes implicating US trade and investment policy display the narrow frame of reference that guides US negotiators and decision-makers. The first episode concerned the terms upon which Congress would grant trade promotion authority to President George W Bush in 2002; the second had to do with failed negotiations towards a free trade and investment agreement between the US and the Southern African Customs Union. The frame for global policy development was defined principally with reference to US economic interests, but not entirely so. There are also imperial ambitions at work,[1] namely, an understanding that treaty partners are states whose citizens do not have the privilege of being US citizens. This is an aberration capable of being corrected by offering up US constitutional standards as global standards. Nor is a cosmopolitan consciousness likely to issue out of the EU. Having obtained European-wide competence to enter into comprehensive trade and investment agreements with non-European states, we find the European Council insisting that investors receive the highest possible protections abroad. The European Council considered and then rejected any dilution of standards that deviated from the standard capital-exporting model. In which case, we would want to adjust Habermas' expectation that it is the states of the global North – ones that have rejected crude ethnic formulations of citizenship in favour of ever-enlarging practices of inclusive citizenship – that will take charge in reforming the institutions of transnational law and erect a new multi-level constitutional edifice to curb the power of footloose capital. Rather than looking to states of the global North, we might instead look to locales on the periphery that, Habermas suggestively hints, are more fully 'exposed to the full force of the imperatives of an increasingly globalized economy' (2008, p. 453).

We turned, then, to examine more closely attempts by actors from within the global South to critically resist transnational legality. We also took the opportunity to consider the role of non-state actors in facilitating critical resistance. Focusing on events in Cochabamba, Bolivia, a much celebrated instance

---

1 This is an imperial ambition that Hardt and Negri associate with the US: an expanding imperial authority which 'does not annex or destroy the other powers it faces but on the contrary opens itself to them, including them in the network' (2000, p. 166).

of resistance to the privatization of the city's water system, we probed the response of the multinational water company after it departed Bolivia. Having launched a claim for some US$25–30 million in damages under a Netherlands–Bolivia bilateral investment treaty (BIT), the investor, without any real connection to the Netherlands, convinced an investment tribunal that there were no impediments to proceeding with adjudication of the merits of the claim. Nor would local or transnational movement activists have any role to play in the proceedings. Undeterred, non-governmental activists, working transnationally and in conjunction with the Bolivian state, successfully convinced the principal US-based investor to back down from its investor dispute. It turns out that activist pressure was effective when it threatened future lucrative contracts in other parts of the world. It also turns out that the circumstances giving rise to successful resistance in this case are hard to replicate. Santos is correct, then, to look to non-state movements of the global South to generate counter-hegemonic strategies that challenge the dominant orthodoxy (Santos, 2004, p. 458; 2007, p. 64). Yet he is overly optimistic about the capacity of local and transnational non-governmental organization movements to overcome transnational legal effects. In particular, he pretty much gives up on states as a locus of resistance. Yet, it is precisely here, at the level of the state, where much work remains to be done – it is the locale where citizens can reverse the seemingly irreversible institutional options of transnational legality.

Transnational legal orders cannot tolerate too much democratic input. Government at national levels is characterized as overloaded with, and overly responsive to, citizen demands and vulnerable to rent-seeking by powerful groups (Crozier et al., 1975, p. 12). It is precisely these sorts of democratic 'defects' that transnational legality is intended to check. Undermining national democratic processes – an important source of the regime's ongoing legitimacy – is awkward, however. Consequently, investment arbitration has sought to claim the high ground of democratic theory as its own, just as high courts do within national legal systems, by invoking concerns with political processes so as to justify investment arbitration's close scrutiny of governmental action. The protection of foreign investors abroad is justified, investment tribunals have ruled, because investors are not represented in host state democratic processes. On this basis, the *Tecmed* tribunal held that denying renewal of a permit to operate a hazardous waste facility in close proximity to the state capital of Hermosillo could not be warranted. Analogizing international investment law to representation-reinforcement review by national courts turns out to be a bad analogy, however. Canvassing the literature on both corporate political activity and 'political risk' reveals that investors have a variety of means available to them to influence political outcomes within host states. This empirical evidence suggests that foreign economic actors typically receive treatment as favourable as that available to local economic actors, oftentimes even better treatment. All of which suggests that international investment law has little to do with democracy promotion and more to do with rendering democracy safe for foreign investors. Wolin turns out to be justified in exhibiting despair about the prospects for democracy in an era when politics is predominantly managed for the benefit of powerful economic actors. Democratic moments, where polities contemplate collective projects that advance the common good, remain fugitive and episodic (Wolin, 1994, p.11; 2004, p.11). Wolin is mistaken, nonetheless, in turning to local 'archaic' social movements to arouse political self-consciousness. Episodic resistance at local levels may be futile against structures of domination operating at national and transnational levels without the helping hand of the state.

Are we left, then, in a situation of despair – left only with 'insurrectionary gesture[s] against a corporatized world with no exits' (Wolin, 1988, p. 179)? The response of Ecuador to neoliberal disciplinarity is instructive in so far as the state has taken a stand in opposition to transnational legal norms, specifically, in the realm of investment rules. Neoliberalism has been productive in this way, generating new subjectivities resistant to its own dictates. Under President Rafael Correa, the state terminated treaty talks, exited from an important international convention (the International Center for the Settlement of Investment Disputes (ICSID)), amended its constitution, and denounced a number of BITS including those with powerful capital-exporting states. On the whole, it could be said that Ecuadorians have been taking care of themselves and of others by adopting Polanyian measures that protect society from the vagaries of economic globalization. The tactics and strategies suggested by Foucault's work on 'care of the self' generate resources for moving in these sorts of directions. Though Foucault does not address specifically how a retrieval of ancient 'practices of the self' will prompt modes of contemporary resistance, his openness to alternative paths – asking why we behave the way that we do and how things could be otherwise – generate resources for thinking and acting differently (Foucault, 1984a; 1988; 2005). There is the perpetual danger, however, of mistaking situations that reinforce extant power relations as opportunities for transformative change – of mistaking what is rigid and immovable for what is plastic and pliable. In this light, Ecuador's perception that Chinese foreign investment should be preferred over traditional sources of capital infusion (both issuing out of capital-exporting states and international financial institutions) seems misguided. The terms upon which Chinese investment is entering host states appear to be little different from those previously on offer. New sources of capital are not yet free of the disciplinary constraints imposed by contemporary international investment law. The state and citizens of Ecuador seem inattentive to the likelihood that they will continue to be vulnerable to new, yet familiar, relations of domination.

Where might we go from here? States, as noted, participate with varying degrees of influence in the authorship of transnational legal norms and institutions. They shape transnational legal regimes in ways that promote the interests of economic actors headquartered within their respective states and the allied interests of employees, consumers and citizens, more generally. Yet, state functions appear to be eroding at the same time as critical supports are required both for the market to operate smoothly and for managing citizen expectations in light of the market's deleterious effects. It is for this reason, that national states, representing the 'strategic codification and institutional integration of power relations' (Jessop, 2011, p. 69), remain 'the most significant site of struggle among competing global, triadic, supranational, national, regional and local forces' (Jessop, 2002, p. 211). States, moreover, provide resources to countervail the loss of democratic accountability at supranational levels. They are, at present, the 'highest instance of formal democratic political accountability' and, thereby, the central political referent at least for the time being (Jessop, 2002, p. 213).

If states are central to the construction and maintenance of transnational legal norms and institutions, as I have argued, states have both the authority and jurisdiction to undo its constraints. Such an outcome requires, of course, mobilization and coordination of political resources within national states at various levels – no small achievement, to be sure. We can reasonably expect democratic publics in some locales to pursue such a political path: to reject the prospect of 'democratic states being turned into debt-collecting agencies on behalf of a global oligarchy of investors' (Streeck, 2011, p. 28). Will foreign investors thereby be rendered unwelcome? One generally should think not. Many states all over the world are desperate for new inward capital to improve public utilities, necessary infrastructure, or simply to keep the economy growing.[2] Short of some new foreign exchange transaction tax that could address disparities in the availability of financing for some of these public infrastructure projects (UNDP, 2011, p. 94), states must find financing somewhere.

We should acknowledge, nevertheless, that the repatriation of authority previously exercised by transnational legality could reasonably result in what Habermas calls a 'renewed closure' (Habermas, 2001a, p. 73).[3] The worry

---

2 In cases where water and sewerage services have been privatized, however, the record reveals that little new private capital flows into these investments (Castro, 2008). See discussion in Chapters 1 and 2.

3 The discourse of closure and openness is redolent in systems theoretical approaches to law (see Luhmann, 2004, p. 80) (discussing 'operatively closed systems' that reproduce themselves). See further discussion in Chapter 2. Both Habermas and Luhmann appear to be building upon Weber's observations about open and closed relationships in (1978, pp. 43ff).

for Habermas is that closure will be pursued 'regressively' or 'defensively', reintroducing the 'nostalgic attitudes of the losers of modernization' associated with failed ethnic nationalist projects of the twentieth century (ibid.). Transferred to the investment law context, this entails not only foreign investors losing their legal entitlements. It also puts a halt to processes promoted by investment law's normative entrepreneurs of extending the reach of transnational legal disciplines to national, and not just foreign, economic actors (Vandevelde, 1998; Hart and Dymond, 2002; Wälde, 2007).

Forms of closure, however, are a persistent phenomenon in self-governing democracies. Paradoxically, the democratic ideal of self-rule and openness to the other through deliberation requires such moments in which the polity constitutes itself or establishes rules and institutions so that it can pursue the deliberative project of self-rule (Keenan, 2003, p. 11; Mouffe, 2005, p. 43). Laying down parameters for the conduct of self-government by definition exclude certain possibilities from political discourse at certain moments. This suggests that not everything can be contested all of the time. Indeed, transnational legality has benefited from this self-limiting feature of democratic practice for some time – globalization is 'inevitable' and 'irreversible,' we are continually reminded. In which case, we should understand that democratic politics requires both openness and closure: the occasional closing down because democracy demands it so that it can then carry on its project of openness. This is the 'irresolution' residing within the idea of self-government itself (Christodoulidis, 2003, p. 413). It is a paradox that democratic politics cannot do away with, even cannot do without.

The exclusion of matters for potential collective concern, however, also turns out to be difficult to do. The smoothing over of ruptures within the socioeconomic fabric seems almost impossible to attain (Laclau and Mouffe, 1985, p. 111).[4] Rather than sweeping away disagreement, the democratic project becomes one of acknowledging power imbalances and bringing into question their operation in official and unofficial encounters with each other (cf. Abensour, 2011, p. 97). In which case, acts of closure do not necessarily preclude a return to openness to others – to the transformative possibilities engendered by encounters with those who are excluded or otherwise outside the sphere of our concern. Polities can be expected to re-engage with the democratic possibility of 'inclusion and generality' and attend to the potential of 'collective self-revisability'.[5] It could be, then, that even moments of closure will give rise to renewed but more modest commitments to foreign investors generated by processes associated with democratic politics. Even

---

4 The universal, Laclau observes, represents an incomplete or unfulfilled 'horizon' that is always receding (1996, pp. 28, 34; Mouffe 1993, p. 141).

5 This is an idea I associate with the work of de Tocqueville (2000) (see Frankenberg, 2000; Schneiderman, 2008, p. 13).

here, citizens have to be attuned to those excluded by any new hegemonic formulation and to the possibility that particularistic remedies are not parlayed into universalistic solutions.

Yet this is precisely how forms of transnational legality, such as the investment rules regime, operate. They amount to particularisms that have attained hegemonic status without any acknowledgment of their contingent origins. As a congery of rules and institutions intended to promote the interests of 'alien' investors, they are presented as universally complete – an exact replica of what is required by customary international law and, consequently, an attempt to 'fix the final meaning of universality' (Keenan, 2003, p. 130). The only 'openness', such as it is, that the regime will tolerate is to embrace all of humanity within its logic. Hence, instruments for 'good governance' associated with investment rules, Wälde argues, should extend to cover all economic actors, including national and not just foreign ones. Wälde applauds the tentative steps that have been taken by investment tribunals to reduce 'the inequality with respect to international protection between domestic and foreign companies' (Wälde, 2007, p. 119). Hart and Dymond also acknowledge their desire to impose investment rule disciplines, which they associate with the 5th and 14th amendments to the US Constitution, on all governments thereby making them 'a critical part of the architecture of rules and procedures for governing the global economy' (Hart and Dymond, 2002, p. 170). This, writes Vandevelde, would create the conditions for an 'enduring' liberal order of investor protection (1998, p. 639).

Revealing no trace of the acts of exclusion that gave rise to the hegemony of international investment law – acts that grant privileged access to defining the content of what is 'universal' to capital-exporting states and their agents – there is little or no room for antagonisms to emerge that give voice to new or differing demands. The system, in this sense, is operationally closed and so, as this book has aimed to elucidate, does not manage opposition very well. There is little pretence here that democratic practice is enhanced by investment rule disciplines, rather, there only is an attempt to forestall further debate by claiming to 'depoliticize' transnational legality.

Rather than domesticating politics via constraints of transnational legality, we should envisage the possibility of opening up the space of politics in realms blanketed by investment disciplines. This is a strategy of resistance that dissolves some of the constraints for those who are the subjects of transnational legality but rendered voiceless by its persistent attempt to foreclose discussion. It requires a voice that only exuberant and uninhibited democratic publics can provide.

Cases Cited

Argentina
Bustos, Alberto Roque v Estadio Nacionale/amapro, CSJN, 26/10/2004, JA (2005-III-189)

Provincia de San Luis v Estado Nacional/amparo, CSJN, 5/3/2003, Fallos (2003–326–417)

Smith, Carlos Antonio v PEN/medidas cautelares, CSJN, 1/2/2002, Fallos (2002–325–28)

Europe
Beyeler v Italy (2001) 33 EHRR 52

Iran Shipping Lines v Turkey (2008) 47 EHRR 24

James and Others v United Kingdom (1986) 98 Eur. Ct H R (ser. A) 9

Lithgow and Others v United Kingdom (1986) 8 EHRR 329

International investment arbitration
Abaclat and Others v Argentina (2011) Decision on Jurisdiction and Admissibility, ICSID Case No ARB/07/5 (4 August)

Aguas del Tunari, SA v Republic of Bolivia (2005) Decision on Respondent's Objections to Jurisdiction, ICSID Case No ARB/02/3 (21 October), *ICSID Review: Foreign Investment Law Journal* 20: 450

Autopista Concesionada de Venezuela CA ('Aucoven') v Bolivarian Republic of Venezuela (2001) Award, ICSID Case Arb/00/5 (27 September 2001); *ICSID Reports* 6: 417–48

Biwater Gauff (Tanzania) Ltd v United Republic of Tanzania (2006) Procedural Order No 3, ICSID Case No ARB/05/22 (29 September 2006) http://italaw.com/documents/Biwater-PONo.3.pdf

Biwater Gauff (Tanzania) Ltd v United Republic of Tanzania (2008) Award, ICSID Case No ARB/05/22 (18 July 2008)

Booker plc v Co-operative Republic of Guyana (2001) ICSID Case No ARB/01/9

Chevron Corporation and Texaco Petroleum Corporation v Republic of Ecuador (2012a) Second Interim Award on Measures, UNCITRAL, PCA Case No 2009–23 (16 February 2001) http://italaw.com/documents/Chevron_v_Ecuador_SecondInterimAward_16Feb2012.pdf

Chevron Corporation and Texaco Petroleum Corporation v Republic of Ecuador (2012b) Third Interim Award on Jurisdiction and Admissibility. UNCITRAL, PCA Case No 2009–23 (27 February) online at http://italaw.com/documents/ChevronvEcuadorThirdInterimAward.pdf

CMS Gas Transmission Company v Republic of Argentina (2005) Award, ICSID Case No ARB/01/08, International Legal Materials 44, 1205–63 (12 May 2005)

CMS Gas Transmission Company v Republic of Argentina (2007) Application for Annulment and Request for Stay of Enforcement of Arbitral Award, ICSID Case No Arb/01/08 (8 September 2007)

Compañía de Aguas del Aconquija SA and Vivendi Universal SA v Argentina (2002) Decision on Annulment, ICSID Case No ARB/97/3

Compañía de Aguas del Aconquija SA and Vivendi Universal SA v Argentina (2007) Award, ICSID Case No ARB/97/3 (20 August 2007)

Compañía del Desarrollo de Santa Elena, SA v Republic of Costa Rica (2000) Award, ICSID Case No ARB/96/1

Enron Corporation and Ponderosa Assets v Argentina (2007) Award, ICSID Case No ARB/01/3

Glamis Gold Ltd v United States (2009) Award, Ad hoc, UNCITRAL Arbitration Rules; International Legal Materials 48: 1038–80

Lanco International Inc. v Argentina (2001) Decision on Jurisdiction, ICSID Case No ARB/97/6 (8 December 1998) International Legal Materials 40: 4457–73

LG&E Energy Corp v Argentine Republic (2006) Decision on Liability, ICSID Case No ARB/02/01 (3 October), ICSID Reports 11: 414

Loewen Group Inc. and Loewen v United States (2003), Award, ICSID Case No ARB(AF)/98/3

Methanex v US (2005) Final Award of the Tribunal on Jurisdiction and Merits (3 August 2005) International Legal Materials 44: 1345–464

Mobil Corporation Venezuela Holdings BV and Others v Venezuela (2010) Decision on Jurisdiction, ICSID Case No ARB/07/27

Mondev International Ltd v United States (2002) Award, ICSID Case No ARB(AF)/99/2, International Legal Materials (2003) 42: 85–120

Occidental Exploration and Production Company v Ecuador (2004) Award. 43 International Legal Materials (2004) 43: 1248

Pope & Talbot v Government of Canada (2002) Award in Respect of Damages, Ad hoc – UNCITRAL Arbitration Rules (31 May); International Legal Materials (2002) 14: 1347–66

Siemens AG v Argentina (2007) Award and Separate Opinion, ICSID Case No ARB/02/8 (6 February 2007)

Suez and Others v Argentina (2010) Decision on Liability. ICSID Case No ARB/03/17 (30 July)

Técnicas Medioambientales Tecmed SA v Mexico (2003) International Legal Materials (2004) 43: 133

Tokios Tokelès v Ukraine (2004) Decision on Jurisdiction. World Trade and Arbitration Materials 16(4): 75

United States

Citizens United v Federal Election Commission, 558 US (2010)

Lochner v New York, 198 US 45 (1905)

Penn Central Transportation Co. v New York City 438 US 104 (1977)

United States v Carolene Products Co., 304 US 144 (1938)

West Coast Hotel v Parrish, 300 US 379 (1937)

Other

Constancia Sugar Refining Co v United States (1909) Before the Spanish Treaty Claims Commission, No 196 (24 March 1909)

Jalapa Railroad and Power Company (1937) Decision No 13-E, American Mexican Claims Report in *American Mexican Claims Commission, Report to the Secretary of State* (Washington: United States Government Printing Office, 1943), pp 538–44

Bibliography

Abensour, M (2011) *Democracy Against the State: Marx and the Machiavellian Moment*, M Blechman and M Breaugh (trans.) (Cambridge: Polity Press)

Ackerman, B A (1985) 'Beyond Carolene Products' 98 *Harvard Law Review* 713–46

Allen, T (2005) *Property and the Human Rights Act 1998* (Oxford: Hart)

Alter, J (2010) *The Promise: President Obama, Year One* (New York: Simon & Schuster)

Alvarez, J E (1992) 'Remarks' 86 *American Society of International Law Proceedings* 550–6

Alvarez, J E (2010) 'The Once and Future Foreign Investment Regime' in M H Arsanjani, J K Cogan, R D Sloane and S Wiessner (eds), *Looking to the Future: Essays on International Law in Honor of W Michael Reisman* (Leiden: Martinus Nijhoff), pp. 607–48

Alvarez, J E and K Khamsi (2009) 'The Argentine Crisis and Foreign Investors: A Glimpse into the Heart of the Investment Regime' in K P Sauvant (ed.) 1 *Yearbook on International Investment Law and Policy* 379

Alvaro, M (2009) 'Ecuador President Seeks to End Investment Protection Agreements' *Dow Jones Newswire* (28 October) www.nasdaq.com/aspx/stock-market-news-story.aspx?storyid=200910281854dowjonesdjonline0-00871&title=ecuador-president-seeks-to-end-investment-protection-agreements

Amoore L, R Dodgson, B Gills, P Langley, D Marshall and I Watson (2000) 'Overturning "Globalization": Resisting Teleology, Reclaiming Politics' in Gills (2000), pp. 12–28

Amsden, A (2007) *Escape from Empire: The Developing World's Journey Through Heaven and Hell* (Cambridge MA: MIT Press)

Anderson, G W (2005) *Constitutional Rights After Globalization* (Oxford: Hart)

Anderson, S (2006) 'Communication Re: Bechtel' (26 October) (on file with the author)

Anghie, A (2004) *Imperialism, Sovereignty and the Making of International Law* (Cambridge: Cambridge University Press)

Aparicio, J R and M Blaser (2008) 'The "Lettered City" and the Insurrection of Subjugated Knowledges in Latin America' 81 *Anthropological Quarterly* 59–94

Appadurai, A (1996) *Modernity at Large: Cultural Dimensions of Globalization* (Minneapolis MN: University of Minnesota Press)

Argentine Republic (2005) 'Application for Annulment and Request for Stay of Enforcement of Arbitral Award in the Proceeding Between CMS Gas Transmission Company and the Argentine Republic' ICSID Case No ARB/01/0 (8 September)

Arrighi, G (2008) *Adam Smith in Beijing: Lineages of the Twenty-First Century* (London: Verso)

Artana, D, F Navajas and S Urbiztondo (1998) *Regulation and Contractual Adaptation in Public Utilities: The Case of Argentina* (Washington DC: Inter-American Development Bank) http://cdi.mecon.gov.as/biblio/docelec/mu2015.pdf

Asamblea Nacional del Ecuador (2009a) 'Comisión de Rlaciones Internacionales analliza tratdos de protección recíproca de inversión' (29 October) www.asambleanacional.gov.ec/200910291330/noticias/boletines/comision-de-relaciones-internacionales-analiza-tratados-de-proteccion-reciproca-de-inversion.html

Asamblea Nacional del Ecuador (2009b) 'Intensifican debate sobre denun-
cia de Tratados de Protección Recíproca de Inversiones' (5 November) www.
asambleanacional.gov.ec/blogs/comision5/2009/11/05/intensifican-debate
-sobre-denuncia-de-tratados-de-proteccion-reciproca-de-inversiones/
Australia, Department of Foreign Affairs and Trade (2011) *Gillard Government Trade
Policy Statement: Trading Our Way to More Jobs and Prosperity* (April) www.dfat.gov.au/
publications/trade/trading-our-way-to-more-jobs-and-prosperity.pdf
Bakan, J (2004) *The Corporation: The Pathological Pursuit of Power* (New York: Free Press)
Balakrishnan, G (ed.) (2003) *Debating Empire* (London: Zed Books)
Balkin, J M (1989) 'The Footnote' 83 *Northwestern University Law Review* 275–320
Bartels, L M (2008) *Unequal Democracy: The Political Economy of the Gilded Age* (Princeton
NJ: Princeton University Press)
Baxi, U (2006) *The Future of Human Rights* (New Delhi: Oxford University Press) (2nd edn)
BBC Monitoring Americas (2007) 'Ecuadorean Attorney General Opposes Bid to End
Bilateral Investment Treaty' (18 May) online at Proquest
Beck, U (1992) *Risk Society*, M Ritter (trans.) (London: Sage)
Beck, U (2005) *Power in the Global Age: A New Global Political Economy*, K Cross (trans.)
(Cambridge: Polity Press)
Becker, F (2007) 'Market Regulation and the Right to Property' 26 *Yearbook of European
Law* 255–96
Becker, M (2008) *Indians and Leftists in the Making of Ecuador's Modern Indigenous
Movements* (Durham: Duke University Press)
Bello, W (2005) *Dilemmas of Domination: The Unmaking of the American Empire* (New
York: Metropolitan Books)
Biggs, M (2002) 'Strikes as Sequences of Interaction: The American Strike Wave of 1886'
26 *Social Science History* 583–617
Birchfield, V (1999) 'Contesting the Hegemony of Market Ideology: Gramsci's "Good
Sense" and Polanyi's "Double Movement"' 6 *Review of International Political Economy*
27–54
Birdsall, N (2002) 'What Went Wrong in Argentina?', remarks to the Center for
Strategic and International Studies Conference 'Argentina: Weighing the Options'
(29 January) www.cgdev.org/doc/commentary/focalpoint_argcrisis.pdf
Biwater (2005) 'City Water and the Government of Tanzania' (2 June), press release,
www.water-technology.net/contractors/construction/biwater/press3.html
Block, F (1987) 'Beyond Relative Autonomy: State Managers as Historical Subjects' in F
Block, *Revising State Theory: Essays in Politics and Postindustrialism* (Philadelphia PA:
Temple University Press)
Blustein, P (2005) *And the Money Kept Rolling In (and Out): Wall Street, the IMF, and the
Bankrupting of Argentina* (New York: Public Affairs)
Borchard, E (1915) *The Diplomatic Protection of Citizens Abroad or the Law of International
Claims* (New York: Banks Law Publishing Co.)
Borchard, E (1939) 'The "Minimum Standard" of the Treatment of Aliens' 33 *American
Society of International Law Proceedings* 51–63
Borchard, E (1940) 'The "Minimum Standard" of the Treatment of Aliens' 38 *Michigan
Law Review* 445–61
Boren, R (1998a) 'Hermosillo Residents Take a Stand' 6(4)(May) *Borderlines* 11
Boren, R (1998b) 'Border Forum: Insights and Perspectives' 6(5)(July) *Borderlines* 16
Boron, A (2005) *Empire and Imperialism: A Critical Reading of Michael Hardt and Antonio
Negri*, J Casiro (trans.) (London: Zed Books)
Bourdieu, P (1997) *Pascalian Meditations* (Stanford CA: Stanford University Press)
Bourdieu, P (1998) *Acts of Resistance: Against the Tyranny of the Market*, R Nice (trans.)
(New York: New Press)

Bourdieu, P (2000) *Pascalian Meditations*, R Nice (trans.) (Stanford CA: Stanford University Press)

Bourdieu, P (2005) *The Social Structures of the Economy*, C Turner (trans.) (Cambridge: Polity Press)

Bowers, S (2003) 'BFG Drops Guyana Claim' *The Guardian*, 18 March www.guardian.co.uk/business/2003/mar/18/debt.development

Braithwaite, J and P Drahos (2000) *Global Business Regulation* (Cambridge: Cambridge University Press)

Brenner, N (1999) 'Beyond State-Centrism? Space, Territoriality, and Geographic Scale in Globalization Studies' 28 *Theory and Society* 39–78

Brodie, J (1996) 'New State Forms, New Political Spaces' in R Boyer and D Drache (eds), *States Against Markets: The Limits of Globalization* (London: Routledge), pp. 383–98

Brown, W (1995) *States of Injury: Power and Freedom in Late Modernity* (Princeton NJ: Princeton University Press)

Brown, W (2006) 'Power After Foucault' in J S Dryzek, B Honig and A Phillips (eds), *The Oxford Handbook of Political Theory* (New York: Oxford University Press), pp. 65–84

Brown, W (2007) 'Democracy and Bad Dreams' 10(1) *Theory and Event*

Buchanan, R (2003) 'Global Civil Society and Cosmopolitan Legality at the WTO: Perpetual Peace or Perpetual Process?' 16 *Leiden Journal of International Law* 673–99

Buchanan, J M and G Tullock (1962) *The Calculus of Consent: Logical Foundations of Constitutional Democracy* (Ann Arbor MI: University of Michigan Press)

Buchanan, R and S Pahuja (2004) 'Legal Imperialism: Empire's Invisible Hand?' in Passavant and Dean (2004), pp. 73–93

Burbach, R (2007) 'Ecuador's Popular Revolt: Forging a New Nation' (September/October) *NACLA Report on the Americas* 4–9

Burchell, G (1996) 'Liberal Government and Techniques of the Self' in A Barry, T Osborne and N Rose (eds), *Foucault and Political Reason: Liberalism, Neo-Liberalism and Rationalities of Government* (Chicago IL: University of Chicago Press), pp. 19–36

Business Report (2003) 'US Wary of SA Empowerment Plans', 5 June www.tralac.org/scripts/content.php?id=1634

Butler, J (2002) 'What is Critique? An Essay on Foucault's Virtue' in D Ingram (ed.), *The Political* (Oxford: Blackwell), pp. 212–28

Butler, J (2004) 'Bodies and Power Revisited' in D Taylor and K Vintges (eds), *Feminism and the Final Foucault* (Urbana and Chicago IL: University of Illinois Press), pp. 183–94

Calhoun, C (2002) 'Constitutional Patriotism and the Public Sphere: Interests, Identity, and Solidarity in the Integration of Europe' in De Greiff and Cronin (2002), pp. 275–312

Calliess, G-P and P Zumbansen (2010) *Rough Consensus and Running Code: A Theory of Transnational Private Law* (Oxford: Hart)

Calvo, C M (1887) *Le Droit International Théorique et Practique* vol. 1 (Paris: Guillaumin et Cie) (4th edn)

Carbonneau, T (2002) 'The Ballad of Transborder Arbitration' 56 *University of Miami Law Review* 773–829

Carr, E H (1939) *The Twenty Year's Crisis, 1919–1939: An Introduction to the Study of International Relations* (London: Macmillan & Co.)

Cass, D Z (2005) *The Constitutionalization of the World Trade Organization* (Oxford: Oxford University Press)

Cassarin, A A and J Delfino and M E Delfino (2007) 'Failures in Water Reform: Lessons from the Buenos Aires's Concession' 15 *Utilities Policy* 234–47

Cassidy, J (2010) 'Annals of Economics: The Volker Rule' *The New Yorker*, 26 July, pp. 25–30

Castells, M (1997) *Power of Identity: The Information Age: Economy, Society and Culture*, vol. II (Oxford: Blackwell)

Castro, J E (2008) 'Neoliberal Water and Sanitation Policies as Failed Development Strategy: Lessons From Developing Countries' 8 *Progress in Development Studies* 63–83

Centre for International Environmental Law, et al. (2007) 'In Case No ARB/05/22 before the International Centre for the Settlement of Investment Disputes Between Biwater Gauff and United Republic of Tanzania Amicus Curiae Submission' (26 March) www.ciel.org/Publications/Biwater_Amicus_26March.pdf

Cerny, P G (1999) 'Globalization and the Changing Logic of Collective Action' in C Lipson and B J Cohen (eds), *Theory and Structure in International Political Economy* (Cambridge MA: MIT Press), pp. 111–41

Cerny, P G (2008) 'The Governmentalization of World Politics' in E Kofman and G Youngs (eds), *Globalization: Theory and Practice* (New York: Continuum) (3rd edn), pp. 221–36

Cerny, P G (2009) 'The Competition State Today: From Raison d'État to Raison du Monde' *Policy Studies* 1–17

Chander, A (2005) 'Globalization and Distrust' 114 *Yale Law Journal* 1193–236

Chang, H-J (2002) 'Breaking the Mould: An Institutionalist Political Economy Alternative to the Neo-Liberal Theory of the Market and the State' 26 *Cambridge Journal of Economics* 539–59

Chatterjee, P (2004) *The Politics of the Governed: Reflections on Popular Politics in Most of the World* (New York: Columbia University Press)

Chen, A (2006) 'Should the Four Safeguards in Sino-Foreign BITs be Hastily Dismantled? Comments on Provisions Concerning Dispute Settlement in Model US and Canadian BITs' 7 *Journal of World Investment and Trade* 899–933

Chevron (2011) 'Caught on Tape', *The Amazon Post*: Chevron's Views and Opinions About the Ecuador Lawsuit (31 January) www.theamazonpost.com/caught-on-tape/caught-on-tape

Chin, C B N and J H Mittleman (2000) 'Conceptualizing Resistance to Globalization' in Gills (2000), pp. 29–45

China Business Newswire (2012) 'Ecuador Inks Hydrpower Project Contract With China's Harbin Electric International' (9 January) online at Factiva

Christodoulidis, E (2003) 'Constitutional Irresolution: Law and the Framing of Civil Society' 9 *European Law Journal* 401–32

Christodoulidis, E (2009) 'Strategies of Rupture' 20 *Law and Critique* 3–262

Chua, A (1995) 'The Privatization-Nationalization Cycle: The Link Between Markets and Ethnicity in Developing Countries' 95 *Columbia Law Review* 223–303

Clarkson, S (2003) *Uncle Sam and US: Globalization, Neoconservatism and the Canadian State* (Toronto: University of Toronto Press)

Clarkson, S and M Mildenberger (2011) *Dependent America? How Canada and Mexico Construct US Power* (Toronto: University of Toronto Press)

Coe Jr, J and N Rubins (2005) 'Regulatory Expropriation and the *Tecmed* Case: Context and Contributions' in T Weiler (ed.) (2005), *International Investment Law and Arbitration: Leading Cases from the ICSID, NAFTA, Bilateral Treaties and Customary International Law* (London: Cameron May)

Colley, L (1992) *Britons: Forging the Nation, 1707–1837* (New Haven CT: Yale University Press)

Conaghan, C M (2008) 'Ecuador: Correa's Plebiscatory Presidency' 19 *Journal of Democracy* 46–60

Conaghan, C M, J M Malloy and L A Abugattas (1990) 'Business and the "Boys": The Politics of Neoliberalism in the Central Andes' 25 *Latin American Research Review* 3–30

Congyan, C (2006) 'Outward Foreign Investment Protection and the Effectiveness of BIT Practice' 7 *Journal of World Investment and Trade* 616–52

Connell, R (2006) 'Northern Theory: The Political Geography of General Social Theory' 35 *Theory and Society* 237–64

Connolly, W E (1993) 'Beyond Good and Evil: The Ethical Sensibility of Michel Foucault' 21 *Political Theory* 365–89

Cooney, P (2007) 'Argentina's Quarter Century Experiment With Neoliberalism: From Dictatorship to Depression' 11 *R. Econ. Contemp., Rio de Janeiro* 7–37

Corbacho, A, M Garcia-Escribano and G Inchauste (2003) 'Argentina: Macroeconomic Crisis and Household Vulnerability' IMF Working Paper WP/03/89 (April) www.imf. org/external/pubs/ft/wp/2003/wp0389.pdf

CorpWatch, Global Exchange and Public Citizen (2003) 'Bechtel: Profiting From Destruction – Why the Corporate Invasion of Iraq Must be Stopped' (June) www. corpwatch.org/article.php?id=6975

Corrigan, P and D Sayer (1985) *The Great Arch: English State Formation as Cultural Revolution* (Oxford: Basil Blackwell)

Cover, R M (1982) 'The Origins of Judicial Activism in the Protection of Minorities' 91 *Yale Law Journal* 1287–316

Coward, M (2005) 'The Globalisation of Enclosure: Interrogating the Geopolitics of Empire' 25 *Third World Quarterly* 855–71

Cox, R W (1992) 'Multilateralism and the World Order', in Cox and Sinclair (1996), pp. 494–523

Cox, R W and T J Sinclair (1996) *Approaches to World Order* (Cambridge: Cambridge University Press)

Crampes, C and A Estache (1996) 'Regulating Water Concessions: Lessons from the Buenos Aires Concession' (September) *Public Policy for the Private Sector*, Note No 91 http://rru.worldbank.org/Documents/PublicPolicyJournal/091crampes.pdf

Crawford, J (2008) 'Treaty and Contract in Investment Arbitration' 24 *Arbitration International* 351–74

Cremades, B M (2005) 'The Resurgence of the Calvo Doctrine in Latin America' 2(5) (November) *Transnational Dispute Management*

Cronin, C (2011) 'Cosmopolitan Democracy' in B Fultner (ed.), *Jürgen Habermas: Key Concepts* (Durham: Acumen), pp. 196–221

Crozier, M J, S P Huntington, and J Watanuki (1975) *The Crisis of Democracy: Report on the Governability of Democracies to the Trilateral Commission* (New York: New York University Press)

Crooks, E and N Mapstone (2012) 'Chevron Case in Ecuador Takes New Twist' *Financial Times*, 5 January, p. 14

Cruikshank, B (1999) *The Will to Empower: Democratic Citizens and Other Subjects* (Ithaca NY: Cornell University Press)

Cutler, A C (2003) *Private Power and Global Authority: Transnational Merchant Law in the Global Political Economy* (Cambridge: Cambridge University Press)

Dale, G (2010) *Karl Polanyi: The Limits of the Market* (Cambridge: Polity Press)

Dardot, P and C Laval (2009) *La nouvelle raison du monde: Essai sur le société néolibérale* (Paris: La Découverte)

Davidson, A I (ed.) (1995) *Philosophy as a Way of Life*, M Chase (trans.) (Oxford: Blackwell)

Davies, R (2012) 'Investment Policy Framework Speech' (27 July) www.trademarksa. org/news/davies-investment-policy-framework-speech

de Gramont A (2006) 'After the Water War: The Battle for Jurisdiction in *Aguas Del Tunari, SA v Republic of Bolivia*' 5(3) *Transnational Dispute Management*

De Grieff, P and C Cronin (eds) (2002) *Global Justice and Transnational Politics* (Cambridge MA: The MIT Press)

De Palma, A (2001) 'Nafta's Powerful Little Secret' *New York Times* (11 March), s. 3, pp. 1, 13 de Vos, H, R Boelens and R Bustamente (2006) 'Formal Law and Local Water Control in the Andean Region: A Fiercely Contested Field' 22 *Water Resources Development* 37–48

Dean, M (1999) *Governmentality: Power and Rule in Modern Society* (London: Sage)

Desbordes, R and J Vauday (2007) 'The Political Influence of Foreign Firms in Developing Countries' 19 *Economics and Politics* 421–51

Desrosiers, É (2002) 'Ottawa entend signer des chapitres 11 partout' *Le Devoir*, 20 November, B1, B2

Dezalay, Y and B G Garth (1996) *Dealing in Virtue: International Commercial Arbitration and the Construction of a Transnational Legal Order* (Chicago IL: University of Chicago Press)

Dill, B (2010) 'Public–Private Partnerships in Urban Water Provision: The Case of Dar es Salaam' 22 *Journal of International Development* 611–24

Dirlik, A (1994) 'The Postcolonial Aura: Third World Criticism in an Age of Global Capitalism' 20 *Critical Inquiry* 328–56

Donzelot, J and C Gordon (2008) 'Governing Liberal Societies – The Foucault Effect in the English-Speaking World' 5 *Foucault Studies* 48–62

Drache, D (2008) *Defiant Publics: The Unprecedented Reach of the Global Citizen* (Cambridge: Polity Press)

Dunn, F S (1932) *The Protection of Nationals: A Study in the Application of International Law* (Baltimore MD: Johns Hopkins Press)

Durkheim, E (1957) *Professional Ethics and Civic Morals*, C Brookfield (trans.) (London and New York: Routledge)

Dumm, T (2000) *Michel Foucault and the Politics of Freedom* (Thousand Oaks CA: Sage)

Eakin, E (2001) 'What is the Next Big Idea? The Buzz is Growing' *New York Times*, 7 July, B7

Economist, The (2008) 'Going Nowhere: Another Leftist Bogs Down', 10 May, p. 48

Economist Intelligence Unit ViewsWire (2007a) 'Ecuador: Investment Regulations' (19 December) online at Proquest

Economist Intelligence Unit ViewsWire (2007b) *World Investment Prospects to 2011: Foreign Direct Investment and the Challenge of Political Risk* (London: Economist Intelligence Unit) http://a330.g.akamai.net/7/330/25828/20070829195216/graphics.eiu.com/upload/WIP_2007_WEB.pdf

Economist Intelligence Unit ViewsWire (2012) 'Ecuador Industry: Big Oil Contracts Are Back' (9 March) online at Proquest

Ecuador Ministerio de Relaciones Exteriores (2004) 'IV.2. 40 Emprasas que más aportaron al fisco durante el 2004' (on file with the author)

Ecuador Ministerio de Relaciones Exteriores (2007) 'Ayuda memoria: Criterios para denunciar y renegociar los acuerdos de promocion y proteccion reciproca de invesriones' (on file with the author)

Ecuador Ministerio de Relaciones Exteriores (2010a) Corte Constitucional, Dictamen No 027-10-DTI-CC, Caso No 0004–10-TI http://186.42.101.3/alfresco/d/d/workspace/SpacesStore/62d8f4a1-3f78-4f8a-b1d3-1604f8e9e2f2/0004-10-TI-res.pdf

El Comercio (2009) 'A punta de anularse 13 acuerdos para proteger la inversion', 28 October ww1.elcomercio.com

Elkins, Z, A T Guzman and B A Simmons (1996) 'Competing for Capital: The Diffusion of Bilateral Investment Treaties, 1960–2000' 60 *International Organization* 811–46

Ely, J H (1980) *Democracy and Distrust: A Theory of Judicial Review* (Cambridge MA: Harvard University Press)

Embassy of Argentina in Washington DC (2011) 'The 2001/2002 Crisis: Impact on Public Utility Operators' www.embassyofargentina.us/v2011/files/sitiowebciadi-v8en.pdf

Emberland, M (2006) *The Human Rights of Companies: Exploring the Structure of ECHR Protection* (Oxford: Oxford University Press)

Emmott, B (2003) 'A Survey of Capitalism and Democracy: Liberty's Great Advance' *The Economist*, 28 June 2003, 4:4

European Commission (2010) 'Communication From the Commission to the Council, The European Parliament, the European Economic and Social Committee and the Committee of Regions: Toward a Comprehensive European International Investment Policy' COM (2010) 343 (Brussels, 7 July 2012) http://trade.ec.europa.eu/doclib/docs/2010/july/tradoc_146307.pdf

Evans, P (2008) 'Is an Alternative Globalization Possible?' 36 *Politics and Society* 271–305

Fachiri, A P (1925) 'Expropriation and International Law' 6 *British Yearbook of International Law* 159–71

Fagre, N and L T Wells Jr (1982) 'Bargaining Power of Multinationals and Host Governments' 13 *Journal of International Business Studies* 9–23

Fairclough, N (2006) *Language and Globalization* (London: Routledge)

Fairclough, N and P Thomas (2004) 'The Discourse of Globalization and the Globalization of Discourse' in D Grant, C Hardy, C Oswick and L Putnam (eds), *The Sage Handbook of Organizational Discourse* (London: Sage), pp. 379–96

Falk, R (1999) *Predatory Globalization: A Critique* (Cambridge MA: Polity Press)

Farber, D A and R E Hudec (1994) 'Free Trade and the Regulatory State: A GATT's-Eye View of the Dormant Commerce Clause' 47 *Vanderbilt Law Review* 1401–40

Fernandes, S and E Rubio (2012) 'Solidarity Within Eurozone: How Much, What For, For How Long?' (February) *Notre Europe* Policy Paper 51 www.notre-europe.eu/uploads/tx_publication/SolidarityEMU_S.Fernandes-E.Rubio_NE_Feb2012.pdf

Finnegan, W (2002) 'Letter from Bolivia: Leasing the Rain' *The New Yorker*, 8 April 2002, pp. 43–53

Fisher-Lescano, A and G Teubner (2004) 'Regime Collisions: The Vain Search for Legal Unity in the Fragmentation of Global Law' 25 *Michigan Journal of International Law* 999–1046

Fitzpatrick, P (2006) '"The New Constitutionalism": The Global, the Postcolonial and the Constitution of Nations' 10 *Law, Democracy and Development* 1–20

Flax, J (2007) 'Soul Service: Foucault's "Care of the Self" as Politics and Ethics' in N Brooks and J Toth (eds), *The Mourning After: Attending the Wake of Postmodernism* (Amsterdam NY: Editions Rodopi)

Forbath, W E (1991) *Law and the Shaping of the American Labor Movement* (Cambridge MA: Harvard University Press)

Ford, N (2005) 'Tanzania: Water Concession Goes Down the Drain' 311(July) *African Business* 50–1

Forero, J and J Partlow (2009) 'Latin America Appears to Warm to IMF' *The Washington Post*, 28 April

Foucault, M (1976) 'Two Lectures' in Foucault (1980c), pp. 78–108

Foucault, M (1977a) *Discipline and Punish: The Birth of the Prison*, A Sheridan (trans.) (New York: Pantheon Books)

Foucault, M (1977b) 'Power and Strategies' in Foucault (1908c), pp. 134–45

Foucault, M (1978) *The History of Sexuality: An Introduction* vol. 1 (New York: Random House)

Foucault, M (1979b) '*Omnes et Singulatim*: Toward a Critique of Practical Reason' in Foucault (2003a), pp. 180–201

Foucault, M (1980a) 'The Masked Philosopher' in Foucault (2003a), pp. 174–79

Foucault, M (1980b) 'Power, Moral Values, and the Intellectual' 4 (Spring) *History of the Present* 1–2, 11–13

Foucault, M (1980c) *Power/Knowledge: Selected Interviews and Other Writings 1972–77*, C Gordon (ed.) (New York: Pantheon)

Foucault, M (1982) 'The Subject and Power' in Foucault (2003a), pp. 126–44

Foucault, M (1983) 'On the Geneaology of Ethics' in Foucault (2003a), pp. 102–25

Foucault, M (1984a) 'The Ethics of the Concern of the Self as a Practice of Freedom' in Foucault (2003a), pp. 25–42

Foucault, M (1984b) 'What is Enlightenment' in Foucault (2003a), pp. 43–57

Foucault, M (1985) *The Use of Pleasure: The History of Sexuality* vol. 2, R Hurley (trans.) (New York: Vintage Books)

Foucault, M (1988) *The Care of the Self: The History of Sexuality* vol.3, R Hurley (trans.) (New York: Vintage Books)

Foucault, M (1990) *The History of Sexuality, An Introduction* vol. 1, R Hurley (trans.) (New York: Vintage Books)

Foucault, M (2000) *Power: Essential Works of Foucault 1954–1984* vol. 3, J D Faubion (ed.) (New York: New Press)

Foucault, M (2001) *Fearless Speech*, J Pearson (ed.) (Los Angeles CA: Semiotexte)

Foucault, M (2003a) *The Essential Foucault: Selections from Essential Works of Foucault, 1954–1984*, P Rabinow and N Rose (eds) (New York: New Press)

Foucault, M (2003b) *Abnormal: Lectures at the Collège de France 1974–75*, G Burchell (trans.) (New York: Picador)

Foucault, M (2005) *The Hermeneutics of the Subject: Lectures at the Collège de France 1981–82*, G Burchell (trans.) (Basingstoke: Palgrave Macmillan)

Foucault, M (2007) *Security, Territory, Population. Lectures at the Collège de France, 1977–78*, G Burchell (trans.) (Basingstoke: Palgrave Macmillan)

Foucault, M (2008) *The Birth of Biopolitics: Lectures at the Collège de France, 1978–79*, G Burchell (trans.) (Basingstoke: Palgrave Macmillan)

Foucault, M (2010) *The Government of Self and Others: Lectures at the Collège de France, 1982–83*, G Burchell (trans.) (Basingstoke: Palgrave Macmillan)

Franck, S (2005) 'Occidental Exploration & Production Co. v Republic of Ecuador. Final Award. London Court of International Arbitration Administered Case No UN 3467' 99 *American Journal of International Law* 675–681

Franck, T M (1995) *Fairness in International Law and Institutions* (Oxford: Clarendon Press)

Frankenburg, G (1992) 'Disorder is Possible: An Essay on Systems, Laws, and Disobedience' in A Honneth, T McCarthy, C Offe and A Wellmer (eds), *Cultural–Political Interventions in the Unfinished Project of Enlightenment* (Cambridge MA: MIT Press), pp. 17–37

Frankenburg, G (2000) 'Tocqueville's Question: The Role of a Constitution in the Process of Integration' 13 *Ratio Juris* 1–30

Fraser, N (2003) 'From Discipline to Flexibilization: Rereading Foucault in the Shadow of Globalization' 10(2) *Constellations* 160–71

Freeman, A V (1938) *The International Responsibility of States for Denial of Justice* (London: Longmans Green & Co.)

Gaillard, E (2007) 'The Denunciation of the ICSID Convention' *New York Law Journal* (June 26) 6–7

Galiani, S, M González-Rozada and E Schrgrodsky (2008) 'Water Expansion in Shantytowns: Health and Savings' in A Chong (ed.), *Privatization for the Public Good? Welfare Effects of Private Intervention in Latin America* (Washington DC: Inter-American Development Bank/David Rockefeller Center for Latin American Studies), pp. 25–41

Gallagher, N and W Shan (2009) *Chinese Investment Treaties: Policies and Practice* (Oxford: Oxford University Press)

Gallagher, K P, A Irwin and K Koleski (2012) 'The New Banks in Town: Chinese Finance in Latin America' (March) *Inter-American Dialogue Report* www.thedialogue.org/PublicationFiles/TheNewBanksinTown-FullTextnewversion_1.pdf

Gardiner, J L, D H Freyer and M E Schnabl (2008) 'Ecuador Attempts to Withdraw Consent to ICSID Jurisdiction for Natural Resources Disputes' *Latin American Law & Business Report*, 31 January

Gardner, J (1997) 'Liberty, Community, and the Constitutional Structure of Political Influence: A Reconsideration of the Right to Vote' 145 *University Pennsylvania Law Review* 951

Gauchet, M (1991) 'Democratic Pacification and Civic Desertion' 29 *Thesis Eleven* 1–13

Gerhart, P M and M S Baron (2004) 'Understanding National Treatment: The Participatory Vision of the WTO' 14 *Indiana International and Comparative Law Review* 505–52

Gibbs, G (2003) 'Big Food Group Attacked for £12m Claim Against Guyana' *The Guardian*, 17 March www.guardian.co.uk/business/2003/mar/17/debt.development

Giles, C and L Barber (2009) 'Zoellick Calls for Global Response to Crisis' *Financial Times*, 19 February

Gill, S (1995a) 'Globalisation, Market Civilisation, and Disciplinary Neoliberalism' 24 *Millenium: Journal of International Studies* 399–423

Gill, S (1995b) 'Theorizing the Interregnum: The Double Movement and Global Politics in the 1990s' in B Hettne (ed.), *International Political Economy: Understanding Global Disorder* (London: Zed Books), pp. 65–99

Gill, S (2003) *Power and Resistance in the New World Order* (Basingstoke: Palgrave Macmillan)

Gill, S (2008) *Power and Resistance in the New World Order* (Basingstoke: Palgrave Macmillan) (2nd edn)

Gill, S and D Law (1988) *The Global Political Economy: Perspectives, Problems and Policies* (Baltimore MD: Johns Hopkins University Press)

Gillman, H (1993) *The Constitution Besieged: The Rise and Demise of Lochner Era Police Powers Jurisprudence* (Chapel Hill: Duke University Press)

Gills, B K (ed.) (2000) *Globalization and the Politics of Resistance* (Basingstoke: Macmillan)

Gills B and J Rocamora (1993) 'Low-intensity Democracy' 13 *Third World Quarterly* 501–23

Gómez, K F (2012) 'Ecuador's Attainment of the Sumak Kawsay and the Role Assigned to International Arbitration' *Yearbook on International Investment Law and Policy 2010–2011* 451–87

Gordon, C (1980) 'Afterword' in Foucault (1980c), pp. 229–59

Gordon, C (2000) 'Introduction' in Foucault (2000), pp. xi–xli

Gordon, W C (1941/1976) *The Expropriation of Foreign-Owned Property in Mexico* (Westport CT: Greenwood Press)

Gramsci, A (1971) *Selections from the Prison Notebooks of Antonio Gramsci*, Q Hoare and G N Smith (trans.) (New York: International Publishers)

Grandin, G (2006) *Empire's Workshop: Latin America, the United States and the Rise of the New Imperialism* (New York: Metropolitan Books)

Greene, J P (2011) *The Constitutional Origins of the American Revolution* (Cambridge: Cambridge University Press)

Greenhill, R and I Wekiya (2004) *Turning off the Taps: Donor Conditionality and Water Privatisation in Dar es Salaam, Tanzania* (London: ActionAid International) www.actionaid.org.uk/_content/documents/TurningofftheTAps.pdf

Greider, W (2001) 'The Right and US Trade Law: Invalidating the 20th Century' *The Nation*, 15 October, pp. 21–9

Grier, K B, M C Munger and B E Roberts (1994) 'The Determinates of Industry Political Activity, 1978–1986' 88 *American Political Science Review* 911–26

Grimm, D (2005) 'Integration by Constitution' 3 *I-CON* 193–208

Gros, F (2005) 'Course Context' in Foucault (2005), pp. 507–50

Gros, F (2010) 'Course Context' in Foucault (2010), pp. 377–91

Guasch, J L (2004) *Granting and Renegotiating Infrastructure Concessions: Doing it Right* (Washington DC: World Bank Publications)

Guess, R (1981) *The Idea of Critical Theory: Habermas the Frankfurt School* (Cambridge: Cambridge University Press)

Guha, R (1983) *Elementary Aspects of Peasant Insurgency in Colonial India* (Delhi: Oxford University Press)

Guhathakurta, S, D Jacobson and N DelSordi (2007) 'The End of Globalization? The Implications of Migration for State, Society and Economy' in G Ritzer (ed.), *The Blackwell Companion to Globalization* (Oxford: Blackwell), pp. 201–15

Habermas, J (1996) *Between Facts and Norms: Contributions to a Discourse Theory of Law and Democracy*, W Rehg (trans.) (Cambridge MA: MIT Press)

Habermas, J (1998a) 'Reconciliation through the Public Use of Reason' in Habermas (1998d), pp. 49–73

Habermas, J (1998b) 'The European Nation State: On the Past and Future of Sovereignty and Citizenship' in Habermas (1998d), pp. 105–28

Habermas, J (1998c) 'Three Normative Models of Democracy' in Habermas (1998d), pp. 239–64

Habermas, J (1998d) *The Inclusion of the Other: Studies in Political Theory*, E P De Greiff and C Cronin (eds) (Cambridge MA: MIT Press)

Habermas, J (2001a) 'The Postnational Constellation and the Future of Democracy' in Habermas (2001c), pp. 58–112

Habermas, J (2001b) 'Learning From Catastrophe' in M Pensky (ed. and trans.), *The Postnational Condition: Political Essays* (Cambridge MA: MIT Press), pp. 38–57

Habermas, J (2001c) *The Inclusion of the Other: Studies in Political Theory* (Cambridge MA: MIT Press)

Habermas, J (2002a) 'On Legitimation Through Human Rights' in Habermas (2002c), pp. 197–214

Habermas, J (2002b) 'The European Nation-State and the Pressures of Globalization', G M Goshgarian (trans.), in Habermas (2002c), pp. 217–34

Habermas, J (2002c) *Global Justice and Transnational Politics*, P De Greiff and C Cronin (trans.) (Cambridge MA: The MIT Press)

Habermas, J (2003) 'Interpreting the Fall of a Monument' 4 *German Law Journal* 701–8

Habermas, J (2006a) 'Does the Constitutionalization of International Law Still Have a Chance?' in J Habermas, *The Divided West* (Cambridge: Polity Press), pp. 115–91

Habermas, J (2006b) 'There are Alternatives!' in Habermas (2006f), pp. 3–15

Habermas, J (2006c) 'Euroskepticism, Market Europe, or a Europe of (World) Citizens' in Habermas (2006f), pp. 73–88

Habermas, J (2006d) 'Does Europe Need a Constitution?' in Habermas (2006f), pp. 89–109

Habermas, J (2006e) 'Constitutional Democracy – A Paradoxical Union of Contradictory Principles?' in (2006f), pp. 113–28

Habermas, J (2006f) *Time of Transitions*, C Cronin and M Pensky (trans.) (Cambridge: Polity Press)

Habermas, J (2007) 'A Political Constitution for the Pluralist World Society?' 34 *Journal of Chinese Philosophy* 331–43

Habermas, J (2008) 'The Constitutionalization of International Law and the Legitimation Problems of a Constitution for a World Society' 15 *Constellations* 444–55

Habermas, J (2009) 'Life After Bankruptcy: An Interview with Jürgen Habermas' 16 *Constellations* 227–34

Habermas, J (2011) 'Europe's Post-democratic Era' guardian.co.uk, 10 November www.guardian.co.uk/commentisfree/2011/nov/10/jurgen-habermas-europe-post-democratic

Habermas J (2012) *The Crisis of the European Union: A Response*, C Cronin (trans.) (Cambridge: Polity Press)

Hadot, P (1995) 'Reflections on the Idea of the "Cultivation of the Self"' in A I Davidson (ed.), *Philosophy as a Way of Life*, M Chase (trans.) (Oxford: Blackwell), pp. 206–13

Hadot, P (2009) *The Present Alone is our Happiness: Conversations With Jeannie Carlier and Arnold I Davidson*, M Djaballah (trans.) (Stanford CA: Stanford University Press)

Hale, R L (1923) 'Coercion and Distribution in a Supposedly Non-Coercive State' 38 *Political Science Quarterly* 470

Hall, S (1982) 'The Rediscovery of Ideology: The Return of the Repressed in Media Studies' in M Gurevitch, T Bennett, J Curran and J Woollacott, (eds), *Culture, Society and the Media* (London: Routledge), pp. 56–90

Hall, S (1996) 'The Meaning of New Times' in D Morley and K-H Chen (eds), *Stuart Hall: Critical Dialogues in Cultural Studies* (London: Routledge)

Halperin, S (2004) 'Dynamics of Conflict and System Change: The Great Transformation Revisited' 10 *European Journal of International Relations* 263–306

Hansen, W L, N J Mitchell and J M Drope (2004) 'Collective Action, Pluralism, and the Legitimacy Tariff: Corporate Activity or Inactivity in Politics' 57 *Political Research Quarterly* 421–9

Hansen, W L and N J Mitchell (2000) 'Disaggregating and Explaining Corporate Political Activity: Domestic and Foreign Corporations in National Politics' 94 *American Political Science Review* 891–903

Hansen, W L and N J Mitchell (2001) 'Globalization or National Capitalism: Large Firms, National Strategies, and Political Activities' 3 *Business and Politics* 1–19 www.bepress.com/bap/vol3/iss1/art1

Harcourt, B E (2011) *The Illusion of Free Markets* (Cambridge MA: Harvard University Press)

Hardt, M and A Negri (2000) *Empire* (Cambridge: Harvard University Press)

Hardt, M and A Negri (2004) *Multitude: War and Democracy in the Age of Empire* (New York: Penguin)

Hardt, M and A Negri (2009) *Commonwealth* (Cambridge MA: Harvard University Press)

Harlow, C (2002) *Accountability in the European Union* (New York: Oxford University Press)

Harlow, C and R Rawlings (2007) 'Promoting Accountability in Multilevel Governance: A Network Approach' 13 *European Law Journal* 542–62

Hart, M and W Dymond (2002) 'NAFTA Chapter 11: Precedents, Principles, and Prospects' in L R Dawson (ed), *Whose Rights? The NAFTA Chapter 11 Debate* (Ottawa: Centre for Trade Policy and Law), pp. 128–70

Harris, P (2006) 'Bechtel, Bolivia Resolve Dispute' *San Francisco Chronicle*, 19 January, A3

Harvey, D (1990) *The Condition of Postmodernity: An Enquiry into the Origins of Cultural Change* (Cambridge: Blackwell)

Harvey, D (2000) *Spaces of Hope* (Berkeley: University of California Press)

Harvey, D (2005) *A Brief History of Neo-Liberalism* (Oxford: Oxford University Press)

Hauriou, M (1923) *Précis de droit constitutuionnel* (Paris: Librarie de la Société du Recueil Sirey)

Hay, C (2005) 'Too Important to Leave to the Economists? The Political Economy of Welfare Entrenchment' 4 *Social Policy and Society* 197–205

Hay, C and D Marsh (2000) 'Introduction: Demystifying Globalization' in C Hay and D Marsh (eds), *Demystifying Globalization* (Basingstoke: Macmillan), pp. 1–17

Hayek, F A (1982) *Law, Legislation and Liberty: The Political Order of a Free People* vol. 3 (London: Routledge & Kegan Paul)

Held, D (1980) *Introduction to Critical Theory: Horkheimer to Habermas* (Berkeley CA: University of California Press)

Held, D (1995) *Democracy and the Global Order: From the Modern State to Cosmopolitan Governance* (Cambridge: Polity)

Held, D, A McGrew, D Goldblatt and J Perraton (1999) *Global Transformations: Politics, Economics and Culture* (Stanford CA: Stanford University Press)

Helleiner, E (2005) 'The Strange Story of Bush and the Argentine Debt Crisis' 26(6) *Third World Quarterly* 951–70

Hettne, B (2010) 'Development and Security: Origins and Future' 41 *Security Dialogue* 31–52

Hess, B (1993) 'The International Law Commission's Draft Convention on the Jurisdictional Immunities of States and Their Property' 4 *European Journal of International Law* 269–82

Higgins, R (1982) 'Certain Unresolved Aspects of the Law of State Immunity' *Netherlands International Law Review* 265–76

Hillman, A J (2003) 'Determinants of Political Strategies in US Multinationals' 42 *Business and Society* 455–84

Hirsch, M (2008) 'Interactions Between Investment and Non-Investment Obligations' in Muchlinski et al. (eds), pp. 154–81

Hirschman, A O (1977) *The Passions and the Interests: Political Arguments for Capitalism Before its Triumph* (Princeton NJ: Princeton University Press)

Hirschl, R (2004) *Towards Jursitocracy: The Origins and Consequences of the New Constitutionalism* (Cambridge MA: Harvard University Press)

Hirst, P Q (ed.) (1989) *The Pluralist Theory of the State: Selected Writings of G D H Cole, J N Figgis, and H J Laski* (London and New York: Routledge)

Hirst, P and G Thompson (1999) *Globalization in Question: The International Economy and the Possibilities of Governance* (Cambridge: Polity Press) (2nd edn)

Hobsbawm, E (1996) 'The Future of the State' in C Hewitt (ed.), *Social Futures, Global Visions* (Oxford: Blackwell)

Horkheimer, M (1972) *Critical Theory: Selected Essays* (New York: Seabury Press)

Hoy, D C (2004) *Critical Resistance: From Poststructuralism to Post-Critique* (Cambridge MA: MIT Press)

Hurst, J W (1956) *Law and the Conditions of Freedom in Nineteenth Century United States* (Madison: University of Wisconsin Press)

Inside US Trade (2002a) 'Baucus, Grassley Split on Government Veto for Investor-State Disputes' (29 March) www.insidetrade.com

Inside US Trade (2002b) 'Kerry Defeat Boosts Industry Case in Interagency Debate' (24 May) www.insidetrade.com

Inside US Trade (2002c) 'Final Trade Package Further Weakens Limits on Investor Protections', 2 August www.insidetrade.com

Inside US Trade (2004a) 'August Round of SACU Talks Delayed, USTR Says No New Date Set', 9 July www.insidetrade.com

Inside US Trade (2004b) 'Slow Pace of SACU FTA Negotiations Raises Doubts Among Supporters', 7 May www.insidetrade.com

Inside US Trade (2004c) 'Administration, Business Pressure SACU for Comprehensive FTA', 10 December www.insidetrade.com

Inside US Trade (2011) 'Member States Mandate Strong Investor Rights for EU-Wide Deals', 22 September www.insidetrade.com

Integrated Regional Information Networks (IRIN) (2005a) 'Tanzania: Government Terminates Firm's Water Contract', 17 May at www.irinnews.org/report.aspx?reportid=54444

Integrated Regional Information Networks (IRIN) (2005b) 'Tanzania: Row Over Water Contract Could Mean Continued Shortages', 18 May www.irinnews.org/report.aspx?reportid=54483

International Center for the Settlement of Investment Disputes (ICSID) (2006) *ICSID Convention, Regulations and Rules* (Washington DC: ICSID)

International Center for the Settlement of Investment Disputes (ICSID) (2007) 'News Release: Bolivia Submits a Notice Under Article 71 of the ICSID Convention', 16 May www.worldbank.org/icsid/highlights/05–16–07.htm

International Center for the Settlement of Investment Disputes (ICSID) (2009) 'Ecuador Submits a Notice under Article 71 of the ICSID Convention', 9 July http://icsid.worldbank.org/ICSID/FrontServlet?requestType=CasesRH&actionVal=OpenPage&PageType=AnnouncementsFrame&FromPage=Announcements&pageName=Announcement20

International Law Commission (ILC) (2006) *Fragmentation of International Law: Difficulties Arising From the Diversification and Expansion of International Law*, Report of the Study Group (finalized by M Koskenniemi) UN Doc. A/CN4/L682 (13 April 2006)

International Monetary Fund (IMF) (1998) 'Argentina: Recent Economic Developments', IMF Staff Country Report No 98/38 (April) www.imf.org/external/pubs/ft/scr/1998/cr9838.pdf

International Monetary Fund (IMF) (2000) 'International Development Association and International Monetary Fund – Tanzania: Decision Point Document Under the Enhanced Heavily Indebted Poor Countries Initiative', 20 March www.imf.org/external/np/hipc/2000/tza.pdf

International Monetary Fund (IMF) (2003) 'Lessons From the Crisis in Argentina' prepared by the Policy Development and Review Department, 8 October www.imf.org/external/np/pdr/lessons/100803.pdf

International Monetary Fund (IMF) (2006) 'South Africa: 2006 Article IV Consultation – Staff Report; Staff Statement; Public Information Notice on the Executive Board Discussion; and Statement by the Executive Director for South Africa', IMF Country Report No 06/237, 23 (September) www.imf.org/external/pubs/ft/scr/2006/cr06327

International Monetary Fund (IMF) (2007) *World Economic Outlook: Globalization and Inequality* (Washington DC: The Fund) www.imf.org/external/pubs/ft/weo/2007/02/pdf/text.pdf

International Organization for Migration (IOM) (2008) *World Migration Report 2008: Managing Labour Mobility in the Evolving Global Economy* (Geneva: IOM) http://publications.iom.int/bookstore/free/WMR_1.pdf

International Organization for Migration (IOM) (2010) *World Migration Report 2010: The Future of Migration: Building Capacities for Change* (Geneva: IOM) http://publications.iom.int/bookstore/free/WMR_2010_ENGLISH.pdf

International Organization for Migration (IOM) (2011) *World Migration Report 2011: Communicating Effectively About Migration* (Geneva: IOM) http://publications.iom.int/bookstore/free/WMR2011_English.pdf

Ismail, F, P Draper and X Carim (2002) 'South Africa's Global Economic Strategy: A Policy Framework and Key Elements' 6 (September–December) *AAPS Newsletter* 7, 10

Jack, I (2001) 'Canada Loses Bid to Change NAFTA Chapter11' *Financial Post*, 5 April

Jack, V (2006) 'Unpacking the Different Waves of BEE' 22 *New Agenda: The South African Journal of Social and Economic Policy* 19–23

Jackson, J H (1997) *The World Trading System: Law and Policy of International Economic Relations* (Cambridge MA: MIT Press) (2nd edn)

Jacques, M (2009) *When China Rules the World: The Rise of the Middle Kingdom and the End of the Western World* (London: Penguin)

Jessop, B (1982) *The Capitalist State: Marxist Theories and Methods* (New York: New York University Press)

Jessop, B (1990) *State Theory: Putting the Capitalist State in its Place* (University Park PA: Pennsylvania State University Press)

Jessop, B (2002) *The Future of the Capitalist State* (Cambridge: Polity Press)

Jessop, B (2008) *State Power: A Strategic–Relational Approach* (Cambridge: Polity Press)

Jessop, B (2011) 'Constituting Another Foucault Effect: Foucault on States and Statecraft' in U Bröckling, S Krasman and T Lemke (eds), *Governmentality: Current Issues and Future Challenges* (New York and London: Routledge), pp. 56–73

Joerges, C (2006) 'European Law as Conflict of Laws' in C Joerges and J Neyer (eds), *'Deliberative Supranationalism' Revisited*, EUI Working Paper Law 20, p. 15

Johnson, S and J Kwak (2010) *13 Bankers: The Wall Street Takeover and the Next Financial Meltdown* (New York: Pantheon)

Johnston, J and G Laxer (2003) 'Solidarity in the Age of Globalization: Lessons from the Anti-MAI and Zapaztista Struggles' 32 *Theory and Society* 39–91

Jones, H S (1993) *The French State in Question: Public Law and Political Argument in the Third Republic* (Cambridge: Cambridge University Press)

Judt, T (2010) *Ill Fares the Land* (New York: Penguin)

Juhasz, A (2006) *The Bush Agenda: Invading the World, One Economy at a Time* (New York: Harper Collins)

Kadens, E (2012) 'The Myth of the Customary Law Merchant' 90 *Texas Law Review* 1153–206

Kant, I (1795/1991) 'Perpetual Peace: A Philosophical Sketch' in *Political Writings*, H B Nesbit (trans.) (Cambridge: Cambridge University Press), pp. 93–130

Kateb, G (2001) 'Wolin as a Critic of Democracy' in A Botwinick and W E Connolly (eds), *Democracy and Visions: Sheldon Wolin and the Vicissitudes of the Political* (Princeton NJ: Princeton University Press), pp. 39–57

Katzenstein, P (1976) 'International Relations and Domestic Structures: Foreign Economic Policies of Advanced Industrial States' 30 *International Organization* 1–45

Katzenstein, P (ed.) (1978) *Between Power and Plenty: Foreign Economic Policies of Advanced Industrial States* (Madison WI: University of Wisconsin Press)

Keane, J (1991) *The Media and Democracy* (Cambridge: Polity Press)

Keck, M E and K Sikkink (1998) *Activists Beyond Borders: Advocacy Networks in International Politics* (Ithaca NY: Cornell University Press)

Keefe, P R (2012) 'Reversal of Fortune' *The New Yorker*, 9 January, pp. 38–49

Keenan, A (2003) *Democracy in Question: Democratic Openness in a Time of Political Closure* (Stanford CA: Stanford University Press)

Kelman, M (1999) *Strategy or Principle? The Choice Between Taxation and Regulation* (Ann Arbor MI: University of Michigan Press)

Kelsey, J (1999) 'Global Economic Policy-Making: A New Constitutionalism?' 9 *Otago Law Review* 535–55

Kennedy, D (1994) 'The International Style in Postwar Law and Policy' *Utah Law Review* 7–103

Kennedy, D (1999) *Freedom From Fear: The American People in Depression and War, 1929–1945* (New York: Oxford University Press)

Klein, N (1999) *No Logo: Taking Aim at the Brand Bullies* (New York: Picador)

Kim, W C (1988) 'The Effects of Competition and Corporate Political Responsiveness on Multinational Bargaining Power' 9 *Strategic Management Journal* 289–95

Klarman, M J (1991) 'The Puzzling Resistance to Political Process Theory' 77 *Virginia Law Review* 747–832

Klug, H (2005) 'Campaigning for Life: Building a New Transnational Solidarity in the Face of HIV/AIDS and TRIPS' in Santos and Rodríguez-Garavito (2005b), pp. 118–57

Korobkin, R (1995) 'The Local Politics of Acid Rain: Public Versus Private Decision-making and the Dormant Commerce Clause in a New Era of Environmental Law' 75 *Boston University Law Review* 751

Korovkin, T (2007) 'The Indigenous Movement and Left-Wing Politics in Ecuador' (unpublished)

Koskenniemi, M (2001) *The Gentle Civilizer of Nations: The Rise and Fall of International Law 1870–1960* (Cambridge: Cambridge University Press)

Koskenniemi, M (2007) 'The Fate of Public International Law: Between Technique and Politics' 70 *Modern Law Review* 1–30

Koskenniemi, M and P Leino (2002) 'Fragmentation of International Law? Postmodern Anxieties' 15 *Leiden Journal of International Law* 553–79

Krasner, S D (1983) 'Structural Causes and Regime Consequences: Regimes as Intervening Variables' in S D Krasner (ed.), *International Regimes* (Ithaca NY: Cornell University Press), pp. 1–21

Kriebaum, U (2008) 'Nationality and the Protection of Property under the European Convention on Human Rights' in I Buffard, J Crawford, A Pellet and S Wittich (eds), *International Law Between Universalism and Fragmentation* (Martinus Nijhoff), pp. 649–66

Kriebaum, U (2009) 'Is the European Court of Human Rights an Alternative to Investor–State Arbitration?' in P-M Dupuy, F Francioni and E-U Petersmann (eds), *Human Rights in International Investment Law and Arbitration* (Oxford: Oxford University Press), pp. 219–45

Krugman, P (2010) 'Making Financial Reform Fool Resistant', *New York Times* 4 April www.nytimes.com/2010/04/05/opinion/05krugman.html

Laclau, E (1996) *Emancipations* (London: Verso)

Laclau, E and C Mouffe (1985) *Hegemony and Socialist Strategy: Towards a Radical Democratic Politics* (London: Verso)

Lafont, C (2008) 'Alternative Visions of a New Global Order: What Should Cosmopolitans Hope For?' 1 *Ethics and Global Politics* 41–60

Lalu, A, K Webb and A Bond (2007) 'Understanding the Codes Before Jumping In' *Business Report*, March 13 www.busrep.co.za/index.php?fSectionId=553&fArticleId =3729349

Lang, A (2011) *World Trade Law After Neoliberalism: Re-imagining the Global Economic Order* (Oxford: Oxford University Press)

La Prensa (2006) 'Temen heredar deudas de Aguas del Tunari', 4 January

La Razón (2006) 'Coordinadora pide rechazar acuerdo con transnacionales', 10 January

Lash, S and J Urry (1994) *Economies of Signs and Space* (London: Sage)

Laxer, G (2001) 'The Movement That Dare Not Speak its Name: The Return of Left Nationalism/Internationalism' 26 *Alternatives* 1–32

Lee, W-C (2010) 'Yours, Mine, or Everyone's Property? China's Property Law in 2007' 15 *Journal of Chinese Political Science* 25–47

Lefort, C (1979) 'The Image of the Body and Totalitarianism' in Lefort (1986), pp. 292–306

Lefort, C (1982) 'Reversibility: Political Freedom and the Freedom of the Individual' in Lefort (1988), pp. 165–82

Lefort, C (1986) *The Political Forms of Modern Society*, J B Thompson (ed.) (Cambridge: MIT Press)

Lefort, C (1988) *Democracy and Political Theory*, D Macey (trans.) (Minneapolis MN: University of Minnesota Press)

Lefort, C (2002) 'Thinking With and Against Arendt' 69 *Social Research* 447–59

Lefort, C (2007) *Complications: Communism and the Dilemmas of Democracy*, J Bourg (trans.) (New York: Columbia University Press)

Lemke, T (2001) '"The Birth of Biopolitics": Michel Foucault's Lectures at the Collège de France on Neo-liberal Governmentality' 30 *Economy and Society* 190–207

Lenaerts, K and A Verhoeven (2002) 'Institutional Balance as a Guarantee for Democracy in EU Governance' in C Joerges and R Dehousse (eds) (2002), *Good Governance in Europe's Integrated Market* (Oxford: Oxford University Press), pp. 35–88

Lessig, L (2011) *Republic Lost: How Money Corrupts Congress – and a Plan to Stop It* (New York: Twelve)

Lévesque, C (2006) 'Influences on the Canadian FIPA Model and the US Model BIT: NAFTA Chapter 11 and Beyond' 44 *Canadian Yearbook of International Law* 249–96

Levmore, S (1990) 'Just Compensation and Just Politics' 22 *Connecticut Law Review* 285–322

Lindblom, C (1977) *Politics and Markets* (New York: Basic Books)

Linera, Á G (2004) 'The "Multitude"' in Olivera and Lewis (eds) (2004), pp. 65–86

Linera, Á G (2006) 'State Crisis and Popular Power' 37 *New Left Review* 73–85

Lipson, C (1985) *Standing Guard: Protecting Foreign Capital in the Nineteenth and Twentieth Centuries* (Berkeley CA: University of California Press)

Loftus, A J and D A McDonald (2001) 'Of Liquid Dreams: A Political Ecology of Water Privatization in Buenos Aires' 13 *Environment and Urbanization* 179–99

Lomnitz, C (2006) 'Latin America's Rebellion: Will the New Left Set a New Agenda?' 31(5) *Boston Review* 7–10

Luhmann, N (1989) *Ecological Communication*, J Bednarz Jr (trans.) (Cambridge: Polity Press)

Luhmann, N (1992) 'Operational Closure and Structural Coupling: The Differentiation of the Legal System' 13 *Cardozo Law Review* 1419–42

Luhmann, N (1995) *Social Systems*, J Bednarz Jr with D Baecker (trans.) (Stanford CA: Stanford University Press)

Luhmann, N (2004) *Law as a Social System*, K A Ziegert (trans.) (Oxford: Oxford University Press)

Lukes, S (2003) *Liberals and Cannibals: The Implications of Diversity* (London: Verso)

Lupel, A (2009) *Globalization and Popular Sovereignty: Democracy's Transnational Dilemma* (London: Routledge)

Lusky, L (1982) 'Footnote Redux: A *Carolene Products* Reminiscence' 82 *Columbia Law Review* 1093–109

Lynch, R A (2011) 'Foucault's Theory of Power' in D Taylor (ed.), *Michel Foucault: Key Concepts* (Durham: Acumen), pp. 13–26

MacCormick, N (1999) *Questioning Sovereignty: Law, State, and Nation in the European Commonwealth* (Oxford: Oxford University Press)

Malesky, E J (2005) 'Rethinking the Obsolescing Bargain: Do Foreign Investors Really Surrender their Influence over Economic Reform in Transition States?' (unpublished) http://nathanjensen.wustl.edu/me/files/WP2_06.pdf

Mance, H (2009) 'Re-Election the Easy Part for Ecuador's Correa' *World Politics Review*, 27 April www.worldpoliticsreview.com/articles/3651/re-election-the-easy-part-for-ecuadors-correa

Mansbridge, J (2012) 'The Importance of Getting Things Done' (January) *PS: Political Science and Politics* 1–8

Marks, S (2000) *The Riddle of All Constitutions: International Law, Democracy and the Critique of Ideology* (Oxford: Oxford University Press)

Marshall, F (2007) 'The Precarious State of Sunshine: Case Comment on the Procedural Orders in the *Biwater Gauff (Tanzania) Ltd v Tanzania* Investor–State Arbitration' 3 *McGill International Journal of Sustainable Development Law and Policy* 181–203

Martin, R (1988) 'Truth, Power, Self: An Interview with Michel Foucault, October 25, 1982' in L H Martin, H Gutman, and P H Hutton (eds), *Technologies of the Self: A Seminar With Michel Foucault* (Amherst MA: University of Massachusetts Press), pp. 9–15

Mathiason, N (2003a) 'After 26 Years, UK Food Group Squeezes Poverty-Stricken Guyana for £12 million' *The Observer*, 16 March www.guardian.co.uk/business/2003/mar/16/theobserver.observerbusiness3

Mathiason, N (2003b) 'Big Food Group Abandons Guyana Compensation Claim', 19 March www.guardian.co.uk/business/2003/mar/19/corporateaccountability.theobserver

Mathiason, N (2003c) 'Big Food Does Big U-Turn' *The Observer* (23 March 2003) www.guardian.co.uk/business/2003/mar/23/corporateaccountability.theobserver

Mbeki, T (2005) 'President of South Africa, State of the Nation Address', 11 February www.anc.org.za/ancdocs

McCann, M (2006) 'Law and Social Movements: Contemporary Perspectives' 2 *Annual Review of Law and Social Science* 17–38

McCormick, J P (2007) *Weber, Habermas, and Transformations of the European State* (Cambridge: Cambridge University Press)

McGinnis, J P and M L Movsevian (2000) 'The World Trade Constitution' 114 *Harvard Law Review* 511–605

McIlroy, J (2004) 'Canada's New Foreign Investment Protection and Promotion Agreement: Two Steps Forward, One Step Back?' 5 *Journal of World Investment and Trade* 621–46

McIlwain, C H (1947) *Constitutionalism: Ancient and Modern* (Ithaca NY: Cornell University Press)

McMichael, P (2003) 'Globalization' in T Janoski, R Alford, A Hicks and M Schwartz (eds) (2005) *The Handbook of Political Sociology* (Cambridge: Cambridge University Press), pp. 587–606

Mehranvar, L (2009) *Constructing and Contesting Hegemony: Counter-Hegemonic Resistance to the International Investment Law Regime* LLM Thesis (Graduate Department of the Faculty of Law, University of Toronto)

Michelman, F (1996) 'Democracy and Positive Liberty' 21 *Boston Review* 3–8

Milberg, W (2009) 'Keynes, Polanyi's Moment' (March) *Policy Notes, New School for Social Research* www.newschool.edu/scepa/publications/#PolicyNotes

Miller, G P (1987) 'The True Story of Carolene Products' *Supreme Court Review* 397–428

Miller, P and N Rose (2008) *Governing the Present* (Cambridge: Polity Press)

Mold, A (2007) 'Between a Rock and a Hard Place – Whither EU Development Policy?' in Mold (ed.) (2007), pp. 237–69

Mold, A (ed.) (2007) *EU Development Policy in a Changing World* (Amsterdam: Amsterdam University Press)

Moon, C W and A A Lado (2000) 'MNC-Host Government Bargaining Power Relationship: A Critique and Extension within the Resource-Based View' 26 *Journal of Management* 85–117

Moore, M (2003) *A World Without Walls: Freedom, Development, Free Trade and Global Governance* (Cambridge: Cambridge University Press)

Morgan, B (2004) 'Water: Frontier Markets and Cosmopolitan Activism' 27 *Soundings: A Journal of Politics and Culture* 10–24

Morgenthau, H J (1948) *Politics Among Nations: The Struggle for Power and Peace* (New York: Knopf)

Mortimore, M and L Stanley (2006) 'Has Investor Protection Been Rendered Obsolete by the Argentine Crisis?' 88 (April) *CEPAL Review* 15–31

Mosley, L (2006) 'Constraints, Opportunities, and Information: Financial Market-Government Relations around the World' in P Bardhan, S Bowles and M Wallerstein (eds), *Globalization and Egalitarian Distribution* (Princeton NJ: Russell Sage Foundation and Princeton University Press), pp. 87–112

Mouffe, C (1993) *The Return of the Political* (London: Verso)

Mouffe, C (2005) *The Democratic Paradox* (London: Verso)

Moustafa, T (2007) *The Struggle for Constitutional Power: Law, Politics, and Economic Development in Egypt* (Cambridge: Cambridge University Press)

Moyers, B (2001) 'NOW with Bill Moyers: Trading Democracy' www.pbs.org/now/print-able/transcript_tdfull.html

Moyo, D (2009) *Dead Aid: Why Aid is Not Working and How There is a Better Way for Africa* (Vancouver: Douglas & McIntyre)

Muchlinski, P (2011) 'Corporations and the Uses of Law: International Investment Arbitration as "Multilateral Legal Order"' 1(4) Oñati Socio-Legal Series ssrn.com

Muchlinski, P, F Ortino and C Schreuer, (eds) (2008) *The Oxford Handbook of International Investment Law* (New York: Oxford University Press)

Mumme, S P (2000) 'Sustainable Development and Environmental Decentralization on the Border: Insights from Sonora' in L A Herzog (ed.), *Shared Space: Rethinking the US–Mexico Border Environment* (La Jolla CA: Centre for US–Mexican Studies) pp. 101–27

Myers, E (2008) 'Resisting Foucauldian Ethics: Associative Politics and the Limits of the Care of the Self' 7 *Contemporary Political Theory* 125–46

Nedelsky, J (2000) 'Communities of Judgment and Human Rights' 1(2) *Theoretical Inquiries in Law*

Negri, A (2008) *Reflections on Empire*, E Emery (trans.) (Cambridge: Polity Press)

Negri, A (2010) 'The Law of the Common' 21 *Finnish Yearbook of International Law* 16–25

Niebuhr, R (1944) *The Children of Light and the Children of Darkness* (New York: Charles Scribner's & Sons)

Neumayer, E and L Spess (2005) 'Do Bilateral Investment Treaties Increase Foreign Direct Investment to Developing Countries?' 33 *World Development* 1567–85

New York City General Assembly (2011) 'Declaration of the Occupation of New York City' (29 September 2011) www.nycga.net/resources/declaration/

Newcombe, A (2007) 'Sustainable Development and Investment Treaty Law' 8 *Journal of World Trade and Investment* 357–407

Nickson, A and C Vargas (2002) 'The Limitations of Water Regulation: The Failure of the Cochabamba Concession in Bolivia' 21 *Bulletin of Latin American Research* 99–120

Nino, C S (1996) *The Constitution of Deliberative Democracy* (New Haven CT: Yale University Press)

Nocera, J (2009) 'A Financial Overhaul Plan, But Only a Hint of Roosevelt' *The New York Times*, 18 June, A1

Nocera, J (2010) 'US Bills Barely Scratch the Surface' *International Herald Tribune*, 5–6 June, pp. 15, 16

O'Leary, A O (2002) 'Women and Environmental Protest in a Northern Mexican City' 6(1)(spring) *Arizona Report* 1, 4–5

Ojeda-Mestre, R (2007) 'Environmental Justice in Mexico: Hopes and Disappointments' 37(2–3) *Environmental Policy and Law* 142–57

Olivera, O and T Lewis (eds) (2004) *¡Cochabamba! Water War in Bolivia* (Cambridge: South End Press)

Olson M (1965) *The Logic of Collective Action: Public Goods and the Theory of Groups* (Cambridge: Harvard University Press)

Orellana, M A (2007) 'Science, Risk and Uncertainty: Public Health Measures and Investment Disciplines' in P Kahn and T W Wälde (eds), *New Aspects of International Investment Law* (Leiden: Martinus Nijhoff Publishers), pp. 671–790

Panitch, L (1996) 'Rethinking the Role of the State' in J Mittelman (ed.), *Globalization: Critical Reflections* (Boulder CO: Lynne Reiner Publishers)

Parvanov, P R and M Kantor (2012) 'Comparing US Law and Recent US Investment Agreements' in *Yearbook on International Investment Law and Policy 2010–2011* (Oxford: Oxford University Press), pp. 741–836

Passavant, P A and J Dean (eds) (2004) *Empire's New Clothes: Reading Hardt and Negri* (New York: Routledge)

Patel, R and P McMichael (2004) 'Third Worldism and the Lineages of Global Fascism: The Regrouping of the Global South in the Neoliberal Era' 25 *Third World Quarterly* 231–54

Paulsson, J (2005) *Denials of Justice in International Law* (Cambridge: Cambridge University Press)

Paulsson, J (2008) 'Avoiding Unintended Consequences' in Karl P Sauvant (ed.), *Appeals Mechanism In International Investment Disputes* (Oxford: Oxford University Press), p. 241

Peck, J (2010) *Constructions of Neoliberal Reason* (Oxford: Oxford University Press)

Peerenboom, R (2002) *China's Long March Toward Rule of Law* (Cambridge: Cambridge University Press)

Peters, A (2006) 'Compensatory Constitutionalism: The Function and Potential of Fundamental International Norms and Structures' 19 *Leiden Journal of International Law* 579–610

Peterson, L E (2002) 'All Roads Lead Out of Rome: Divergent Paths of Dispute Settlement in Bilateral Investment Treaties' (November) International Sustainable and Ethical Investment Rules Project http://oldsite.nautilus.org/archives/enviro/PetersonFinalFormatted_2_2.PDF

Peterson, L E (2008) 'Ecuador Will Denounce At Least Nine Bilateral Investment Treaties' *Investment Treaty News*, 5 February www.iisd.org/pdf/2008/itn_feb5_2008.pdf

Pettigrew, P (2001) 'We Need to "Clarify" NAFTA to Fix Tribunal Errors' *Financial Post*, 23 March, C19

Pew Research Centre (2011) *23-Nation Pew Global Attitude Survey*, 13 July www.pewglobal.org/files/2011/07/Pew-Global-Attitudes-Balance-of-Power-U.S.-Image-Report-FINAL-July-13-2011.pdf

Piore, M J (2009) 'Second Thoughts: On Economics, Sociology, Neoliberalism, Polanyi's Double Movement and Intellectual Vacuums' 7 *Socio-Economic Review* 161–75

Plato (2003) *Socrates and Alcibiades*, D M Johnson (trans.) (Newburyport MA: Focus)

Poirier, M R (2002) 'The Virtue of Vagueness in Takings Doctrine' 24 *Cardozo Law Review* 93–191

Polanyi, K (1944/2001) *The Great Transformation: The Political and Economic Origins of Our Time* (Boston MA: Beacon Press)

Posner, R (2009) *A Failure of Capitalism: The Crisis of '08 and the Descent into Depression* (Cambridge MA: Harvard University Press)

Poulantzas, N (1978) *State, Power, Socialism* (London: New Left Books)

Powell, A (2002) 'Argentina's Avoidable Crisis: Bad Luck, Bad Economics, Bad Politics, Bad Advice' *Brookings Trade Forum* 1–58

Poynter, T A (1982) 'Government Intervention in Less Developed Countries: the Experience of Multinational Companies' 13 *Journal of International Business Studies* 9–25

Praider Fodéré, P (1885) *Traité de Droit International Public* tome I (Paris: A Durand et Pedon-Lauriel Éditeurs)

Prestowitz, C (2003) *Rogue Nation: American Unilateralism and the Failure of Good Intentions* (New York: Basic Books)

Quint, D (2000) e-mail to Jim Shultz, The Democracy Center, from Didier Quint, Managing Director, International Water Ltd LLC, 30 April http://webshells.com/cgi-bin/councilor/intbd/cgi-bin/intbd.cgi?action=read&id=215

Rabinow, P (1997) 'Introduction: The History of Systems of Thought' in Foucault (1997), pp. xi–xlii

Rabinow, P (2003) *Anthropos Today* (Princeton NJ: Princeton University Press)

Rajagopal, B (2003) *International Law From Below: Development, Social Movements and Third World Resistance* (Cambridge: Cambridge University Press)

Rancière, J (1999) *Disagreement: Politics and Philosophy*, J Rose (trans.) (Minneapolis MN: University of Minnesota Press)

Rancière, J (2006) *Hatred of Democracy*, S Corcoran (trans.) (London: Verso)

Ratner, S R (2008) 'Regulatory Takings in Institutional Context: Beyond the Fear of Fragmented International Law' 102 *American Journal of International Law* 475–528

Reuters (2012) 'Ecuador Signs First Large-Scale Mining Contract', 6 March online at Factiva

Ricardo, D (1912) *The Principles of Political Economy and Taxation* (London: JM Dent & Sons)

Rice, X (2007) 'The Water Margin' *The Guardian*, 16 August www.guardian.co.uk/business/2007/aug/16/imf.internationalaidanddevelopment

Rittich, K (2006) 'The Future of Law and Development: Second-Generation Reforms and the Incorporation of the Social' in D M Trubek and A Santos (eds), *The New Law and Economic Development: A Critical Appraisal* (Cambridge: Cambridge University Press)

Roberts, A (2010) 'Power and Persuasion in Investment Treaty Interpretation: The Dual Role of States' 104 *American Journal of International Law* 179–225

Robinson, I (1993) 'Neo-Conservative Trade Policy and Canadian Federalism: Constitutional Reform by Other Means' in D M Brown (ed.), *Canada: The State of the Federation 1993* (Kingston: Institute for Intergovernmental Relations)

Robinson, W I (2008) *Latin American and Global Capitalism: A Critical Globalization Perspective* (Baltimore MD: Johns Hopkins University Press)

Robinson, W I (2001) 'Social Theory and Globalization: the Rise of the Transnational State' 30 *Theory and Society* 157–200

Rodríguez-Garavito, C A and L C Arenas (2005) 'Indigenous Rights, Transnational Activism, and Legal Mobilization: The Struggle of the U'wa People in Colombia' in Santos and Rodríguez-Garavito (eds) (2005b), pp. 241–66

Rodrik, D (1997) *Has Globalization Gone Too Far?* (Washington DC: Institute for International Economics)

Romero, S (2009) 'As Oil Wealth Slips, So Fade Venezuela's Hopes of Extending Sway in the Region' *The New York Times*, 20 May, A6

Rosanvallon, P (2008) *Counter-Democracy: Politics in an Age of Distrust*, A Goldhammer (trans.) (Cambridge: Cambridge University Press)

Rosatti, H D (2003) 'Los tratados bilaterales de inversión, el arbitraje internacional obligatorio y el sistema constitucional argentino' *La Ley*, 15 October, No 198

Rose, B (2004) 'US Groups in SA Say Empowerment Deters Investment' *Business Day*, 14 December www.businessday.co.za

Rose, C (2000) 'Property and Expropriations: Themes and Variations in American Law' 1 *Utah Law Review* 1–38

Rose, N (1999) *Powers of Freedom: Reframing Political Thought* (Cambridge: Cambridge University Press)

Rose, N and P Miller (1992) 'Political Power Beyond the State: Problematics of Government' in Miller and Rose (2008), pp. 53–83

Rose, N, P O'Malley and M Valverde (2006) 'Governmentality' 2 *Annual Review of Law and Social Science* 83–104

Rose-Ackerman, S and J L Tobin (2009) 'Do BITs Benefit Developing Countires?' in C A Rogers and R P Alford (eds), *The Future of Investment Arbitration* (Oxford: Oxford University Press), pp. 131–43

Rosenau, J N and E-O Czempiel, (eds) (1992) *Governance Without Government: Order and Change in World Politics* (Cambridge: Cambridge University Press)

Rosenfeld, M (1995) 'Book Review: Law as Discourse: Bridging the Gap Between Democracy and Rights' 108 *Harvard Law Review* 1163–89

Rudolf, B (2000) 'Beyeler v Italy' 94 *American Journal of International Law* 736–40

Ruggie, J G (1998) *Constructing the World Polity: Essays on International Institutionalization* (London: Routledge)

Ruonavaara, H (1997) 'Moral Regulation: a Reformulation' 15 *Sociological Theory* 277–93

Salacuse, J W (2010) 'The Emerging Global Regime for Investment' 51 *Harvard Journal of International Law* 427–73

Sampliner, G H (2003) 'Arbitration of Expropriation Cases under US Investment Treaties – A Threat to Democracy or the Dog that Didn't Bark?' 18 *ICSID Review: Foreign Investment Law Journal* 1

Santos, A (2006) 'The World Bank's Uses of the "Rule of Law" Promise in Economic Development' in D M Trubek and A Santos (eds), *The New Law and Economic Development: A Critical Appraisal* (Cambridge: Cambridge University Press), pp. 253–300

Santos, B de S (1995) *Toward a New Legal Common Sense: Law, Globalization, and Emancipation* (London: Butterworths)

Santos, B de S (2001) '*Nuestra America*: Reinventing a Subaltern Paradigm of Recognition and Redistribution' 18 *Theory, Culture and Society* 185–217

Santos, B de S (2002) *Toward a New Legal Common Sense: Law, Globalization and Emancipation* (London: Butterworths Lexis Nexis) (2nd edn)

Santos, B de S (2004) 'A Critique of Lazy Reason: Against the Waste of Experience' in Immanuel Wallerstein (ed.), *The Modern World-System in the Longue Durée* (Boulder CO: Paradigm), pp. 157–97

Santos, B de S (2006) *The Rise of the Global Left: The World Social Forum and Beyond* (London: Zed Books)

Santos, B de S (2007) 'Beyond Abyssal Legal Thinking: From Global Lines to Ecologies of Knowledges' 30 *Review* 45–89

Santos, B de S and L Avritzer (2005) 'Introduction: Opening Up the Canon of Democracy' in B de S Santos (ed.), *Democratizing Democracy: Beyond the Liberal Democratic Canon* (London: Verso), pp. xxxiv–lxxiv

Santos, B de S and C A Rodríguez-Garavito (2005a) 'Law, Politics and the Subaltern in Counter-Hegemonic Globalization' in Santos and Rodríguez-Garavito (eds) (2005b), pp. 1–26

Santos, B de S and C A Rodríguez-Garavito (eds) (2005b) *Law and Globalization from Below: Toward a Cosmopolitan Legality* (Cambridge: Cambridge University Press)

Sassen, S (1996) *Losing Control? Sovereignty in an Age of Globalization* (New York: Columbia University Press)

Sassen, S (2000) 'Territory and Territoriality in the Global Economy' 15 *International Sociology* 372–93

Sassen, S (2004) 'Local Actors in Global Politics' 52 *Current Sociology* 649–70

Sassen, S (2006) *Territory, Authority, Rights: From Medieval to Global Assemblages* (Princeton NJ: Princeton University Press)

Sawyer, S (2004) *Crude Chronicles: Indigenous Politics, Multinational Oil, and Neoliberalism in Ecuador* (Durham NC: Duke University Press)

Saxegaard, M (2004) 'Creditor Participation in the HIPC Debt Relief Initiatives: The Case of Guyana' 32 *Georgia Journal of International and Comparative Law* 725–31

Schaefer, T 'Engaging Modernity: The Political Making of Indigenous Movements in Bolivia and Ecuador, 1900–2008' 30 *Third World Quarterly* 397–413

Scheuerman, W E (2002) 'Between Radicalism and Resignation: Democratic Theory in Habermas' *Between Facts and Norms*' in R V Schomberg and K Baynes (eds), *Discourse and Democracy: Essays on Habermas' Between Facts and Norms* (Albany NY: State University Press of New York), pp. 61–85

Scheuerman, W E (2008) 'Review Essay: Global Governance Without Government?' 36 *Political Theory* 135–51

Scheuerman, W E (2011a) *The Realist Case for Global Reform* (Cambridge: Polity Press)

Scheuerman, W E (2011b) 'Realists Against the Nation-State' 20 *Transnational Law and Contemporary Problems* 67–105

Schill, S W (2007) 'Tearing Down the Great Wall: The New Generation Investment Treaties of the People's Republic of China' 15 *Cardozo Journal of International and Comparative Law* 73–118

Schill, S W (2012) 'Cross-Regime Analysis Through Proportionality Analysis: The Case of International Investment Law, the Law of State Immunity and Human Rights' 27 *ICSID Review* 87–119

Schmitt, C (1999) 'Ethic of State and Pluralistic State' in C Mouffe (ed.), *The Challenge of Carl Schmitt* (London: Verso), pp. 195–208

Schnabl, M E and J Bédard (2007) 'International Law: The Wrong Kind of Interesting' *National Law Journal*, 30 July 2007

Schneiderman, D (1996) 'NAFTA's Takings Rule: American Constitutionalism Comes to Canada' 46 *University of Toronto Law Journal* 499–537

Schneiderman, D (1998) 'Harold Laski, Viscount Haldane and the Law of the Canadian Constitution in the Early Twentieth Century' 48 *University of Toronto Law Journal* 521–60

Schneiderman, D (2000) 'Constitutional Approaches to Privatization: An Inquiry into the Magnitude of Neo-Liberal Constitutionalism' 63 *Law and Contemporary Problems* 83–109

Schneiderman, D (2001) 'Investment Rules and the Rule of Law' 8 *Constellations* 521–37

Schneiderman, D (2004a) 'Habermas, Market-Friendly Human Rights, and the Revisibility of Economic Globalization' 8 *Citizenship Studies* 419–36

Schneiderman, D (2004b) 'Globalisation, Governance and Investment Rules' in J N Clarke and G R Edwards (eds), *Global Governance in the Twenty-First Century* (Basingstoke: Palgrave Macmillan), pp. 67–91

Schneiderman, D (2006) 'Constitution or Model Treaty? Struggling Over the Interpretive Authority of NAFTA' in S Choudhry (ed.), *The Migration of Constitutional Ideas* (Cambridge: Cambridge University Press), pp. 294–315

Schneiderman, D (2008) *Constitutionalizing Economic Globalization: Investment Rules and Democracy's Promise* (Cambridge: Cambridge University Press)

Schneiderman, D (2009) 'Promoting Equality, Black Economic Empowerment, and the Future of Investment Rules' 25 *South African Journal on Human Rights* 246–79

Schneiderman, D (2010a) 'Judicial Politics and International Investment Arbitration: Seeking an Explanation for Conflicting Outcomes' 30 *Northwestern Journal of International Law and Business* 383–416

Schneiderman, D (2010b) 'Investing in Democracy? Political Process and International Investment Law' 60 *University of Toronto Law Journal* 909–40

Schneiderman, D (2011) 'Revisiting the Depoliticization of Investment Disputes' in *Yearbook on International Investment Law and Policy 2010–2011* (Oxford: Oxford University Press), pp. 693–714

Schneier-Madanes, G (2001) 'From Well to Network: Water Supply and Sewerage in Buenos Aires (1993–2000)' 8 *Journal of Urban Technology* 45–63

Scoffield, H (2000) 'Mexico Holds Firm on NAFTA Investment Rules' *The Globe and Mail*, 2 September, B3

Scott, J (1985) *Weapons of the Weak: Everyday Forms of Peasant Resistance* (New Haven CT: Yale University Press)

Seattle to Brussels Network (2011) 'EU Investment Policy – Text of the Mandates' www. s2bnetwork.org/themes/eu-investment-policy/eu-documents/text-of-the-mandates. html

Sell, S K (2003) *Private Power, Public Law: The Globalization of Intellectual Property Rights* (Cambridge: Cambridge University Press)

Sen, A K (1990) 'Rational Fools: A Critique of the Behavioral Foundations of Economic Theory' in J Mansbridge (ed.), *Beyond Self-Interest* (Chicago IL: University of Chicago Press)

Sen, K (2011) '"A Hard Rain's a-Gonna Fall": The Global Financial Crisis and Developing Countries' 16 *New Political Economy* 399–413

Shaffer, G C (2003) *Defending Interests: Public–Private Partnerships in WTO Litigation* (Washington DC: Brookings Institution Press)

Shamir, R (2005) 'Corporate Social Responsibility: A Case of Hegemony and Counter-Hegemony' in Santos and Rodríguez-Garavito (eds) (2005b), pp. 92–117

Shan, W (2007) 'From "North–South Divide" to "Private-Public Debate": Revival of the Calvo Doctrine and the Changing Landscape in International Investment Law' 27(3) *Northwestern Journal of International Law and Business* 631–64

Shihata, I F I (1986) 'Towards a Greater Depoliticization of Investment Disputes: The Roles of ICSID and MIGA' 1 *ICSID Review: Foreign Investment Law Journal* 1–25

Shihata, I F I (1991) 'The World Bank and "Governance" Issues in its Borrowing Members' in 1 *World Bank in a Changing World: Selected Essays* (Dordrecht: Martinus Nijhoff), pp. 53–96

Shultz, J (2002) *The Democracy Owners' Manual: A Practical Guide to Changing the World* (New Brunswick NJ: Rutgers University Press)

Shultz, J (2003) 'The Water is Ours Dammit!' in Notes from Nowhere (ed.), *We Are Everywhere: The Irresistible Rise of Global Capitalism* (London: Verso), pp. 265–77

Shultz, J (2008) 'The Cochabamba Water Revolt and its Aftermath' in J Shultz and M Draper (eds), *Dignity and Defiance: Stories from Bolivia's Challenge to Globalization* (Berkeley CA: University of California Press)

Silbey, S S (2005) 'After Legal Consciousness' 1 *Annual Review of Law and Social Science* 323–68

Sklair, L (2002) *Globalization: Capitalism and its Alternatives* (Oxford: Oxford University Press)

Slemon, S (1990) 'Unsettling the Empire: Resistance Theory for the Second World' 30(2) *Journal of Postcolonial Writing* 30–41

Solanes, M (2006) 'Efficiency, Equity and Liberalisation of Water Services in Buenos Aires, Argentina' in OECD Trade Policy Studies, *Liberalisation of Universal Access to Basic Services: Telecommunications, Water and Sanitation, Financial Services and Electricity* (Paris: OECD and the International Bank for Reconstruction and Development and The World Bank), pp. 149–71

Somek, A (2010) 'The Argument From Transnational Effects I: Representing Outsiders Through Freedom of Movement' 16 *European Law Journal* 315

Sornarajah, M (1997) 'Power and Justice in Foreign Investment Arbitration' 14 *Journal of International Arbitration* 103–40

Sornarajah, M (2008) 'A Coming Crisis: Expansionary Trends in Investment Treaty Arbitration' in K P Sauvant (ed.), *Appeals Mechanism in International Investment Dispute* (Oxford: Oxford University Press), pp. 39–80

Sornarajah, M (2011) 'The Descent into Normlessness' in C Brown and K Miles (eds), *Evolution in Investment Treaty Law and Arbitration* (Cambridge: Cambridge University Press), pp. 631–57

Soule, S A (2009) *Contention and Corporate Social Responsibility* (Cambridge: Cambridge University Press)

South Africa, Department of Trade and Industry (DTI) (2009) 'Bilateral Investment Treaty Policy Framework Review: Government Position Paper' (June) www.thedti.gov.za/ads/bi-lateral_policy.pdf

South African Development Community (SADC) (2012) 'SADC Model Bilateral Investment Treaty Template with Commentary' (July) (Gaborone, Botswana: SADC) www.iisd.org/itn/wp-content/uploads/2012/10/SADC-Model-BIT-Template-Final.pdf

Southey, C (2007) 'South Africa Exempts Foreign Groups on Black Empowerment' *Financial Times*, 15 December, p. 7

Spector, H (2008) 'Constitutional Transplants and the Mutation Effect' 83 *Chicago–Kent Law Review* 129–45

Spivak, G C (1988) 'Can the Subaltern Speak?' in C Nelson and L Grosberg (eds), *Marxism and the Interpretation of Culture* (Urbana IL: University of Illinois Press), pp. 271–313

Spivak, G C (1999) A *Critique of Postcolonial Reason: Toward a History of the Vanishing Present* (Cambridge MA: Harvard University Press)

Stabroek News (2003) 'Jagdeo Thanks Lobbyists against Welsh Supermarket Chain', 23 March www.landofsixpeoples.com/news301/ns303234.htm

Steger, M B (2008) *The Rise of the Global Imaginary: Political Ideologies from the French Revolution to the Global War on Terror* (Oxford: Oxford University Press)

Stern, B (2007) 'Civil Society's Voice in the Settlement of International Economic Disputes' 22 *ICSID Review: Foreign Investment Law Journal* 280–348

Stevens, C (2007) 'Creating a Development-Friendly EU Trade Policy' in Mold (ed.) (2007), pp. 221–36

Stewart, F (2009) 'Relaxing the Shackles: The Invisible Pendulum' 21 *Journal of International Development* 765–71

Stiglitz, J E (2002a) *Globalization and its Discontents* (New York: WW Norton & Co.)

Stiglitz, J E (2002b) 'Argentina, Shortchanged: Why the Nation That Followed the Rules Fell to Pieces' *Washington Post*, 12 May

Stiglitz, J E (2009) 'The Global Crisis, Social Protection and Jobs' 148(1–2) *International Labor Review* 1–13

Stiglitz, J (2010a) 'Build Strong Rules for Finance System' *Politico*, 12 April www.politico.com/news/stories/0410/35636.html#ixzz0mzH2NXUM

Stiglitz, J E (2010b) *Freefall: America, Free Markets, and the Sinking of the World Economy* (New York: WW Norton & Co.)

Stokes, S (2001) *Mandates and Democracy: Neoliberalism by Surprise in Latin America* (New York: Cambridge University Press)

Stopford, J and S Strange (1991) *Rival States, Rival Firms: Competition for World Market Shares* (Cambridge: Cambridge University Press)

Strange, S (1982) '*Cave! Hic Dragones*: A Critique of Regime Analysis' 36 *International Organization* 479–96

Strange, S (1988) *States and Markets* (London: Pinter) (2nd edn)

Strange, S (1996) *The Retreat of the State: The Diffusion of Power in the World Economy* (Cambridge: Cambridge University Press)

Strange, S (1997) 'The Problem or the Solution? Capitalism and the State System' in S Gill and J Mittelman (eds), *Innovation and Transformation in International Studies* (Cambridge: Cambridge University Press)

Streeck, W (2011) 'The Crises of Democratic Capitalism' 71(September–October) *New Left Review* 5–29

Streeck, W (2012) 'Markets and Peoples' 73 (January–February) *New Left Review* 61–71

Summers, L H (2009) 'Summers Remarks at Council on Foreign Relations', 12 June http://blogs.wsj.com/economics/2009/06/12/summers-remarks-at-council-on-forei gn-relations/

Sunday Times (2004) 'SACU-US Talks Seesaw Back Towards Pessimism', 20 September www.tralac.org/scripts/content.php?id=2923

Supiot, A (2012) 'Under Eastern Eyes' 73 *New Left Review* 29–36

Tarrow, S (2003) '"Global" Movements, Complex Internationalism, and North–South Inequality' http://falcon.arts.cornell.edu/sgt2/contention/documents/columbia-harvard.oct%2010.doc

Tarrow, S (2005) *The New Transnational Activism* (Cambridge: Cambridge University Press)

Tarrow, S and D McAdam (2005) 'Scale Shift in Transnational Contention' in D della Porta and S Tarrow (eds), *Transnational Protest and Global Activism* (Lanham: Rowman & Littlefield), pp. 121–47

Tarullo, D K (1987) 'Beyond Normalcy in the Regulation of International Trade' 100 *Harvard Law Review* 546–28

Teubal, M (2004) 'Rise and Collapse of Neoliberalism in Argentina: The Role of Economic Groups' 20 *Journal of Developing Societies* 173–88

Teubner, G (1983) 'Substantive and Reflexive Elements in Modern Law' 17 *Law and Society Review* 239–86

Teubner G (1988) 'Introduction to Autopoietic Law' in G Teubner (ed.), *Autopoietic Law: A New Approach to Law and Society* (Berlin: Walter de Gruyter), pp. 1–11

Teubner, G (1997a) '"Global Bukowina": Legal Pluralism in the World Society' in G Teubner (ed.), *Global Law without a State* (Aldershot: Dartmouth), pp. 3–28

Teubner, G (1997b) 'Altera pars audiatur: Law in the Collision of Discourses' in R Rawlings (ed), *Law, Society and Economy* (Oxford: Oxford University Press), pp. 149–76

Teubner, G (2004) 'Societal Constitutionalism: Alternatives to State-centred Constitutional Theory?' in C Joerges, I-J Sand and G Teubner (eds), *Transnational Governance and Constitutionalism* (Oxford: Hart), pp. 3–28

Teubner, G (2010) 'Societal Constitutionalism and the Politics of the Common' 21 *Finnish Yearbook of International Law* 2–15

Teubner, G (2011a) 'Constitutionalizing Polycontextuality' 20 *Social and Legal Studies* 210–29

Teubner, G (2011b) 'A Constitutional Moment? The Logics of "Hitting the Bottom"' in P Kjaer, G Teubner and A Frabbajo (eds), *The Financial Crisis in Constitutional Perspective: The Dark Side of Functional Differentiation* (Oxford: Hart)

Teubner, G (2012) *Constitutional Fragments: Societal Constitutionalism and Globalization* (Oxford: Oxford University Press)

Thacker, S C (2000) *Big Business, the State, and Free Trade: Constructing Coalitions in Mexico* (Cambridge: Cambridge University Press)

Thomas, L and J Leape with M Hanouch and R Rumney (2005) 'Foreign Direct Investment in South Africa: The Initial Impact of the Trade, Development and Cooperation Agreement between South Africa and the European Union' (October) (London: Centre for Research into Economics and Finance in Southern Africa, London School of Economics) www.lse.ac.uk/Depts/CREFSA/pdf/CREFSA_BusinessMap_FDI_in_ South_Africa_October_2005.pdf

Thompson, E P (1975) *Whigs and Hunters: The Origin of the Black Act* (New York: Pantheon)

Tilly, C and S Tarrow (2007) *Contentious Politics* (Boulder CO: Paradigm)

Tocqueville, A de (2000) *Democracy in America*, H C Mansfield and D Winthrop (trans.) (Chicago IL: University of Chicago Press)

Tomuschat, C (2009) 'The European Court of Human Rights and Investment Protection' in C Binder, U Kriebaum, A Reinisch, S Wittich (eds), *International Investment Law for the 21st Century: Essays in Honour of Christoph Schreuer* (Oxford: Oxford University Press), pp. 636–56

Trade and Environment Policy Advisory Committee (TEPAC) (2004) *Report on The US–Australia Free Trade Agreement*, 12 March

Trakman, L E (1983) *The Law Merchant: The Evolution of Commercial Law* (Littleton CO: Fred B Rothman & Co.)

Trebilcock, M and R Howse (1998) 'Trade Liberalization and Regulatory Diversity: Reconciling Competitive Markets with Competitive Politics' 6 *European Journal of Law and Economics* 5–37

Tribe, K (2009) 'The Political Economy of Modernity: Foucault's Collège de France Lectures of 1978 and 1979' 38 *Economy and Society* 679–98

Tribe, L H (1980) 'The Puzzling Persistence of Process-Based Constitutional Theories' 89 *Yale Law Journal* 1063–80

Tushnet, M V (1979) 'Rethinking the Dormant Commerce Clause' *Wisconsin Law Review* 125–65

Ugarteche, Ó (2012) 'What Accounts for South America's Resilience?' 45(2) *NACLA*

Unger, R M (1996) *What Should Legal Analysis Become?* (London: Verso)

Unger, R M (1998) *Democracy Realized* (London: Verso)

Unger, R M (2007) *Free Trade Reimagined: The World Division of Labor and the Method of Economics* (Princeton NJ: Princeton University Press)

United Nations (2009) *Report of the Commission of Experts of the President of the United Nations General Assembly on Reforms of the International Monetary and Financial System*, 21 September www.un.org/ga/econcrisissummit/docs/FinalReport_CoE. pdf

United Nations Conference on Trade and Development (UNCTAD) (2001) *Investment Policy Review: Ecuador* (Geneva: United Nations)

United Nations Conference on Trade and Development (UNCTAD) (2004) *World Investment Report 2004: The Shift Toward Services* (New York and Geneva: United Nations)

United Nations Conference on Trade and Development (UNCTAD) (2006) *World Investment Report 2006: FDI From Developing and Transition Economies: Implications for Development* (New York and Geneva: United Nations)

United Nations Conference on Trade and Development (UNCTAD) (2007) *World Investment Report 2007: Transnational Corporations, Extractive Industries and Development* (New York and Geneva: United Nations)

United Nations Conference on Trade and Development (UNCTAD) (2008) *World Investment Report 2008: Transnational Corporations and the Infrastructure Challenge* (New York and Geneva: United Nations)

United Nations Conference on Trade and Development (UNCTAD) (2009a) *World Investment Report 2009: Transnational Corporations, Agricultural Production and Development* (New York and Geneva: United Nations)

United Nations Conference on Trade and Development (UNCTAD) (2009b) *Trade and Development Report 2009* (New York and Geneva: United Nations)

United Nations Conference on Trade and Development (UNCTAD) (2011) *World Investment Report 2011: Non-Equity Modes of International Production and Development* (New York and Geneva: United Nations)

United Nations Conference on Trade and Development (UNCTAD) (2012) *World Investment Report 2012: Toward a New Generation of Investment Policies* (New York and Geneva: United Nations)

United Nations Development Programme (UNDP) (2005) *Human Development Report 2005: International Cooperation at a Crossroads: Aid, Trade and Security in an Unequal World* (New York: UNDP)

United Nations Development Programme (UNDP) (2009) *Human Development Report 2009: Overcoming Barriers: Human Mobility and Development* (New York: UNDP)

United Nations Development Programme (UNDP) (2010) *Human Development Report 2010 – The Real Wealth of Nations: Pathways to Human Development* (New York: UNDP)

United Nations Development Programme (UNDP) (2011) *Human Development Report 2011 – Sustainability and Equity: A Better Future for All* (New York: UNDP)

United States Department of State (2004) 'US Trade Representative Zoellick Holds Talk in Cape Town' transcript of joint press conference, 17 February http://usinfo.state.gov/ei/Archive/2004/Feb/18-911614.html

United States Department of State (2005) '2005 Investment Climate Statement – South Africa' www.state.gov/e/eb/ifd/2005/42112.htm

United States Department of State (2009) '2009 Investment Climate Statement – Ecuador' www.state.gov/e/eeb/rls/othr/ics/2009/117668.htm

United States Department of State (2011) '2011 Investment Climate Statement – Ecuador' www.state.gov/e/eb/rls/othr/ics/2011/157270.htm

United States Senate Permanent Subcommittee on Investigations (2011) 'Wall Street and the Financial Crisis: Anatomy of a Financial Collapse' (chair S Levin) 13 April www.hsgac.senate.gov/subcommittees/investigations/media/senate-investigations-subcommittee-releases-levin-coburn-report-on-the-financial-crisis

United States Trade Representative (USTR) (2004) '2004 US Model Bilateral Investment Treaty' www.ustr.gov/sites/default/files/U.S.%20model%20BIT.pdf

United States Trade Representative (USTR) (2006) 'US-SACU Agree to Pursue Concrete Steps to Deepen Trade and Investment Relations' (18 April 2006) www.ustr.gov/Document_Library/Press_Releases/2006/April/US-SACU_Agree_to_Pursue_Concrete_Steps_to_Deepen_Trade_Investment_Relations.html

United States Trade Representative (USTR) (2012) '2012 US Model Bilateral Investment Treaty' www.ustr.gov/sites/default/files/BIT%20text%20for%20ACIEP%20Meeting.pdf

Urry, J (2005) 'The Complexities of the Global' 22 *Theory, Culture, and Society* 235–54

Vagts, D F (1961) 'The Corporate Alien: Definitional Questions in Federal Restraints on Foreign Enterprise' 74 *Harvard Law Review* 1489–551

Valverde, M (2007) 'Genealogies of European States: Foucauldian Reflections' 36 *Economy and Society* 159–78

Valverde, M (2009) 'Jurisdiction and Scale: Legal "Technicalities" as Resources for Theory' 18(2) *Social and Legal Studies* 139–57

Valverde, M (2010) 'Specters of Foucault in Law and Society Scholarship' 6 *Annual Review of Law and Social Science* 3.1–15

Van Harten, G (2007) *Investment Treaty Arbitration and Public Law* (Oxford: Oxford University Press)

Van Harten, G (2008a) 'Investment Provisions in Economic Partnership Agreements' www.epa2007.org/upload/PDF/EPAs_and_%20investment.Van%20Harten.pdf

Van Harten, G (2008b) 'Policy Impacts of Investment Agreements for Andean Community States' www.ssrn.com

Van Harten, G (2010) 'Investment Treaty Arbitration, Procedural Fairness, and the Rule of Law' in S Schill (ed.), *International Investment Law and Comparative Public Law* (Oxford: Oxford University Press), pp. 627–57

Vandevelde, K J (1992) 'The BIT Program: A Fifteen-Year Appraisal' in *American Society of International Law, Proceedings of the 86th Annual Meeting* (Washington DC: ASIL), pp. 532–40

Vandevelde, K J (1998) 'The Political Economy of a Bilateral Investment Treaty' 92 *American Journal of International Law* 621–41

Vandevelde, K J (2007) 'Bilateral Investment Treaties – Investor–state arbitration – Jurisdiction – Choice of Forum clauses – Corporate Nationality – Control of Investment' 101 *American Journal of International Law* 179–84

Vázquez, C M (2003) 'Trade Sanctions and Human Rights – Past, Present, and Future' 6 *Journal of International Economic Law* 797–839

Veitch, S (2007) *Law and Irresponsibility: On the Legitimation of Human Suffering* (Oxford: Routledge Cavendish)

Vernon, R (1971) *Sovereignty at Bay: The Multinational Spread of US Enterprises* (New York: Basic Books)

Vertovech, S (2009) *Transnationalism* (London: Routledge)

Veyne, P (1986) 'The Final Foucault and His Ethics' in Davidson (ed.) (1995), pp. 225–33

Veyne, P (2010) *Foucault: His Thought, His Character*, J Lloyd (trans.) (Cambridge: Polity Press)

Vidal, J (2005) 'Flagship Africa Scheme Collapses' *The Guardian*, 25 May, p. 1 www.guardian.co.uk/politics/2005/may/25/uk.world

Vincentelli, I (2008) 'The Uncertain Future of ICSID in North America' ssrn.com/abstract= 1348016

Vis-Dunbar, D and L E Peterson (2008) 'Tanzania declares victory in contractual dispute with water services company' *Investment Treaty News,* 11 January www.iisd.org/itn/wp-content/uploads/2010/10/itn_jan11_2008.pdf

Vis-Dunbar, D, L E Peterson and F C Diaz (2007) 'Bolivia Notifies Bank of Withdrawal from ICSID, Pursues BIT Revisions' *Investment Treaty News*, 9 May www.iisd.org/pdf/2007/itn_may9_2007.pdf

Vogel, D (1989) *Fluctuating Fortunes: The Political Power of Business in America* (New York: Basic Books)

Wade, R (2008) 'Financial Regime Change?' 53(September–October) *New Left Review* 5–21

Wagner, J M (1999) 'International Investment, Expropriation and Environmental Protection' 29 *Golden Gate University Law Review* 465–527

Wai, R (2003) 'Countering, Branding, Dealing: Using Economic and Social Rights in and around the International Trade Regime' 14 *European Journal of International Law* 35–84

Wälde, T (2007) 'The Specific Nature of Investment Arbitration' in P Kahn and T W Wälde (eds), *New Aspects of International Investment Law* (Leiden: Martinus Nijhoff Publishers), pp. 43–119

Walker, N (2002) 'The Idea of Constitutional Pluralism' 65 *Modern Law Review* 317–59

Walker, N (2005) 'Europe's Constitutional Momentum and the Search for Polity Legitimacy' 3 *I-CON* 211–38

Walker, N (2008) 'Beyond Boundary Disputes and Basic Grids: Mapping the Global Disorder of Normative Orders' 6 *I-CON* 373–96

Wallach, L and M Sforza (1999) *Whose Trade Organization? Corporate Globalization and the Erosion of Democracy* (Washington DC: Public Citizen)

Wallerstein, I (1974) *The Modern World-System I: Capitalist Agriculture and the Origins of the European World-Economy in the Sixteenth Century* (San Diego CA: Academic Press)

Walsh, M W and C Hulse (2009) 'AIG Bonuses of $50 Million Will Be Repaid' *New York Times*, 23 March

WaterAid (2008) 'Why Did City Water Fail? The Rise and Fall of Private Sector Participation in Dar es Salaam's Water Supply' (May) (Dar es Salaam: WaterAid) www.wateraid.org/documents/plugin_documents/city_water_report_online_version.pdf

Weber, M (1978) *Economy and Society: An Outline of Interpretive Sociology* vol. 1 (Berkeley CA: University of California Press)

Weiler J H H (2001) 'The Rule of Lawyers and the Ethos of Diplomats: Reflections on WTO Dispute Settlement' in R B Porter, P Sauvé, A Subramanian and A B Zampetti (eds), *Efficiency, Equity, Legitimacy: The Multilateral Trading System at the Millennium* (Washington DC: Brookings Institute), pp. 334–50

Weiss, L (2005a) 'Global Governance, National Strategies: How Industrialized States Make Room to Move Under the WTO' 12 *Review of International Political Economy* 723–49

Weiss, L (2005b) 'The State-Augmenting Effects of Globalisation' 10 *New Political Economy* 345–53

Wells, L T and R Ahmed (2007) *Making Foreign Investment Safe: Property Rights and International Sovereignty* (Oxford: Oxford University Press)

Wenyon, S and C Jenne (1999) 'Water and Sewerage Privatization and Reform' in F Basañes, E Uribe and R Willig (eds), *Can Privatization Deliver? Infrastructure for Latin America* (Washington DC: Inter-American Development Bank), pp. 173–216

White, D (2005) 'Tanzanian Spat Puts Focus on Aid Dilemma' *Financial Times*, 29 June, p. 7

Wickham, G (1990) 'The Political Possibilities of Postmodernism' 19 *Economy and Society* 121–49

Wiley, J (2006) 'Sheldon Wolin on Theory and the Political' 38 *Polity* 211–34

Wilkins, M (1989) *The History of Foreign Investment in the United States to 1914* (Cambridge: Harvard University Press)

Williams, B (1975) 'The Truth in Relativism' NS 75 *Proceedings of the Aristotelian Society* 215–28

Williams, R (2011) 'Presentation to "Rethinking Investment Treaty Law – A Policy Perspective"', London School of Economics, Department of Law, 23 May www2.lse.ac.uk/newsAndMedia/videoAndAudio/channels/publicLecturesAndEvents/player.aspx?id=1014

Williams, R (1961) *The Long Revolution* (Harmondsworth: Penguin)

Wolf, M (2004) *Why Globalization Works* (New Haven CT: Yale University Press)

Wolf, M (2009) 'To Nationalise or Not to Nationalise is the Question' *Financial Times*, 4 March

Wolin, S S (1960) *Politics and Vision: Continuity and Innovation in Western Thought* (Boston: Little, Brown & Company)

Wolin S S (1982) 'What Revolutionary Action Means Today' in C Mouffe (ed.), *Dimensions of Radical Democracy: Pluralism, Citizenship, Community* (London: Verso), pp. 24–53

Wolin, S S (1988) 'On the Theory and Practice of Power' in J Arac (ed.), *After Foucault: Humanistic Knowledge, Postmodern Challenges* (New Brunswick NJ: Rutgers University Press), pp. 179–201

Wolin, S S (1989) *The Presence of the Past: Essays on the State and the Constitution* (Baltimore MD: Johns Hopkins University Press)

Wolin, S S (1994) 'Fugitive Democracy' 1 *Constellations* 11–25

Wolin, S S (2001) *Tocqueville Between Two Worlds: The Making of a Political and Theoretical Life* (Princeton NJ: Princeton University Press)

Wolin, S S (2004) *Politics and Vision: Continuity and Innovation in Western Thought* (Princeton NJ: Princeton University Press) (expanded edn)

Wolin, S S (2008) *Democracy Inc.: Managed Democracy and the Specter of Inverted Totalitarianism* (Princeton NJ: Princeton University Press)

Wong, E (2008) 'Booming, China Faults US Policy on the Economy' *New York Times*, 17 June, A1

Wood, E M (2003a) 'A Manifesto for Global Capitalism?' in G Balakrishnan (ed.), *Debating Empire* (London: Verso), pp. 61–82

Wood, E M (2003b) *Empire of Capital* (London: Verso)

World Bank (1999) *Bolivia: Public Expenditure Review*, Report No 19232-BO (Washington DC: World Bank)

World Bank (2003) 'Project Appraisal Document on a Proposed Credit in the Amount of SDR 45.0 Million (US$ 61.5 Million Equivalent) to the United Republic of Tanzania for the Dar es Salaam Water Supply and Sanitation Project', Report No 2549-TA, 10 April www.worldbank.org/afr/padi/TZ_PAD.pdf

World Bank (2006) 'The United Republic of Tanzania Dar es Salaam Water Supply and Sanitation Project Restructuring (Credit 3771-TA)', 17 February 2006 www-wds.worldbank.org/external/default/WDSContentServer/WDSP/IB/2006/02/21/0000903 41_20060221103939/Rendered/PDF/35322.pdf

World Bank (2011) 'Implementation Completion and Results Report (IDA-37710 and IDA-3771A) on a Credit in the Amount of SDR 45 Million (US$ 61.5 Million Equivalent) to the United Republic of Tanzania for a Dar es Salaam Water Supply and Sanitation Project', Report No ICR00001361, 31 May www-wds.worldbank.org/external/default/WDSContentServer/WDSP/IB/2011/08/12/000333037_201108120 10851/Rendered/PDF/ICR13610P059070e0only0900BOX361525B.pdf

Yackee, J W (2008) 'Bilateral Investment Treaties, Credible Commitment, and the Rule of (International) Law: Do BITs Promote Foreign Direct Investment?' 42 *Law and Society Review* 805–31

Yackee, J W (2012) 'Controlling the International Investment Law Agency' 53 *Harvard Journal of International Law* 391–448

Zaldumbide-Serrano, J P (2008) 'Windfall Profit Tax in Ecuadorian Petroleum Industry' 5(2)(April) *Transnational Dispute Management*

Zamosc, L (2004) 'The Ecuadorian Indian Movement: From Politics of Influence to Politics of Power' in N G Postero and L Zamosc (eds), *The Struggle for Indigenous Rights in Latin America* (Brighton and Portland: Sussex Academic Press)

Zibechi, R (2005) 'Subterannean Echos: Resistance and Politics "*desde el Sótano*"' 19 *Socialism and Democracy* 13–39

Zibechi, R (2009) 'Cochabamba: From Water War to Water Management' *Americas Program Report*, 28 May www.cipamericas.org/archives/1723

Zibechi, R (2011) 'Ecuador: The Construction of a New Model of Domination', upsidedownworld.org, 5 August http://upsidedownworld.org/main/ecuador-archives-49/3152-ecuador-the-construction-of-a-new-model-of-domination

Zizek, S (2009) 'Post Wall' 31 *London Review of Books*, 19 November, p. 10

Zoellick, R (2002) 'Free Trade, Free People' *Wall Street Journal*, 4 November, A15

Zumbansen, P (2002) 'Piercing the Legal Veil: Commercial Arbitration and Transnational Law' 8 *European Law Journal* 400

Zumbansen, P (2006) 'Transnational Law' in J Smits (ed.), *Encyclopedia of Comparative Law* (Cheltenham: Edward Elgar), pp. 738–54

Index

Printed and bound in Great Britain by
TJ International Ltd , Padstow, Cornwall